A ROSIE LIFE IN ITALY 4

POTATOES, PIZZA & POTEEN

ROSIE MELEADY

ENVY PUBLISHING

To Mam

Thank you for a great childhood

1

GOODBYE

"**D**o you want a wine gum? Ah go on take one, you can't refuse, they were his favourite."

My cousin Rob is offering around the bag of wine gums he has retrieved from the coffin.

The posh relatives politely take one but I can see the discomfort on their faces as they chew the hard jellies that were just beside Dad's corpse. It's not like they were in his hands—a set of rosary beads were there as is customary in Ireland.

The Elf on the Shelf above the coffin is not customary. That has been there since the previous Christmas and we only noticed it after they had removed the lid of the coffin, but it suits his personality so we left it there. He'd prefer it to a cross—that would look morbid.

"The beads were a set belonging to our daughter Eileen," my mother explained to anyone who was listening the day before, when Dad was being laid out in the sunroom. Not that there was anyone, other than the undertakers, to listen as there was only me in the room and Dad of course, but he wasn't being very responsive.

He looks so peaceful wearing his good blazer, the same one he wore to my wedding twenty-five years ago. His hair feels soft and clean. I wonder how the undertakers make them have a little smile, a look of contentment.

The journalist was coming out in me; I wanted to ask the undertakers if their embalming training is similar to those who work in creating wax works for museums.

"He's better from this side," said the younger undertaker who, I heard through the grapevine, was keen to take over the family business. Perhaps both he and his father did a side, and he wanted us to say "oh yes, this is definitely his better side now. In life it was his right side, but in death the left is definitely his best side."

The son would then walk smugly off and say to his ageing father, "you see they prefer my work. It's time for you to step down and hand over the reins of the business."

Rob reaches me with the bag of wine gums and winks at me with his cheeky half-smile. I am the only person not to take one. The one good thing about having to fly back from Italy for my dad's funeral is that I get to spend time with family and friends I haven't seen in a very long time.

"They are nearly all gone, leave some for him," I say in all seri-ousness, feeling a little annoyed that the bag of wine gums I had bought was nearly empty.

Rob is my Mam's sister's son who is the same age as me. We practically grew up in each other's pockets. My aunt was quite ill after having him, so he was with us for most of his first year of his life and after that he was always over at our house, staying over and hanging out.

We went to school together, clubbing and holidays. He was like a brother and sister combined, a best friend who was always watching out for me during my teens and early twenties and there for me when life went ass ways.

My Mam once told me, when she'd had a few too many, that he was her favourite. She forgets he is not biologically hers and just considers him one of her boys. Her favourite one.

"Rob works for a billionaire you know," she boasts to her in-laws, as if Rob was the billionaire, while they sip their tea and she gulps her whiskey. "So do all the people in McDonalds," whispers Rob to me, over-hearing her boasting.

He married twice and has three kids with three different women. They all adored him. Even his ex's. During Covid, along with my brother Jim, he was my parent's lifeline and here he was now, getting ready to carry Dad, along with my brothers, to Dad's final resting place.

Rob would be my emotional support substitute during the funeral since Ronan, my husband, needed to stay in Italy and look after the pets. Dad's death had been too sudden for us to arrange pet sitters.

The posh relatives left before my daughter Izzy, and niece Jessie arrived. They are both overcome with emotion seeing their much-loved grandad, who they both grew up around.

"Who bought the wine gums?" asks Jessie.

"Ronan asked me to put them in with Dad from him," I answered softly. "It was an ongoing joke about Dad since

Ronan approached him and asked his permission to marry me. Dad's response was to hold out a packet to him and offer, 'do you want a wine gum?'"

"They are the wrong brand. He didn't like those ones," says Jessie.

"Well, in that case, I'll take one."

The bag with the few that are left is put back into the coffin.

"He looks great. I really can't believe how well he looks," gushes Izzy. "I was worried it would freak me out seeing him in his coffin, but he really looks fantastic."

"Izzy, enough of the gushing compliments," I say, pulling them both close to me, a cocktail of emotions mixing within me. I am delighted they could make it and to have them both close during this time, but like a gone-off strawberry dipped in chocolate, the shell is sweet but the reason we are together is bitter. "He might look fantastic, but ... he's still dead."

They both stand on either side of the open coffin, their hands resting gently on his.

"I wonder what foundation they used. It goes great with our family's skin tone," Jessie says through the tears pumping out of the blue eyes she had inherited from him.

These two together are like a comedy act, born nine months apart, with Jessie's brother born six months before Izzy, and her sister born five months before Luca. It was as though their mother Ingrid and I caught pregnancy off each other.

Jim and Ingrid were Ronan and my best friends. We all lived close to each other so that the kids grew up together. And, in doing so, Izzy and Jessie were best mates and her sister and Luca were best friends. They went to school together and stuck together like glue. Like me and Rob.

Now that it was just us, the women of the family, and the matriarch, my mother, we begin to discuss the details of the funeral.

Mam's smart speaker has been playing Mario Lanza in the background since the previous day.

"So what about music? We need something to play him out of the church," I say.

"I think Ave Maria. The Mario Lanza version. Alexa, play Ave Maria by Mario Lanza," Mam orders. The song starts. It's booming. Mam is singing along and then she interrupts herself, "Although he couldn't stand Mario Lanza."

"What? Alexa shut up," I shout. The music abruptly stops.

"But you always had him playing in the house."

"I love him. Your dad just put up with him for me. He couldn't stand him. His favourite was Nat King Cole. He died of gluttony. Can you imagine?"

"Who did? Grandad?" asks Jessie. I can see the shock on her face, looking at our much-loved waif of a man, we'd nicknamed the leprechaun, as he was so slight and small.

"No, Mario Lanza. Couldn't stop eating."

"Sounds like a good way to die. I might try it myself," I say, walking over to blow out the candle beside Dad for a while. We needed to keep him cold, didn't want him melting.

"You are not far off," Mam says, poking my slightly protruding belly as I walk by. The girls' eyes widen. Body shaming is not a concept my mother is familiar with.

I'm googling as I walk and ignore her jibes.

"I think we should play him out to this." A cartoon sketch of a boy and girl playing in a garden is on my phone and the words of 'Daisy Daisy' sing out. I am joking, of course. But then Mam says, "Yes, that's it. We should play that. It's his song." We're all laughing at the thought.

"Will the priest allow it?" asks Izzy.

"Well, what's he going to do about it?" I say. "Throw us out of the church faster than we are already walking towards the door? That's what I say to my wedding couples. Choose what you want when leaving the church. He can't throw you out, as you are already leaving."

"Who is singing it?" asks Mam. "It sounds like Nat King Cole."

"It is!"

"I didn't know he did a version of that! I don't think your dad knew either. How strange. His favourite singer singing his favourite song." She's pleased with the choice.

I go into the sunroom the following morning. The scent in the room brings back memories of the few previous wakes I attended. The very sweet, distinct scent of a relieved soul being released from its decaying body.

"Hi Dad, how are you doing?" I have a little laugh with him at the stupidity of my question. "Do you want a cup of tea?" I look at him lying there and go over and stroke his hair.

He's not in his body, but I can feel he's around and can hear me.

His little smile is still there on his face. "Big day today," I say. His last words to me, on the last day I saw him alive, before I left for Italy two months previously, ring in my ears. "I'm going to miss you terribly."

"Me too Dad. Me too," I whisper.

2

READY TO GO

When booking the afters of the funeral, they never mentioned a guest limit. I had no idea how many would turn up twenty, thirty, fifty?

"I don't know. How do you judge these things? It's not like a wedding where we can send out invites and RSVPs and with Covid it's hard to know who will travel," I say to the restaurant receptionist as I try to estimate the numbers for soup and sandwiches—the traditional pub meal after a burial in Ireland.

It turns out, a lot of people want to say goodbye to Dad. I recognise some of his old workmates, including his friend Danny, who I used to think was Moonface from Enid Blyton's Faraway Tree. He never will know how much he meant to my brain as a child.

There are my brother's friends; Tony's backroom motorbike gang, Peter's hut friends and Jim's attic friends. Cousins who knew my dad longer than I did, with their now adult children, his last sister of six siblings and my old school pal Denise. All our close and extended family except for Ronan.

Surrounded by all the familiar faces I grew up with, speaking a language I understand about times that were precious memories to us all, I'm surprised at how well I am holding it together.

People at the funeral stand around drinking, chatting like normal. While it is a sad occasion, it feels warm and cozy, surrounded by love and familiar faces. I can see their smiles.

Seventy unmasked people standing so close, socialising as if Covid didn't exist. This wouldn't happen in Italy at the moment. Actually, I do not know what a funeral is like in Italy and I'm not keen to learn anytime soon.

Looking around at all the familiar faces of relatives and friends, I can't help but think if Mam stayed in Ireland she would have a support network, it would not just be me she would be relying on. Taking her back to Italy meant there was no support, but she and I felt it was definitely the right choice for us all at this moment.

As with all Irish funerals, the get together continues back at the house, but we limit it to just direct family. We play charades with rebel Irish songs as background music.

The copious pints of Guinness I drank after the funeral have caught up with me. I'm tired and a little overwhelmed. I watch Mam basking in all the love and attention. She's doing okay, so I step out into the garden through the now empty conservatory where Dad last lay that morning.

It's a dark crisp November night, Rob is taking a walk in the back garden, having a smoke.

"Look what I found," he calls over. I go over to where Rob is and see a hedgehog rummaging in the grass.

"I haven't seen an unrolled hedgehog in years," I say as I get a flashback to Dad waking me one night when I was about three and carrying me out to the garden to show me the baby hedgehogs coming out for the first time from under Peter's hut.

"It's Da," states my four pints of Guinness and large gin and tonic. "He's come back as a hedgehog. It must be his spirit animal."

"Or maybe it's just a hedgehog, come to eat the bits of chicken that were thrown out earlier?" Rob says.

"That would seem more logical, but I think it's Da," I hiccup.

For two days after the funeral, the house is a buzz of activity with my brothers over from New York and down from the north and Rob up from Cork.

I've started to deal with the paperwork that needs to be done and am waiting for a registered document to arrive. So when I hear a knock on the door early the following morning, I know it is the postman.

"A registered letter." He hands it to me. "Permission to sign for you?" he smiles unmasked, not even arm's length away. "Because of Covid and all that," he says, as if I needed further explanation. It must have been my shocked face at his stupidity.

In Italy, the always masked delivery services drop the delivery inside your gate and move back to their van to allow you to take the package, and they sign on your behalf so that you do not have to come within Covid hopping distance. The same with the post service.

Here, in Ireland, the guy standing at my parents' door, seems to have missed the point of postal services being given permission to sign because of Covid. He is handing me the letter at the same distance I could sign for it myself, and him all the time, breathing out his possible Covid infested breath on each person he delivers to that day.

"He got a cold, but it went onto his chest and he got a pain in his ribs from coughing," says Mam when asked what caused Dad's death.

"He's had a rattle in his chest for years. I called the doctor to make an appointment but he said if he had a cough he couldn't see him without a proper Covid test. I did one of those on him that you get in the chemist, I don't know if I did it right but it showed negative but the doctor said he needed to go down to the hospital and get a PCR test. How was I meant to get him in the car and bring him half an hour in his condition? He was too sick."

"Would the doctor not do a house call?" I had asked her.

"Doctors stopped doing house calls in Ireland many years ago. And he wouldn't see him without a PCR test."

"So, what were you supposed to do?"

"He said if he has a cough and a pain, I should call an ambulance and get him brought to the hospital. Well, I wasn't going to let that happen. I knew I definitely would never see him again then. You know what the hospitals are like. The doctor prescribed an antibiotic for him and he seemed to improve a little for a couple of days."

"So no one did a proper Covid test on him?"

"No, sure the doctor couldn't even come after he had died. We had to find a care doc to sign the death cert, otherwise he would have been sent for a postmortem and everything and that would take forever."

Either of my parents needing to go to the hospital in Ireland was one of my worst fears during Covid. I can't help but feel that Dad could have possibly survived if they had just come and given him an oxygen tank beside his bed at home for a few days.

I was in our house in in Umbria when I got the call that I knew would come someday. The Irish system left my dad to die of a shortness of breath and possibly Covid.

I didn't go hysterical. I sobbed for a bit, then handed my laptop to Luca to book the flight home as my hands were trembling too much.

I gathered myself up. Washed clothes and baked them in front of the fire to dry for the morning.

While packing to go back to Ireland, something fell off my bedroom dressing table as I grabbed my travel wash bag. It was an old Miraculous Medal I had found in the Sighing House the day we bought it eighteen months ago. Dad loved the symbolism of Miraculous Medals and had a deep devotion to the image of Our Lady etched on them. I hadn't seen one in years. I put it in my wash bag.

I'd put it in with Dad in his coffin so he could have a little piece of Italy, a little piece of the house where he was to come and live the following spring, completing my Italian dream.

It was now time to focus on Mam and getting her back to Italy with me, where I could look after her, keep her company and, at eighty-five years of age, give her a new start.

———

On the first day of quiet after everyone had gone home after the wake, I went into a cleaning frenzy. It's what I do at the end of a wedding season, the end of a book, the end of a stage in my life.

Mam is all business too. "We should probably clear out his stuff," she calls to me from the bedroom.

I had already bundled his coats into a bag and put it in a corner for the recycling bin.

"Okay. Do you need a hand?" I call out ahead of myself, already bringing her in a roll of plastic bags.

"No, I can do it." She opens the wardrobe, grabs the five hangers holding up Dad's three shirts and two pairs of trousers, folds them over on themselves and stuffs them into one bag. "Done. That wasn't too difficult, was it?"

Dad was a man of few possessions.

"It's not going to take much to prepare to go away. I won't be bringing much. I can shop over there."

I'm thinking about how problematic that will be. Sizes are smaller in Italy, I am a UK size 12-14. In Italy I've bought clothes labelled UK size 16 that wouldn't be close to closing on me and that's the biggest size a lot of shops stock. As Mam is a size 20 midriff, finding clothes shops she can browse was going to be difficult.

"Perhaps we should go shopping before we go to Italy?" I suggest.

Mam's face lights up. "Well, his money is mine now!"

Dad was indeed the saver and my mother was definitely the spender in their relationship.

"When will we leave for Italy?" asks Mam as we drive to the shopping centre.

"Whenever you feel ready to."

"I think I'll be ready in a few days. No point hanging around here getting miserable, like the weather. The weather is better in Italy, isn't it?"

"Everything feels better in Italy, Ma."

3

SIGNS

We go to the store that has several boutiques on one floor, all with the style of clothes Mam likes. It's her favourite place to shop and today she is going to shop unrestricted. Within half an hour, I have become a walking clothes horse.

An assistant comes to help and removes several layers from my arms, putting them beside the till. My mother quickly replaces these with several more layers.

"I think we have enough now Ma, we will not be able to fit all this in one suitcase."

"Then we'll buy another suitcase," she says, laughing, completely loving her unadulterated shopping spree for the first time in her eighty-five years.

By the time we are paying, I realise I do not have enough arms nor strength to carry all the bags, so I tell the assistant to store half of them for me and I'll come back later.

I drop Mam home and go back into town after lunch, which is 2pm in Ireland, not 4pm like Italy. Ingrid has come in too, but goes in the opposite direction to get a scheduled eye test.

I am glad to get out and have some time to myself for a wander through the familiar cobbled streets; lined with the shops where I bought my kids their school uniforms and shoes, book shops I loved to linger in, and the familiar coffee shop I'd meet friends in.

Everyone is oblivious that I was standing beside a grave the day before, weeping goodbye to the physical remains of my father. It makes me feel more sympathetic to each individual I see. Who knows what they went through the day before or in their lifetime?

Armed with the overstuffed bags of Mam's shopping, I leave the mall and realise I didn't ask Ingrid which opticians she was going to. There are several on the same street as the clothes shop. I peer in the window of the one right next to the mall, to see if I can spot her and I am faced with a ceramic ornament beside a glasses display. It's a hedgehog smiling at me.

I walk down the street and remember I want to buy a birthday card for my friend. Italy lacks a good selection of greeting cards; Hallmark has failed miserably to establish itself there, as have fast-food chains and branded coffee shops. Italians don't seem to be fooled by consumerism. They prefer quality that lasts.

The same goes for the season of Christmas. Christmas spirit starts later in Italy than other parts of the western world, but lasts longer and is much less commercialised. They wait until the sixth December to turn on the Christmas lights and the celebrations go on until the sixth January.

Here in Ireland, it's mid-November, and already the shops are thriving with every gift possible for the person who already has everything. The constant need to buy for Christmas is shoved in your face at every opportunity.

I go into a card shop and the first card I spot has a hedgehog on it. "Dad," I mutter to myself and smile at the coincidence of his newly acclaimed spirit animal popping up in front of me. "I'm heading back to the carpark, follow me when you are ready," texts Ingrid.

I swivel around and head back up the street. I am familiar with this town and know a shortcut to the carpark. The bags are weighing me down so much they are burning into my finger joints.

There are crowds of people out, and no one is wearing a mask. Back in Italy, people still need to be masked outside. It's the first time I have seen a street of facial expressions in two years. Happy, worried, bored. I cut down the pedestrian street lined with some of my favourite shops.

Even though I'm on a time limit before the bag handles sever my fingers off, I take a moment to savour the familiarity, the voices speaking, rushed words I can understand.

Snippets of conversation feed my story creating mind. I don't have this pleasure in Italy. Italy enlivens other senses though; the sound of cicadas, toads and medieval drumming and the heavy scent of jasmine, rosemary and lavender in the summer, fermenting grapes in the autumn and roasted chestnuts in the winter. I don't get any of that in Ireland.

"Excuse me, can I share this with you?" I glance toward a gangly, well-dressed man with a shock of thick white hair and a kind face. A woman slows and takes what the man is offering and moves on with a smile and a nod. The curly haired, designated bag holder woman with him also has a welcoming face. They are standing in off the path in a doorway beside the catholic church that will host carols from next week—the sign beside them announces. I still can't read signs quickly in Italy.

People are rushing by, not looking. He says it again, but this time to me. There is enough space between us for two busy people to fit through. I am tempted to just nod a quick smile and not to stop my pace, but something compels me to hesitate. Perhaps it's hearing someone speak to me and me not having to think of the words, perhaps it's just me feeling sorry for them trying to share their enthusiasm with an ignoring crowd. "Go on then," I say, taking the two horizontal steps needed to be beside him and to rest one of my group of bags on the ground.

"It's the power of prayer. It really is miraculous. This is the prayer." On a small square piece of paper he has the 'Our Father' printed in bold black ink, my favourite prayer when sung at mass growing up. "And this, this is the rosary." He hands me a small plastic bag with a small circle of white plastic beads enough for one decade of the rosary and a small cross in the middle to know where to stop and start when you keep them in your pocket.

A familiar blue picture of Our Lady of Lourdes is the backing for the beads.

"Let me give you this as well." He delves into his pocket and withdraws a small plastic baggy, the same type and size you see cocaine dealers use on TV. "It's truly miraculous, it's Our Lady and the power of this prayer is truly—"

In the bag there is another small, printed picture and prayer serving as a backup to a Miraculous Medal hanging on a pale blue piece of wool. A copy of the same medal I brought from the house in Italy for Dad.

I remember being handed the same package by a visiting missionary to our school when I was about ten and it was always tradition for my grandmother and mother to give a Miraculous Medal to newborn babies of the family.

" I know Our Lady... she was a favourite of my dad... He died the other day. Buried yesterday," I blurt out.

The man pauses. "Oh, I am truly sorry."

He means it.

The woman has sympathy and a touch of pain for me in her eyes. I have said "My dad died" for the first time, and my mouth was so hungry for me to say it out loud that is has gobbled up all my other words. With the little coke bag in my already crowded hand, I nod and quickly walk away without thanking them.

My eyes are stinging, like when I was a teenager and tried cheap eyeliner for the first time, giving me an eye infection for a week. The busy people walking towards me are blurry. They divide and flow past the tugboat like woman weighed down by a cargo of shopping bags and a scrunched-up face. I take deep breaths. "Don't think about it, don't think about it." I get myself back under control. I have myself composed before I get to the carpark but Ingrid sees my eyes.

"Are you okay?" She smiles, knowing too well what I am going through.

"You were right about the triggers happening when you least expect it. I did okay at the hedgehog but fell at the Miraculous Medal."

4

DELIVERIES

"You know you will have to feed Ma?" Rob sniggers. "I'm serious." My cooking has always been the butt of their jokes.

My sister was the hostess with the mostest, and I could never live up to her standards. Rob loves cooking and was always keen to know what we were cooking in Italy for the first few months we moved there, but he soon stopped asking after he tired of hearing spaghetti bolognese or chicken with rice repeatedly.

"Can you even poach an egg?"

"Of course I can."

I can because in the top drawer in Mam's kitchen I have seen a packet of 'Poachies; fail proof poached eggs in eight minutes. As Seen on TV!'

"Do you want tea?" I ask.

Before Rob answers, I am already in my mother's kitchen retrieving the 'Poachies' and slipping them into my suitcase, as I don't actually know how to poach an egg—Mam's favourite breakfast food.

A perk of being a wedding planner is that I get to experience amazing food in Italy, as I am invited to eat at Michelin star restaurants and hotels catered by amazing chefs. And as I do weddings, the caterers I use always have to be fantastic, so I get to eat some very nice dinners during the wedding season.

However, that's not everyday life. I never caught the Italian cooking bug. Yes, we have found some great restaurants and even our local pizzerias serve pizza worthy of a last meal on the green mile. But we mostly cook at home, especially in the last two years, and our cookery efforts are quite limited. It's not because I am a terrible cook, it is because when I go to the supermarkets in Italy, I am a bit stumped. The supermarkets are very different from the big chains at home in Ireland.

In Ireland, you can walk miles of aisles and come out with an overloaded trolley of fruit and veg imported from around the world with ready-made kits and sauces so you can create eclectic, exotic meals quickly and easily, accompanied by wines from the same places. Even the potatoes are often imported.

In Italy, it is different. Wine from another country, other than Italy, is unheard of, so I needed to give up my liking for Australian and New Zealand wines. The basics like tacos, tortillas, sweet and sour sauce just do not exist in most shops. Actually, any sauce other than something tomato or basil-based does not seem to exist in our local shops in Italy. As for fruit and veg, most are near zero kilometres, meaning they are grown locally.

Other than bananas and pineapples, the odd rack of Sicilian lemons was as far-flung as you got in the fruit and veg aisle.

Most other fresh produce is farmed locally and within the seasons. Asparagus in autumn? Are you damn crazy? That's a spring vegetable picked in the local forests. Blood oranges in summer? Hold my drink while I laugh so hard. Oranges are a winter fruit, you silly woman.

So, back in Italy, we go to the supermarkets that stock limited supplies in our eyes, and we walk the aisles of different shaped pastas and jars of various tomato sauce. We look at the quirky cheeses and choose the safe bet of mozzarella. We visit the meat fridges and frown at the fully skinned rabbits, the boney chickens not plumped by pumped-in water, and choose a styrofoam tray of minced cow and go home and cook up yet another spaghetti bolognese.

I knew good Italian food existed, but I didn't know how to put the pieces together. Yes, I had recipe books written in English, but finding the required ingredients in the local shops meant translating everything I needed, and then, inevitably not finding some key ingredients, so we'd end up with dishes that 'had potential' but were never tried again.

We couldn't go out to eat because of Covid, and I think I would rather eat dog food, which also had a full aisle to itself including orange flavoured mix and pasta for dogs, rather than eat spaghetti bolognese again.

I begin to sweat; I don't know if it's a midlife hot flush or the pure terror of not living up to the dining expectations of my 85-year-old mother who was moving in with me for the first time since I'd become an adult.

So, I text Karen. "I need to learn to cook... bloody hell, why can't I cook in the country most famous for cooking? And I need to learn Italian... what if Ma needs a doctor? I would have no clue what to say or how to call one... why can I not speak Italian after four years of living in Italy? Am I bloody thick? I can't even find an egg poacher."

"Deep breaths," pops up on my screen. Karen knows me so well. She can sense my panic.

"There is a food delivery company, they are all over Europe I think; you choose recipes from their site and they deliver you all the ingredients and recipe cards. I have never used them, but I've seen them advertise on social media and they look good. I'll try to find it and send you the link."

I put an order in. It's in Italian which sometimes might as well be Chinese to me. But I think I have found my way around the site.

The two weeks following the funeral are filled with paperwork regarding pensions, the funeral, bank accounts, their will, bills and ensuring Mam has everything she needs like her prescription, new glasses, her European health card, as well as arguing with her over the stuff she's packing.

"I have a cheese grater and a potato peeler. You don't need to pack them."

While trying to organise everything for my mother to move to Italy at short notice, there is also the ever-looming concern of trying to sort out our car back in Italy. My car insurance is nearly up and changing the plates on our Irish car over to Italian ones still hasn't happened yet.

"I went up about it, but the woman just started asking for my cock again," says Ronan, giving me the latest update of his adventures at the car registration office back in Italy. "She said they have changed the system because stolen cars are being brought in from eastern Europe."

"So they make it more difficult for everyone rather than just ensuring the paperwork we all do, including the Eastern European importers, is correct?" I am not looking for an answer, just expressing my frustration. I love Italy, but the bureaucracy behind trying to get things done is soul draining.

"We need a plan, as you have to pick us up from the airport in three days' time."

"I'll do car hire. There's a place in town I'll go to."

Ronan goes to the car hire place with a courtyard full of cars. It has a sign on the door saying it is closed until the spring. He calls the number, as he knows the guy can speak English.

"I need a long-term rental."

"Sorry we are closed."

"But I have business for you. After Covid, do you not want it?"

"Sorry we are closed until Spring," he repeats.

Ronan turns to the yogis—my group of expat friends from yoga who are a gold mine of info and help—Sherwin has a car hire contact based at the airport.

"Ah, you are a friend of Sherwin, so I will give you the best deal," he greets Ronan with, and gives Ronan a car out of season for €340 for two weeks. That should get us through to when the car changeover finally happens.

"The electric chair has arrived," says Ronan only days after I ordered it from Germany, as every Italian site would take at least twenty days. "It's not the type of electric chair I had in mind for my mother-in-law." I am lucky to have such an understanding husband who is looking forward to welcoming my mother to live with us permanently at the drop of a hat.

I've a heap of other online orders being delivered to Italy before we get back to make Mam's life in Italy more comfortable; a shower chair, a disability frame for the bathroom, bedside table, side table, sheets and pillows.

Daily, I am checking in with Ronan about deliveries.

"Another box of food has arrived," is his usual response.

I must have pressed the button too many times on the order from the place Karen told me about. So far, five boxes of ingredients with recipes have arrived. I cannot remember the path I took to ordering them. Cancelling will have to wait until I get back.

Leaving Ireland was relatively easy. Ingrid and Jim drove us to the airport, and we had booked disability assistance.

Arriving at the airport, an assistant takes Mam's massive suitcase to be checked in only to return to say it is 10kg over and they charge €10 per kg. So €100 later, the bag—mostly full of things Mam does not need in Italy, but she has insisted on bringing — is checked through.

She is deposited in a wheelchair and whisked through security to the boarding gate at breakneck speed, with me hot on her heels.

We flew to Pisa as the time of the plane was more reasonable than Rome and I thought the drive through the Tuscan countryside might be nicer than the motorway for Mam. I was right. Ronan arrives at the airport in a very nice Fiat to collect us.

Mam cries when she sees Ronan and I cry too. We had said goodbye to Dad, who Ronan loved so much, without him there, and now we were embarking on our new adventure together. Well, that's what we thought.

Luca decided to stay on in Ireland an extra week. He has a girl-friend there and has converted to being a complete hippy. No surprise there, as it was how me and Ronan were at his age.

He's turned into a complete socialist, vegetarian, wanting to campaign about everything. He's added in the whole hatred of the system and has 'radical' thoughts about how disgusting it is that his friends have to work in a pizza takeaway for just a minimal wage.

"It's because they are still studying and don't have a quali-fication."

I find myself saying; "When I was your age, I would have been delighted to get a job in a takeaway, but there were literally no jobs to get. We had a choice of London or America after school. I collected aluminium cans from the field-drinking sites around where I lived after each weekend and sold them for 50p a sack. That is how I got my money for my train ticket to Germany, where I had my first real job cleaning toilets in a hotel and I was delighted about it."

The 'when I was your age' statement whizzes me into an old age category.

He's moaning because there are no secondhand clothes shops in Italy. When he's in Ireland, that's where he goes with his friends to buy clothes, so as not to buy into the whole fast fashion industry.

It's weird when your teenage kids start lecturing you on beliefs that have always been just part of your life, not a big statement gesture. They just never realised it.

I've always loved secondhand shops. It's like going on a treasure hunt. I still have a top I wear which I bought in a Boston church sale when I was twenty-one. In Italy, particularly in the south, taking secondhand clothes is a no no, unless it is passed down from immediate family. You are extremely poor if you wear secondhand clothes. Even if you have a baby and all your friends have older babies, Italians would not take hand-me-downs.

I've chatted with my Italian friends, Ben and his wife Ellie, about this. "We love to buy classy, beautiful things that last. We are used to beauty, and it is in our DNA. I suffer when I see people wearing shoes that are not well made or with good material. I notice it immediately and suffer," Ben says, as if I was making him wear cheap shoes that were three sizes too small for him for the rest of his life.

"Charity shops like you have in Ireland or the UK would not work at all in Italy. Good quality clothes from family and friends are okay, as this sounds hygienically acceptable to us," adds Ellie. "We do like vintage clothes and antiques. We go to the mercatino dell'antiquariato for these. Italians value old things and we are happy to pay a lot for them, but we always try to 'fare l'affare'. Get a discount. But we buy stuff we intend to keep forever."

Helga shares my love of secondhand shops and briefly looked into setting up a charity shop in Italy. "Unfortunately, even charities are taxed high in Italy, even if they are non-profit. And the regulations involved in setting up in retail is bloody expensive. Unless this all changes, we won't have charity or second-hand shops in Italy."

I'll just have to leave hippy me aside in Italy and get more class.

5

NEW WHEELS

I t's a beautiful sunny winter's day as we drive through the Tuscan countryside. I thought Mam would be wondrous about the towns perched on hills built on the side of precipices, where villages melt on to rocks, but she's more fascinated about the tilled fields.

"Look at how straight that tilling is, how fine the soil is. I wonder what they will grow in it?" she says in amazement, looking over the undulating burrowed field where a queue of white egrets hop along behind the tilling tractor.

For the whole two-hour journey, her fascination with the fields grow. You'd swear she was a farmer back in Ireland.

We're nearly home.

"There's that car again, the Ferrari with the horrible wrap," I say, pointing out the parked car with the woman sitting in.

We've been puzzled by this woman who we see parked under the bridge regularly. She sits and talks on her phone or just adjusting things in her modern Ferrari. I've seen her standing outside the car the odd time; long silky black hair and dressed in a way only a beautiful Italian can dress.

"It's so weird. What do you think she is, an escort or drug dealer?" Ronan is thinking out loud and not waiting for me to answer. "She must do great business under the bridge to afford a Ferrari, I give her that. But why would anyone buy a Ferrari and then put a horrible wrap on it that looks like cheap gift wrap?"

"Ronan, don't be such an arse. If it was a guy, would you presume he was selling his body or illegal drugs?"

"Well, whether it be a man or woman, I would think they had no morals if they did that to their car. I mean, what the hell?"

I won't let Ronan brand a woman as being an escort or drug dealer just because she is driving a Ferrari. However, while I am not a car fanatic, I do think covering a Ferrari in plastic camouflage wrap is beyond any belief of any taste. She's really letting the side down.

Arriving at the front door, two very excited dogs, Paddy and Looney, greet us, along with Spooky, our very affectionate tailless black cat.

"The house is huge," is Mam's first response, although she has seen it many times by video tour. She plonks herself into the throne-sized electric armchair, orders a glass for the bottle of whiskey Ronan left for her, and puts her feet up. Ma has arrived and is ready to be served.

But she will have to wait. I'm running around the house like a lunatic taking all the newly decorated rooms in; the hall is more pinky than the cappuccino colour I ordered, but other than that I'm loving the transformation that Alex, Ivor and Ronan have done while I've been away.

The bedrooms are now painted beautifully, and with the warmth of the radiators and polished doors with door handles that work, they feel fresh, cozy, and inviting. All they are missing is furniture and character. That is our next step.

I show Mam her room and bathroom. Ronan constructed the brass Aladdin's bed in Mam's room as I had requested. "Oh, that's too big. It will have to go. I don't need a bed that big."

"Oh, okay. I thought you'd like it."

"Ah no, I'll get myself a single bed. Where's the dining room?"

"I don't have one. Well, not yet. It's an odd house as I don't have a room big enough downstairs for a dining room, I don't think."

"But where's the dining table for Christmas dinner?" she asks.

"I think there is a table upstairs we can use."

"Ah, we have to have a table, Rosie. I want to decorate it! Let's have a look at where we can put it..." She is shuffling around, finding her way around the rooms. "You can put one in the hall, make it the banqueting hall," she decides. "I'm surprised you don't have a table."

"Ma, this house was completely different when I left it three weeks ago. It was a building site in recovery."

"Well, you'll have to get a table."

"Yes, I know! There are a lot of things we have to get. Furnishing the house is our next step, but I'm only in the door. Give me a chance!"

The pressure is on. She has only been here five minutes, and she has already turned into an Italian. Italians always eat at a table. They would never eat sitting on the sofa watching TV, for example. Not that we like to do that either. However, the breakfast bar in the kitchen or the upside-down cardboard box acting as a coffee table in the sitting room are currently our only dining surface options.

When the kids were small, we got a huge oval table from a secondhand yard and it was where we'd eat and chat. I really miss having that central hub. So if we are going to get a table, it is going to be a proper big table where we can gather with friends and family and have that sense of togetherness again.

"Anyway, even if you don't have a dining table, what are you making me for dinner? I'm starving."

Usually on a day like this, Ronan and I would head to a favourite restaurant so we don't have to cook after all the driving and travelling, but I know Mam is too tired from travelling to go sit in a restaurant. She needs to raise her feet and rest her back.

"Let me just get changed and washed up and I'll have a look. Don't worry, I'll feed you," I say, joking, but I am worried. I don't know what I am going to feed her.

"Okay, so where are these food boxes?" I say to Ronan, unsure of what to expect. I don't have to ask twice. In the corner of the kitchen, there are five boxes stacked on top of each other. "I took all the frozen stuff and perishables out of each and piled them in the fridge, but we are running out of space."

"This looks easy and quick," I say, choosing a carbonara-style recipe from one box. In the fridge, I find the corresponding numbered ingredients.

Ricotta and Pecorino cheese, pancetta, walnuts and spaghetti.

I use the very cool translating app where I hold my phone screen over a paragraph of writing and it magically translates it, giving me the step-by-step preparation instructions in English.

However, I give reading it aloud in Italian a go, while I put the water on to boil and mix the ricotta with half the pecorino and chop the walnuts.

The instructions say don't salt the boiling water until you are just about to put the pasta in. And to keep some of the pasta water aside to add to the cheese sauce to make it the right consistency. Two cooking tips I did not know before. Within thirty minutes, I present Mam and Ronan with a delicious carbonara garnished with walnuts.

"Hmmm. Wasn't expecting this. That's way too much for me..." says Mam looking at her plate of unfamiliar deliciousness.

"You don't have any potatoes, no?"

"Give it a go," I say.

Five minutes later, I hear her scraping her plate.

"That was surprisingly good. I wasn't expecting to like it. Especially as you made it, haha," she says, handing me the empty plate.

The following day, Karen comes to visit and I decide to make another pasta dish from the magic deliveries. She helps me figure out how to cancel my online order of food boxes as yet another one arrived that afternoon.

I've chosen a recipe that includes a pasta called "Strozzapreti."

"Strozzapreti?" says Karen, looking at the packet.

"You know that means 'Priest Strangler'? I've heard about this pasta. The Church used to take all the eggs produced by the peasants, leaving them to make pasta and a living solely on water, salt and flour. So people used to make this pasta for when the clergy would come by.

The priests expected to be fed well, so the women who made the pasta by hand would speak its name as a type of curse against the clergymen who they were preparing it for. They hoped that the long, corkscrew shape would make it difficult to swallow the pasta quickly without choking."

We google it to make sure I am not going to feed Mam something she could choke on. And it is confirmed, that while no official records of such choking events can be found, people in Italy have entertained the idea for centuries.

Numerous stories, plays, jokes, and songs, including an eight century Neapolitan comedy, use phrases like "macaroni-strozza-preti," which means "priest stranglers of macaroni."

In a play called Della Porta, a character named La Sorella says: "Come on, the master is awaiting you at the table with a plate of extraordinarily large macaroni that will strangle you as soon as it's put into your mouth."

In her drama La Cucina Napoletana, Caròla Francesconi tells the story of a hungry priest who sits down to dinner at a parishioner's house in a poor section of town. After being served by the housewife, he suffocates on a helping of gnocchi after trying to eat it too fast.

Strozzapreti, becomes one of my favourite go-to pastas.

Mam again clears her plate. "Hmmm, that was very nice. Different. But do you not have potatoes here?"

"I'm sensing you are not that fond of my pasta dishes?" I say.

"No, they are nice. I am just wondering, do you not have potatoes? Some chips would be nice. I love a nice big pot full of chips or mash."

"Tomorrow I'll bring you to the supermarket and you can buy all the potatoes and whatever else you want."

"Oh, don't go out of your way for me. What day do you usually do your grocery shopping on?"

"I don't have a particular day, Ma. We just buy what we need when we need it."

"What? What sort of planning is that?" She guffaws as if we are complete morons. "Oh, I'll organise you. Wait and see. Don't you worry." It sounds like a threat.

The supermarket does not impress Mam.

"They've no Bisto? That chicken is very expensive and yellow and skinny."

"That's because it's not pumped up with water in a factory to make it look bigger than it is, which is what they do back home, I believe. "

"They've no cheddar cheese. They've no ordinary white sliced pans? Where are the sausages?... They look horrendous. How am I going to make coddle out of them?"

I am glad they are horrendous in her eyes. I have always hated salty coddle–a traditional Dublin soup-like meal made from boiled sausages, rashers, onions and potatoes. My dad loved it.

"Where are the bags of spuds? ... Is that it? Can you not get a bigger sack of spuds? Sure, I'd eat all of them in one go myself," she says, looking at the net bag with about ten potatoes in it.

Flashbacks came flooding back to when we were growing up in Dublin and the vegetable delivery man would deliver two four stone bags of spuds each week for the eight of us to eat our way through, living in our little bungalow. Two full colanders of peeled potatoes steamed and then mashed five days per week served with a lamb or pork chop, piece of meat or chicken.

On Sundays, a roast chicken or roast beef with mashed and roast potatoes. A stew on Monday. On Fridays Mam's famous homemade chips with fresh cod bought direct from the fishermen in Howth that morning.

I then show her the full rabbits they sell, stripped of their skin and ears and cellophaned onto a large styrofoam tray.

"Oh God, what would you do with that? And the chicken breasts, they are just sold on the bone or in such thin slices. I'll get some on the bone, better than the wafers. I'll keep them in the freezer and boil them up whenever I need them."

"Boiled chicken?"

"Yes, with some boiled potatoes."

"That's a lot of boiling."

The only thing that impressed her is the price of whiskey.

"Only €16 a bottle! This is great. Get me three just in case they run out."

Karen has come to help me navigate a few things I need to get for Mam. The first being a wheelchair, so I can take her out for walks along the lake.

"We'll find a Sanitaria shop near you," says Karen. "There's one in practically every town in Italy and they sell all the disability aids and supplies you need, but first we'll try the pharmacy, the bigger ones often have wheelchairs to hire and some sell them."

So, we go to the big pharmacy in town that has a wholefood section for celiacs, much to Karen's approval. They sell orthopaedic shoes, walking sticks and an entire wall of different types of incontinence pads with wonderful illustrations and photos modelling the different styles on each package. Some look quite sexy.

The pharmacy has a wheelchair available to buy. Great. They wheel it out and the assistant says she thinks it's €130, but she needs to check. It has been used as a hire out, so has a few scratches and a strap is missing from the footrest, but we don't need that.

Then the head pharmacist comes out and looks up the price. These models are €290 new she explains.

"So how much can we have it for?"

"€290."

"But it is not new. It is secondhand."

"We do not have secondhand prices, only new."

"Okay then, we will leave it and go buy a new one for the new price somewhere else," I say.

A twenty-minute drive later, we are wheeling out a brand-new wheelchair of the same brand from the Sanitaria shop, which is an Aladdin's cave of equipment and aids for the elderly and disabled. She even gave us a discount, so we got it for €260.

Ronan is so excited at the arrival of the new toy, "Can I have a go?"

"No! Ma first." I tell him off. Mam sits herself in the unfolded wheelchair in the hallway and Ronan takes control.

"It's grand, isn't it?" he says, spinning Mam around at high speed. She's laughing like a schoolgirl while I am shouting at him to stop. It's my 85-year-old mother he has in the chair, but they are not listening, just laughing hysterically. Two Aquarians without a care in the world, other than an anxious Piscean to watch out for them.

White Walnut Pasta

Serves: 4

200g Ricotta

2 handfuls of chopped walnuts

80g Grated pecorino

Spaghetti (enough for 4 people)

200g Pancetta (chopped up small or cubed)

Method:

Cook the pasta according to the instructions on the packet. Add a pinch of salt to the boiling water before adding in the pasta. Chop the walnuts.

Heat a pan and fry the pancetta in its own fat for 3-4 minutes. Add half the walnuts and continue to fry for about 2 minutes.

In a bowl, mix the ricotta and pecorino. Add some of the pasta water to make it a thick creamy texture.

Turn off the heat and add the pasta into the pan of pancetta and walnuts and toss together. Then add the creamy ricotta and pecorino. Stir until the pasta is evenly coated.

If needed, add a little more of the pasta water to make it into a creamier consistency.

Add some salt and pepper to taste if needed. Divide between four plates and sprinkle with some grated pecorino and chopped walnuts.

6

CHIPS & NETTLES

The week that follows is full-on. There is a Christmas tree to be found and decorating to be done before the kids arrive home.

Luca is arriving back the following day and even though he has only been gone an additional week to us, I want to have the house decorated to welcome him home. I have missed his wit and view of the world.

Like me, Mam loves decorating for Christmas or any seasonal occasion; any excuse for a big get together in her eyes is good. I take out the Christmas decoration boxes I had brought from Ireland to check what we had. The first thing Mam asks is, "where's your crib?"

"We don't have one."

"You have to have a crib."

Growing up, the crib was the centrepiece in our entrance hall during Christmas. A place where I would hide all the good things I'd done, written on tiny bits of paper to make baby Jesus happy for his birthday. Christmas without a crib is sacrilege in Mam's eyes.

So off we go, with Ronan driving, to one of the big DIY shops that has a whole Christmas decoration section. The Italians don't just have simple cribs with the holy family; they build nativity scenes, whole towns like mini movie sets. There are not just figurines to choose from but surrounding buildings, props like elephants, cats, watermills, wells and lighting.

Mam is in her element with the vast range of figurines that take up an entire aisle. "We need the holy family, three wise men and shepherds," she says, while I have already trollied a Christmas gnome that will look great in the hallway.

"Let's get this set of three that includes a shepherd," I say. She agrees without really looking. She is more concerned about which size baby Jesus to get.

The other two figures in the packet of shepherd cast members I have chosen are a shepherdess girl with a vessel of wine on her head and the other is a shepherd-looking character with a pizza in his hand. We are in Italy, after all.

Mam, of course, wants to buy the gaudiest clashing-coloured ornaments while I would like something slightly colour themed. She wins and in a very short time, our trolley is stuffed with garlands, gnomes, candles, baubles, boxes of lights, Christmas fake flowers and a gang of nativity scene characters.

"Can we buy a bed here?" asks Mam, who keeps mentioning how ridiculous the double bed is in her room.

"Not here. We'd need to go to the furniture shop. We can stop at it on the way home as we need to get a new sofa too."

There is no way I'm having another Christmas with the diarrhea sofa and I wouldn't have enough time to re-upholster the one that I had salvaged from the house. A new blue velvet sofa that we could all fit on was on all our wish lists since we lost our home to the bank in Ireland over eight years ago.

"That one will do," Mam says to the first single bed she sees.

"Well, the mattress is sold separately to the beds here, so choose the mattress you want then the bed."

"Sure they are all the same. Just something firm and in single size."

"I think a single is going to be too small for you, Ma."

"No, it's not. It's what I want. Now here's the money, just get it." So I pay for the bed and the mattress. Both will be delivered in two days. It's a Christmas miracle we don't have to wait the usual standard twenty days.

Looking around the sofas for sale, there is nothing I like in this store. Besides, their sofa delivery time is at least twenty days, so that won't do. Ronan is impatient as always and tries to persuade me to agree to an ugly-looking sofa that is available to take today. He's using the same line as Mam, "This one will do."

But this is something I am not compromising on. "I'll check online for something like the couch we all liked when we looked together two years ago. It needs to be blue velvet."

Next, we take Mam to the homeware store for her to buy whatever she wants for her room to make it her own. She decides on a plastic set of drawers like you'd keep vegetables in. I had forgotten my mother's love affair with plastic and kitchen gadgets. Her cupboards at home are stuffed with them. That will not happen here, so I steer her away from the plastic gadget aisles.

"That was a good day's shopping, time for whiskey!" proclaims Mam, settling herself into her electric throne.

Ronan and I leave Mam to sort through her purchases while we go to buy the Christmas tree with the van. We learnt too late the year before where we can buy decent sized Christmas trees and not the tiny ones most Italians seem happy with. It was just after we spent €120 for a live tree that promptly died in the Mediterranean summer heat, but did the honourable thing of lasting long enough for our Summer Christmas when Izzy could get back after Covid flight restrictions were lifted. We find a good-sized one that will fit in our hallway for our first real Christmas in the house. Yes, we moved in the previous Christmas eve, but it was such a dreadful week that I just threw the decorations up out of necessity rather than with love or any attention.

Having Mam here to decorate the house and the tree for our first proper Christmas in the house is such a comfort. I don't have to worry about her anymore. I can look after her here.

After living in bungalows most of my life, I have always wanted to 'deck the halls' of a house and now, with a series of winding bannisters in my very own house, I can actually do it. The ivy on the old shed is perfect for the task. I cut a heap, choosing the longest stems with profusions of berries, and then soak it overnight in an old tub in the garden.

The following day, I leave it out to dry before bringing it into the house, insect-free and hydrated enough to last at least two weeks of the Christmas season.

Mam helps me wire together a long garland. Remembering what she taught me during her stint as a florist, I shear off the leaves and spray the berries gold, before adding touches of snow spray after I have wired it to two flights of bannisters.

Next, I wind the long string of fairy lights and dot very convincing, realistic silk flowers through it. I do the same for our huge stone mantlepiece in the sitting room, before hanging two stockings on each side, as we have always done for our kids.

Fairy lights are laced through the growing trailing Devil's Ivy that always seems to grow profusely in every house I own due to my lack of care.

The front door still needs to be refurbished and the garland I have had since our first house in Ireland is looking a bit sad. So, Mam takes it in hand and with the smell of freshly cut cypress, some Christmas baubles and a string of battery lights, she makes it look new again.

Mam sings along to the Christmas carols while she sets up the Christmas nativity scene, including the pizza delivery Shepherd, on the drinks trolley she spent several days cleaning and polishing. The hearth glowing orange, fairy lights twinkling everywhere and Christmas spice essence burning in the defuser, the house feels soaked in Christmas spirit.

It's been a tough twelve months for Mam... her best-friend-sister died the previous Christmas morning, her last brother passed away only a few months ago... also her beloved dog and companion for sixteen years and of course my dad only weeks before. And yet she remains upbeat and ready to share a smile with whoever needs it. She's definitely an inspiration.

That evening, I order a sofa online after much deliberating. It is from a French shop and I'm sure it is the same sofa we had all agreed was the perfect sofa for us about two years ago. Blue velvet, deep cushioned seats and a chaise end for me to fall asleep on while everyone else enjoys a movie. It will arrive in the shop for collection or delivery the day before Izzy is due to arrive.

For dinner, I make tortillas with mince and lots of tasty ingredients as instructed by the recipe sheet. It's absolutely delicious.

Mam gobbles it up again, protesting and telling me off for giving her way too much, but clears her plate none the less. I've also made chips, oven chips, sprinkled with spices, but they haven't crisped up. I am not sure what went wrong as I followed the instructions on the recipe sheet, but they are pale and look in need of some Viagra.

"Did you like your dinner, Ma?"

"The mince was nice... but the chips... do you not have a chip pan?"

Mam loves her chips. Growing up, her chip pot was famous. A cast-iron pot that never got washed. The oil changed about once a month, but the pot never saw water or soap.

She has a thing against properly cleaning anything that you use oil on or in. "What are you doing putting the frying pan in the dishwasher?" she screeched, laughing at me only the day before.

"To clean it?"

"Just give it a rub with some kitchen paper. You don't put frying pans in dishwashers, it will remove the glaze and make everything you fry on it stick."

"Well, I'd prefer a clean frying pan that some things stick to, than a sticky frying pan with things stuck to it," I answered, closing the dishwasher with the frying pan safely impounded.

"You have to have a deep fat-fryer," she states.

Even the words 'deep fat fryer' make me want to throw up. I hate the dirty, smelly, greasy things.

Even though the kitchen cupboards are heaving with foodstuffs for the few days of Christmas, Mam is still finding we are missing crucial additional ingredients to make it perfect.

So, the following morning, before Luca arrives back, we go to the supermarket again. It's a bit of an ordeal each time and takes three times longer than me going by myself or a lot longer than if I did my usual and just gave Ronan a list and stayed at home.

"I need to get a deep-fat fryer; do they sell them here?" Mam asks while in the supermarket to buy the immediate need for CIF cleaning cream and a mop.

"No, Ma, we'd need to go to the electric shop for something like that."

"Do they not sell electric stuff here? Or clothes?" she says, thinking of the mega stores back in Ireland that sell everything, including kitchen basin sinks.

"No, just groceries and some cleaning stuff."

"That's stupid."

"You don't have a microwave either," she adds.

I am unsure if she is blaming me or Italy for this flaw. But I can see her disdain growing. I hate microwaves nearly as much as I hate deep-fat fryers and chip pans.

"Do you even have nettles in Italy?"

I don't know how she just jumped out of the frying pan conversation into nettles.

"I think so, but not in a shop."

"Of course not in the shop," she scoffs, "but in the garden. I need them for my arthritis."

While she is searching the shelves for her favourite brand of whiskey, I google to see if nettles are native to Italy and sure enough it was probably the Romans who brought the seeds with them to the British Isles two thousand years ago, as they used nettles to tenderise meat. My search also suggests that the Roman soldiers used to lash themselves with nettles to increase blood flow and keep warm in the damper climate of the British Isles.

Mam has a great belief in nettles ever since her hand had just about closed up and stopped functioning a few years ago because of arthritis. Rob had told her he heard, while travelling in South America, about Native Americans who stung themselves deliberately with nettles to counter joint pain.

So, when Mam was walking up the lane near her house the following day with her dog, the pain in her fingers was so severe that when she saw a bunch of nettles, she stuck her hand in them. By the time she got home, five minutes' walk away, her hand had completely relaxed and all the pain was gone. She did it regularly and her arthritis in her hands doesn't bother her anymore.

"You'll have to bring me to the electric shop tomorrow to buy my deep-fat fryer. I can't live without me chips," she says as we arrive back home just in time for Ronan to leave to go collect Luca from the train.

The house is slowly coming together and tomorrow I will unpack my incense burner and Christmas spice aromatherapy oil to fill the house with Christmas smells.

Although my dream of lovely scents is being dampened by the thoughts of the impending deep-fat fryer, lacing my Christmassy aromas with eau-de-chipper.

7

FLUFFY BREAD

"**A**ll you two have been doing since I got to Italy is screwing, screwing and screwing," Mam says with disgust from her chair.

We were putting another flatpack together. This time a coffee table. It's badly needed since Ronan hit his clumsy work boot off the edge of the gold-tinted, glass-topped, tubular-legged table we had when he was crossing his legs, smashing it into several pieces.

It was a welcomed loss as it was the one he had brought in from the 'definitely to be dumped pile' of furniture left in the house a year ago, as a temporary solution to our sitting room furniture dilemma. I had not only lost my coffee table but my work desk and dining table, in one fell swoop of a boot. One of the empty delivery boxes, with a Mexican throw over it, had become a replacement 'temporary' table for months.

So, while online ordering our blue velvet sofa, I also ordered a coffee table on casters with deep shelves underneath where I can clear away my laptop and notebooks each evening, a desk for my office and bedside tables. I didn't expect the coffee table, desk and bedside tables to all arrive as flat packs the following day.

Having Luca back adds another element of life to the house. Over dinner we discuss Mam's nettle cure for her arthritis. Luca immediately looks it up and informs us that scientific studies have found that while the stinging obviously hurts, people suffering arthritic discomfort in their hands get relief after nettle stings, as the nettles have tiny hairs that are essentially little hypodermic needles waiting to inject their contents into the skin. Inside them is a fluid containing formic acid, histamine, acetylcholine, and serotonin.

"I remember getting stung as kids and while we wept my granny would say, 'you won't get arthritis when you are older,'" I say while eating yet another one of my delicious concoctions inspired by the recipe boxes. "So there is truth in the old wives' tale."

There was no such luck with cactus spines. As kids, we would regularly have hands like baby porcupines from my brother Peter's cacti fascination. He had a greenhouse full of cacti and baby cacti specimens being nurtured on every windowsill in the house, which regularly got knocked. I'd try to clean it up before he saw, resulting in being gouged by painful, hair-thin spines that felt like glass splinters. There won't be any cacti in this house, even though there is a garden centre dedicated to them only ten minutes away. Every time I pass it, I shudder.

Now that the rooms are finished on two floors, it is easier to see how they will flow. The desk I ordered will match the blue wardrobe in our bedroom. It arrives in a thousand bits, needing to be assembled like the coffee table and the various bedside tables.

"I am so sick of assembling furniture. Does nowhere sell modern solid assembled furniture anymore?" I say while I try to work out yet another set of instructions to see why I have several screws and pieces left over.

Ronan puts together the desk as a surprise for me. I am far more fussy about assembling these things than he is. I read instructions for a start. He had to follow instructions on this one as there were a zillion pieces, but he over tightened some screws splitting the wood. And the drawer, with a plastic bag of bits left over, doesn't quite sit right. I try to look happy about his surprise, but inside I'm crying about the imperfections. I just wanted a nice desk.

"Why are you putting it in the bedroom?" Ronan asks as I push it across the hallway.

"Because all those rooms will be bedrooms for our retreats or bed-and-breakfast, or whatever we decide to do."

"Rosie, that won't be happening this summer, so you have a whole eighteen months at least before that. Spread yourself out a bit, adopt one room as your office. You have a tough summer with all the weddings ahead, so make yourself a comfortable room away from the bedroom."

He's right.

I deserve a pleasant office. I choose my favourite room—the one across the hall on the first floor with the French doors onto its own balcony. With the desk moved in, I begin to locate boxes with all my precious things in, such as my crystals, ornaments, mementos—things I have not had a space for in about twenty years.

I clear the free-standing bookshelf I had in another room holding files of accounts and a whole host of other boring necessary stuff I need to go through, some unlooked at since shipped from Ireland, which could probably just be shredded.

I set the bookshelves up in my study and I fill them with my favourite inspirational books and my years of notebooks packed with business and book ideas. On the new deep shelf that Alex the Albanian built in the space that was once a fireplace, I neatly layout hobbies I have had no time to touch; watercolours and oils, the embroidery project I started during lockdown, upholstery fabric, wrapping paper, coloured card and ribbons. It feels so good to at last be able to unpack stuff into dust-free, fresh rooms.

With my desktop computer set up and my pens in my slightly wonky drawer, I already feel better prepared to face the work year ahead that burnout has blitzed. However, there is something hanging in the back of my mind. My Mam is downstairs on her own. She is used to having the constant company of my dad. I can't leave her just sitting there by herself.

So I close the door of my lovely office for now to go and take my place on the end of the diarrhea sofa with my laptop. At least I have a coffee table now.

Just as I am going downstairs, our Italian friend Lucia calls, "Is it okay I come visit you and your Mamma? To pay my respects, as I have not seen you since your dad died."

"Yes, of course. We would love to see you."

"I want to buy your Mamma a present. How about Ciabatta?"

I'm thinking it an odd choice, "You don't have to buy a gift but—"

"Does she already have ciabatta?"

I look towards the bread bin. "No, not at the moment..."

"Okay, I will bring some furry ciabatta."

Okay, now it is weird. Is mouldy bread a traditional grieving gift to give in Italy?

"I will see you at four after lunch."

After four is near dinner time in our minds, especially my mother's who during my teen years usually had dinner on the table at 5.10pm when Dad would arrive in from work, having given her own mother a potato-laden dinner in bed at 4pm.

She would keep three dinners warm above steaming pots of water to give my brothers as they all arrived in starving between 5.30pm and 7pm every evening.

While the Italians traditionally have long, two-hour dinners together, we had stretched out dinner times too, but each person gobbling down their dinner individually. Except Sundays, Easter and Christmas Day when we all ate together. My Mam's whole adult life revolved around organising dinners starting at 3pm and ending at 7pm.

Lucia arrives, masked and giving me a careful hug, keeping her head and much of her body away from me. I'm so sick of Covid's social distancing.

She sits away from Mam and chats to her, sympathising as Mam recounts how Dad died before her eyes. Lucia reveals the gift bag at an appropriate time to stop us all spiralling into puddles.

I am hanging around as I am dying to hear Lucia's explanation of the mouldy bread Italian grieving gift tradition.

Mam pulls out a pair of slippers. "Rosie said you did not have ciabatta, so I got you a furry pair to keep your feet warm and cozy."

"I thought ciabatta was bread?" I say.

"Sì! The bread you know is nicknamed Ciabatta because it looks like a slipper, not the other way around... did you think I was bringing your mamma bread?"

"No, no, no... yes." I am terrible at lying.

"Rosie, Dio! You really have to learn Italian."

She was not wrong.

8

CAT JEANS

Next on the house furnishing list is a dining table. We have been watching out for a suitable secondhand one online. I want a big dining table, one that becomes the heart of the house. Although the only room we can currently fit a table in is the drafty hallway.

Unlike the previous year, we now have gas and working radiators. The house is warm. Even the hallway feels tepid, not like the icy tundra of last year. It's because of the sizeable gaps around the large, solid wood, ancient front double doors.

We still hang the heavy curtain to stop the north wind whistling through. When clearing the house, I found a bedspread in a cupboard sealed in a zipped polythene bag so it is clean but not fresh enough to use on beds. Instead, I am going to use it as a draft excluder.

"Here, give that to me," says my mother as she watches me stuff it under the large gap. She sits down, rolls it into a giant sausage roll and, with her embroidery thread, sews along the seam to hold it all together to make a perfectly sized giant draft excluder for the gap under our double front doors.

There's still a lot to be done to the house, including the top floor and big bathroom, the gardens of course, not to mention the smaller east wing roof, which still needs to be replaced. Along with light fittings, furnishings, doors and windows needing fixing. But at least this year we are warm and are starting to be dust and mould free.

I'm conscious the gas is on a lot to keep the house warm for Mam. We have all the piping in place for the solar panels on the roof. I see ads for solar panels all the time on social media, but because of my Italian tongue-tied problem, I can't independently call about them and understand what the deal is. There is no point in asking Danny to come back to do it, so I decide to consult one of the yogis who has solar panels.

Coming back from the shop, having bought more stuff from Mam's growing list of bizarre needs, I take a detour and call in to Blodwyn and Ivan, the Welsh sheep-turned-olive farmers. We call Ivan, Welsh Ivan so not to confuse him with Romanian Ivor, the builder, during conversations.

Just as I arrive, Blodwyn is hauling a black garbage bag up her driveway, streaks of blood left in her wake. "Jezuz, she's killed Welsh Ivan." I'm thinking I should just turn around and pretend I didn't see her. But it's too late, she has spotted me.

"Hello!" she calls out, still reefing the bag up to her back door. "It's half a cinghiale one of the hunters gave me."

"Half a wild boar? Does it have half a head?"

"No head, just two legs and lots of meat for a good barbecue next spring." Blodwyn has no issue with the idea of butchering an animal into freezable sections. "It once had four legs, so probably a similar layout to a sheep, I'd imagine."

"I wanted to ask you about your solar panels. Our original plumber put in all the piping but never finished the job so there are now just different coloured random plastic tubes protruding from our roof and I'm thinking it will help fuel our hot water supply if we do decide to run retreats or a BnB next year."

"Oh, beware of solar panels," she says, leaving her kill outside the back door while she puts on the kettle.

"We got two put on our roof and in July and August, the months you really just want cold showers here, the water is so hot the overflow kicks in. It was only months after we finished the house that we experienced the full whack of them, and realised that the plumber who installed them, thought it would be a good idea to have the overflow directed into our radiators. So our heating is on full blast during the forty degree days of July and August," she says, scrubbing her hands before pouring the tea.

"We eventually tracked our plumber down and his solution to the excess hot water was to suggest leaving the taps running, which sort of counters the eco-friendly idea of the panels, doesn't it? So my advice would be to get one solar panel and don't get the overflow attached to your heating."

I have a quick cup of tea and get out of there as fast as I can, in case she asks me to help carve up the carcass on her back step.

Back home, Ronan has put together the last of the flat packs, which is a clothes rack for Luca's room. Having somewhere to hang our clothes is such a novelty.

One of my biggest life transformations since moving into the house happened before my sudden departure to Ireland, when Alex the Albanian moved the wardrobe I had refurbished into our bedroom. For the first time in a long time, I had my clothes out of plastic garbage sacks and hanging in a wardrobe.

Pre the Sighing House, the house we rented from Giovanni included the fifty-plus-year-old, veneered bedroom set with bed, dresser, drawers and the horror wardrobe.

The wardrobe was like a giant coffin that wanted to kill you. A heavy, solid wood, with woodworm included. It had a heavy mirror on the front of the door, which glared at me as soon as I sat up in the morning—not a good look.

If the bottom drawer was open at the same time as the door, the whole lot wobbled towards you with the potential to kill you but with a neat result of in-coffining you at the same time—saving time and money.

It was also unbelievably dark inside, no matter which way we angled it to catch the window light. When Spooky was recovering from her surgery after having her tail amputated, she used to climb into it as her safe place. You'd just see her green eyes in the blackness and hear her purring.

Ronan's hearing wasn't the best since the medieval trumpet incident, so sometimes he thought he could hear her purring and several times he found he was gently petting a pair of jeans in the black hole of a wardrobe rather than our cat during her recovery.

It wasn't the only time a pair of jeans was mistaken as a cat at Giovanni's. There was also the time I video chatted with Ronan while I was home in Ireland and I could see something strange in the background on the bed. There were our two cats curled up asleep and at first I thought a folded black pair of jeans, but then it moved. I looked closer as Ronan chatted away.

"Ronan, is that another cat on the bed?"

"Yes, the two cats are on the bed. I know you prefer them not on the bed but—"

"Ronan, there are three?"

"What the?"

Yes, while I was away, a neighbourhood black cat had been coming in, pretending to be one of ours to be fed and pampered. Clever enough not to appear at the same time as the others, except this time it forgot. The dogs soon discovered the infiltrator and kept the big tom away from our girls.

After two years of leaving our clothes dispersed around the bed, floor and anywhere other than the coffin wardrobe at the rental and then a year of plastic bags and suitcase storage to avoid the ongoing rubble and dust, having somewhere to hang clean clothes was life changing.

It also means I no longer have clothes hidden that I live in hope to fit back into 'next year'—they are all exposed. They are still waiting, as I am, on the day when I will find just lettuce and water so delicious that it is all I will eat for three months.

But the pluses outweigh the negative. Retrieving clothes in the morning that smell fresh and clean rather than smelling like I was taking them from a corpse that previously occupied the coffin wardrobe, was a huge plus in my life.

However, with the threat of a deep-fat fryer coming into the house, I knew this joy was going to be short-lived, as I was sure that smell would not only overpower my Christmas spice aromatherapy, but it would also seep upstairs and I'd be putting on a battered cod outfit each morning.

A saving grace, however, is that Rob has persuaded Mam to get an air fryer instead. He assures me they don't smell much and are a lot cleaner. I had researched these before and had tried to convince Mam but she was having none of it, until Rob mentions it. Then, of course, they are the best things since sliced bread.

That evening Rob calls, "Don't tell your Mam but I'm in hospital. I'm okay, they are just running tests. Apparently I'm very anemic. I got a pain the day after you left and went to the doctor and he sent me to the ER. They left me sitting on a plastic chair for ten hours before I was seen to and then they offered me a bed. I wasn't going to stay, but how could I refuse? It's a rarity to get one in an Irish hospital these days." He could still joke.

"But that was over a week ago?"

"I know. They are sending me home in a day or two. They are just trying to figure out what's wrong. I feel fine now, but might as well get the full MOT while I'm here."

As my brothers and Rob can't get away without calling Mam every day, I tell Mam that Rob dropped his phone down the toilet and is waiting to get a new one, that is why he hasn't called.

I try not to worry. He's being looked after, he'll be okay. And I focus on my mantra in dire situations, "It's grand, everything will be fine."

9

AIR DRYERS & FRYERS

L uca is finding it difficult to settle back into his art course and to live life without his friends. Covid lockdowns were extra harsh for his age group.

The other students on his course are a lot older than him. It's like they all did a degree already and are now doing the course they always really wanted to do.

Most of the first year of classes were by Zoom because of Covid and because he didn't have a Green Pass, he couldn't go on the train when the second year started so it has been difficult for him to get into the swing of it.

He procrastinates about course work by helping us pull the house together.

Ronan and I have been sending each other pics of secondhand dining tables we have found online. None quite tick all the boxes for both of us, until Ronan spots a post about a long, thick wooden table. It's exactly what we both want, and it is for sale about twenty miles away for €150.

"I am the house behind the church," the seller instructs.

So that is where we go and drive into a small courtyard of a house joined to the back of a church. The guy greets us and leads us to a door of another small storage building joined to the church. The table is perfect, solid wood and heavy as hell. Which is probably not the best description considering we are buying it from a church.

"Are you wanting to get rid of them too?" I ask, pointing at two ornately carved dining chairs.

"And what about this?" asks Ronan, pointing to the three-seater matching carved bench also with a leather seat.

"Yes, those can go too, all for a quick sale of €300."

"It's a deal at €280 if you include them too," I say, pointing to four wooden chairs with woven seats.

"Va bene," he says happily.

I am quietly thrilled about the deal we just got. An antique dining table and seating for eight people for under €300. We will be having a proper Christmas banquet this year. We take the chairs and Ronan returns with Luca to get the table.

It's Luca that points out that it's weird the guy wanted a quick sale when the stuff has been clearly lying there for some time, based on the layer of dust on them. And that he was packing his car up with suitcases when they returned to collect the table.

"Are you sure we haven't just unknowingly robbed a church? Are you sure that guy had a right to sell that stuff? Maybe he was just staying there as a BnB guest and discovered the storage room?"

"I don't know," says Ronan. "He could have been telling me he was a master thief in Italian for all I know. The good thing is we now have a table to eat off."

We need a dining room, but it is surprising in a house of twenty-two rooms we have nowhere to currently put the dining table and chairs other than the hallway. The neat room sizes of the Sighing House are an advantage as it is easier to heat but a disadvantage when it comes to large furniture.

It always takes me a while to settle into a house and figure out the best layout and use for each room, based on the flow of where we are drawn to sit and how we move around the house. Until we figure out the best layout for this house, we'll have the dining table in the hall.

"The Great Banqueting Hall," cheers Mam. "I'll take on the role of chief table polisher. Buy me some Mr Sheen when you are out today."

My mother overestimates how often I go out. I would happily stay home for a week, working and writing without going outside the gate and leave the shopping and everything else to Ronan. Covid lockdowns suited me.

My mother is the opposite. She likes to be out and about, poking around shops buying plastic containers, snacks for a potential party and mops, which we now have four varieties of, but she still hasn't found the particular type she wants. It's one she saw on an American shopping channel that you can use to clean windows too.

"Let's go to the chip pan shop. I want to buy one of those air dryer things Rob said are great."

Having Mam here is definitely testing my ability to drive on the motorway more. However, with the left-hand drive rental car it is much easier than trying to come off the slipways onto speeding lanes of traffic in a right-hand drive with a dodgy frozen shoulder my neck can't turn to look over.

We drive out to Media World where there is an aisle full of air fryers. We go for a recognisable brand and put it in the trolley along with a hair dryer, which, according to my mother, is another thing I cannot live without in the house. "Ha, we are buying an air dryer and a hair dryer."

"It's an air fryer, Ma."

"Same thing, an air fryer and an air dryer. I'm a poet and I don't know it. Now where are the deep-fat fryers?"

"What? You don't need a deep-fat fryer with an air fryer, that's the whole point. The air fryer is the healthier alternative to a deep-fat fryer."

"Now listen here, I want a deep-fat fryer. If this thing doesn't make chips like I want them, I don't want to have to come out all this way again."

She won't listen to logic of buying one or the other. So I give up and prepare myself to welcome two smelly frying machines into my house.

The dining table physically fits in the hallway, but it obviously isn't the best place for it. However, Ronan and I convince ourselves it will do for now. With the Christmas tree up and decorated banister backdrop it will make a great Christmas dinner setting. The house deserves a table like this and we will find the right place for it with time.

The new Omicron virus is ripping through the UK. There are new startling headlines about it every day. Izzy is due to fly here on Monday and I am terrified the Italian government will ban flights in from the UK again. It all feels like deja vu.

In Ireland, pubs and nightclubs must close before 11pm now because apparently Covid goes ape-shit after that time. Well, that is not what they are saying. When asked about the logic of it, the government official says that it's to make people more aware.

But the nightclubs come up with an Irish solution. Instead of opening at 10pm, they open at 6pm and there are queues to get into them. So clubbers are now going directly from work to nightclubs on empty stomachs and getting sloshed earlier.

In the meantime, Italy has re-introduced mask wearing outside on the street as well as inside any building or transport. And that the more sturdy face masks are to be worn on trains and at events.

They have also announced we'll soon need to have the super plus Covid pass to show we have had the booster vaccine to go into bars, restaurants and on transport. So our Green Pass we waited so long to get will soon be invalid.

But I will not think about that now. Izzy is coming tomorrow and so is the blue velvet sofa.

10

SMOKING SOFA

With Izzy's arrival only a matter of hours away and the impending delivery of the blue velvet sofa, just like we dreamed of having before we ever bought the house, I get the lads to lift the diarrhea sofa outside with its perished foam and ever dusty cushions.

It served us well for the last year, but I take great delight in bashing it with a sledgehammer.

I email the shop as directed when buying, about the time of the sofa arriving so we can collect it or organise a delivery.

"I'm sorry but they did not include it in the delivery to our store," Davide, the helpful assistant, emails back.

"But I have cleared out the sitting room," I say, looking at the large empty space the sofa used to be, while still holding the sledgehammer. "When is the next delivery?"

"Our next delivery to the store will be after the Christmas break." Judging by how long Christmas breaks go on in Italy, this might mean February.

"What? But we now have nothing to sit on for Christmas," I say.

"Well, you could take the display model."

"Do we get a discount, as it's a display model?"

"No."

This doesn't surprise me. It is common for stores in Italy to say no about discounts on display models, whereas other countries would knock off at least ten percent. And you won't see 'Sale' signs plastered all over Italian shops on a regular basis either. Shops are only allowed to have two sales per year, and it seems many just don't bother. There's no big hype time like January sales, although Black Friday is catching on.

I grudgingly say we will have a look at it and let them know if we'll take it. But if I am paying €1500 for a new sofa, I want exactly that; a new sofa.

Ronan and I trundle off in our loyal 25-year-old van to the French shop, where we saw the sofa two years previously, leaving Mam in Luca's care.

There's the blue sofa looking as pretty as ever. It doesn't have any signs of wear and tear. This, with the thought of Izzy arriving and having nothing to sit on for the entire Christmas period, gets me over my reluctance and so I email 'Davide' from the store.

"We are here in the store and we will take the display model."

We eventually find an assistant who can help us. "Davide said we can take the display model so we are here to collect it," I say using my ever useful Google Translate. My email has got Davide arriving from the back office of the storerooms in a bit of a panic.

"There is Davide now," says the assistant as we all stand beside the blue velvet sofa.

"We'll take it," says Ronan to the trendy-looking nerdy guy.

"But it's not ready." He speaks good English thankfully.

"When will it be ready? What needs to be done to it?"

"Well, I need someone to take it apart and then wrap it in cellophane."

"You get the cellophane," Ronan says to Davide as he flattens himself on the floor under the sofa and starts unscrewing the L part of the chaise lounge sectional from the three-seater section. I'm already removing the cushions.

"There, that's done," Ronan says, wriggling from under it and sitting upright on the floor in the centre of the showroom. "It only has two screws."

"But what about delivery?" Davide is standing staring, holding the cushion I have handed him. We paid in full for a blue velvet sofa and as far as we were concerned, this is now the one we paid for. It's ours to take apart.

"We have a van outside. Here, grab the end Davide, and help me out with it," says Ronan, reaching down to take the end of one section.

"Wait, we are going outside now?"

"Yes, to the van."

"Okay, wait," says Davide, laughing a little. "I need to get my coat."

It's a warm winter sunny day but Davide is not taking any chances in just a sweater.

He really isn't used to someone making decisions so fast and not doing it the Italian way of having to have long monologues within conversations about what is happening next.

By the time he returns, Ronan and I have packed all the back cushions into the van.

Davide has brought a long roll of cellophane and the three of us work together to completely wrap the two separated sections in a protective layer.

Like when we collected the bed base and Ronan deconstructed the inside of the camper with his boot, this guy is finding our 'let's do it now' attitude highly amusing.

Again, Ronan practically knows the guy's entire life story by the time they have carried part two of the sofa out. The three of us then play a giant game of Tetris trying to make the sofa pieces fit in our van around all the things Ronan did not think of removing before we left to collect the sofa, such as a chainsaw and rubbish bin. But our old van doesn't let us down. She seems to take a deep breath to give us that extra inch we need to finally get the sofa in.

Back home, I leave Ronan and Luca to take the two main pieces out. I don't want to be there interfering and being a pain in the ass, I am sure they can do it perfectly well without me. Instead, I focus on prepping the sitting room for the arrival of the sofa I have been waiting for several years to get.

Many times, while sitting uncomfortably on the diarrhea sofa with the perished foam that moulded too quickly to the shape of my posterior, I have dreamed of sitting with my feet up on the chaise part of the sofa that I have already claimed as my space.

As soon as he gets out of the van, Ronan does his usual and lights up a cigarette. He has a cigarette hanging out of the side of his mouth while carrying in the first part. He knows better than to smoke in the house so flicks the cigarette away. I watch it fly through the air and land perfectly on sofa part number two. Still lit.

I can't get the words out quick enough, tripping over all the Fs and Blinding words I am roaring at him, "Relax, will you," he says, thinking I am commenting on the way he has just banged sofa part number one off the French door he is carrying it through. It takes up all the doorway so I can't get past. Luca sees what I am trying to find the fucking words for as the smoke spirals up.

There is only one thing for it. I run to the open window, use my Mam's chair as a trampoline onto the windowsill and I jump-fall outside to where the sofa is sitting with a smouldering whiff rising from the centre. The plastic wrap is shrivelling fast like a reverse film of a flood happening. In the meantime, Luca has found the words to tell Ronan his lit cigarette has just set the sofa on fire.

They both reach me as I throw the cigarette to the side and pound the smoking plastic with my fist. We are all working to tearing the cellophane off to the tune of my Fs and roars of "Can I not have anything perfect in this world?"

"You have me," chimes in Ronan. He is lucky Luca is the one with the flick knife slicing through the plastic to reveal a burn hole in the velvet.

"Ah it's grand, it's only a small hole and on the back, no one will see it," says Ronan, trying to sound casual and an 'aren't we lucky' air to his voice, but he knows I'm ready to explode.

A low grinding scream makes its way through my clenched teeth, but he gets there before me.

"Relax, it's fine. Now let's get it inside before we have to go collect Izzy," he says, trying to brush off his major mess up.

Only for the joy of Izzy arriving, diluting my feelings of anger, the sofa gets away with just a burn mark on its back instead of Ronan's blood being added.

We just about get the sofa screwed back together with the burn mark facing the wall, a quick sit on it for a tryout before the three of us are back in the car on our way to the airport. It's time for Christmas to really start.

11

CHRISTMAS BOMB

The final touch of Christmas spirit arrives in the form of the whirlwind energy that is Izzy. Thankfully, the new Covid variant has not kept her away this year and we have some making up to do for last year.

Izzy has brought over a suitcase of gifts and we both go into our rooms to wrap our presents separately before piling them under the tree. We both love well wrapped presents in co-ordinated colours and ribbons.

I've bought Mam a sack of wool and needles, enough to knit a blanket and keep her busy for a few months of winter evenings. We got Izzy a cashmere cardigan from the local cashmere shop and Luca a new digital drawing board along with books and art equipment for everyone.

Izzy has bought me a one-thousand-piece jigsaw—my must-do Christmas activity–and Ronan an autobiography of someone he's been talking to her about as well as The Beatles White Album for the record player we have set up in the corner of the sitting room. She brought Mam a cozy dressing gown.

Luca has gifted the family the Italian version of one of the games we used to love to play when they were kids. Monopoly. We all had our favourite piece in our Irish version, but now we need to choose new Italian favourites; A gondola for me, a football for Ronan, a pizza slice for Luca, a cappuccino cup for Izzy and the bicycle for Mam.

Hearing my mother chat with Izzy and Luca in the evenings warms my heart as I make another meal she'll agree she is surprised at enjoying. Surprised because I made it and it doesn't contain potatoes. Tonight, it's the strangled priest dish again.

One of the things that made me fall in love with Italy was seeing three or sometimes four generations out in the villages squares socialising and enjoying life together. And now I have it. Mam has Mario Lanza playing as I'm making dinner while she's telling Izzy stories about her and my dad dating and Luca stories of war rations and life in the 40s and 50s.

It's how I wanted things to be, like the Italians, like when I was growing up; three generations in the one house supporting each other like a human ecosystem.

Shelly and Sherwin come over for a Christmas Eve drink and spot the Monopoly board out on the table.

"Rosie you should be the bike," Mam says aloud as she takes another slurp of her whiskey in her electric chair, where she is filling the biggest pot we have in the house full of the potatoes she is busy peeling. "Rosie was known as the bike with the basket around town when she was growing up."

"Mam!" I say, shocked.

Shelly is in knots of laughter, while Sherwin doesn't know where to look.

"What?" Mam looks up from her task. "You were known for your old-fashioned black bone rattler bike with the basket on the front that you carried your school bag in."

"Being known for my bike around the town and being known as the bike around town are two very different things," I correct her, my neck reddening less now that everyone is laughing.

"We are having Welsh Ivan over for Christmas dinner as Blodwyn is in Wales with her mother," I tell Shelly as she joins me in the kitchen where I'm trying to make a dessert for Christmas day. "I didn't know what to make for Christmas dessert. Our usual would be a sherry trifle but I haven't seen sherry nor trifle making things in Italy so I have gone for a Christmas Bomb recipe by Jamie Oliver."

"Oh, I am sure it will be delicious," says Shelly, enthusiastically.

But I'm having serious doubts. I am not known for my dessert making skills. I'm still working on it after they leave; layering ice cream and fruit in a sponge finger lined bowl. I put it in the freezer and remind Ronan to remind me to take it out before we serve dinner the following day, as Jamie instructs.

The following day is Christmas! Ronan looks after the Brussels sprouts and turkey, Izzy is looking after the gravy and Yorkshire puddings, Mam is taking care of the potatoes and I am doing the vegetables and stuffing.

Luca is setting the table and keeping the music going. My kids are not fond of Christmas carols so Irish music is blasting through the house, with certain songs that are associated with

Dad and Eileen quickly skipped past to save me and Mam weeping into our carrots and potatoes.

Welsh Ivan arrives with gifts, prosecco, wine and a traditional Panettone made by the local baker. He's even brought a few Christmas crackers to pull to get the dinner started. The only thing we can't get in Italy, besides Christmas crackers, is a ham like we'd get back home. We'd normally slow cook it in honey and mustard with cloves until it crumbled and melted in your mouth.

We do the typical Irish thing; no courses. We just pile everything on our plates at once; roast potatoes, mashed potatoes, slices or legs of turkey, stuffing, green beans, carrots done in orange, Brussels sprouts, two types of stuffing and Yorkshire puddings and then we flood everything with gravy. This would shock an Italian, and I think it even shocks Welsh Ivan.

Mam says grace. We make her speed through it and immediately start pulling crackers and joking to save her from tears and getting sentimental. Prayers tend to have that effect on her.

We have Christmas songs playing low, a small standalone oil flame fire heater lighting in the corner that has heated the hallway sufficiently to make it cozy, the tree is looking great and twinkling along with the fairy lights on the bannisters and throughout the downstairs.

Paddy, looking like a golden Irish wolfhound with his paws crossed under the tree and Looney looking at least the colour she is supposed to be after a bath, finish the perfect picture. My Mam, Izzy, Luca, Ronan and a friend having Christmas dinner around a big table. It's been a long time since we had dinner like this. Cheers, Slainte, Lechyd da, ring around the table but we all say together in our new homeland's language; 'Salute'.

Somehow a conversation about wrapping presents and cars leads Welsh Ivan to telling us that there is a Ferrari testing factory up on the hill and they put the cars in wraps so the new colours and designs are not leaked.

"Ahh, that explains Ronan's prostitute, drug dealer friend in the camouflage-wrapped Ferrari under the bridge. She's a Ferrari engineer!" I exclaim, so happy Ronan's stereotyping has been exposed as completely inaccurate.

But I have no time to gloat as Ronan backfires with, "Did you take the dessert out of the freezer?"

"Oh, bloody hell!"

As I lift the glass bowl out, it looks like it has been dipped in dry ice as smokey tendrils waft around it like some kind of frozen potion.

The Christmas ice cream dessert bomb is as hard as stone and inedible, but we all agree we are all too full to even try it.

Over the next couple hours, as Mam teaches my kids how to play poker with Monopoly money, she smokes her annual Christmas cigar and makes a good road into the whiskey several people have given her as gifts, the bomb melts into a sloppy mess.

Ronan drives Welsh Ivan home and we all settle down to watch a Christmas classic while nibbling reluctantly on the said mess. The ingredients cost an arm and a leg so there's no way I am letting it go to waste.

Watching TV with Mam here is a challenge. She does not have the same taste as us and insists on staying up until 10pm every night which cuts into our family winter TV watching time from 8pm to 10pm. Our usual routine is for me to fall asleep to around 9.30pm and slink off to bed to leave Luca and Ronan to chat and watch what they like, which would again be different to my taste.

Mam's on our territory now so there is no turning out the TV when sex, drugs or fighting happen as we watch The Great, The Sopranos or Withnail and I.

Instead, she'll just do a running commentary of questions like; "That's terrible, why would anyone want to watch that?" Or "Are they all prostitutes now with their sex lives on TV?"

"You can have a sex life without being a prostitute," comments Luca, much to Mam's tutting, which triggers Luca to roll his eyes so much that I'm afraid he'll get eye strain. Mam's relentless comments to every program we put on drives Luca to spend more time on the second floor and give up family TV time. I can see Ronan is missing the usual lengthy conversations he would have with Luca during their late night TV sessions. But I can't worry about that at the moment, I have a grieving mother to keep amused.

I try her with the Great British Bake Off. "Who in their right mind would make that? What's wrong with just a normal cake or apple tart?"

As she is a painter, I thought she'd enjoy watching Portrait of an Artist: "Oh my God, that is terrible, I would kick someone if they painted that of me. Blues and reds and shit, not even an eyeball in one eye. I don't know what they are all on about with the colour."

But as it's Christmas, I put on some of the 'Carry On' films that I grew up on, with Kenneth Williams, Barbara Windsor, Sid James and all the familiar cast. It's 'Carry On Camping'; the one where Babs Windsor's bikini flies off while she exercises and

Sid James' married man character is chasing the character Windsor is playing.

Considering he's in his late 50s and Babs is playing the part of a teenage schoolgirl, makes Izzy nearly retch with the creepiness and consistent flow of sexual innuendo, while Luca's mouth nearly stays permanently agape at how blatant sexism is portrayed.

"How can you be shocked at what we watch, when you like this awful un-PC stuff?" laughs Luca.

"Ah, it's all a bit of a laugh. Better than the stuff you watch nowadays," says Mam laughing her heart out.

Tasty Strangled Priests

Serves: 4

Strozzapreti pasta (enough for 4 people)

500g Mushrooms

2 Cloves of garlic

80g Pecorino

200g Pancetta

500g Cherry tomatoes

Method:

Cook the pasta according to the packet instructions. Slice the mushrooms and chop the cherry tomatoes into quarters.

Add the pancetta to a dry pan and fry in its own fat for about 5 minutes (until it is starting to crisp a little).

Add the mushrooms and use a garlic press to mince the garlic or finely chop it and add to pan. Fry for 5 minutes. Keep it stirred.

Add the tomatoes and cook for another 6 to 8 minutes over a medium heat. Turn off the heat and add the cooked pasta to the pan. Stir until coated with the sauce.

Sprinkle in the grated pecorino (keep some aside for garnish) and stir until the cheese has melted into the mixture.

Serve into 4 pasta bowls and garnish with the remaining pecorino.

12

PLAGUES & POTATOES

The following day, Alex the Albanian and his beautiful wife arrive with a saffron food hamper and a gift box of wines. I haven't seen Alex since I got back from Ireland and it's strange seeing him in normal clothes rather than plaster and paint covered overalls. He scrubs up well.

I give him a tight hug and a thank you for making the empty shell into a welcoming home for me and my Mam's return.

"So, when can we start work on the house again? We can start this week? We don't do all this extended Christmas stuff, we want to work. We're very busy but we will fit you in."

I don't feel quite ready for hammering and dust again but I also know it's difficult to get anyone in construction at the moment and I do want to get the top floor finished so Luca will have his own space and we can start laying out the house the way we want it.

"Okay start this week, but let's agree on what has to be done and what it will cost first."

"Okay tomorrow we'll meet at dawn," Alex announces. I'm imagining him arriving on horseback and me needing a sword ready to duel.

The following morning I'm preparing Mam's breakfast—poached eggs on toast, which I have now mastered, and tea—when I hear the gate being opened at 7.30am. The winter sun is just about up enough to light the driveway.

"Looks like it's going to be a nice day. Do you not have washing to hang out? Such a shame to waste a day like that," calls out Mam from her room, giving me a subtle instruction to hang out her laundry.

Ivor gives me a beaming smile and a 'buongiorno' while making his way up to the top floor with a rope. He lowers a bucket down from the front balcony which Alex fills with tools and Ivor hoists up. Then Alex and a junior assistant march up all four flights of stairs carrying large sheets of plasterboard, bags of plaster and a set of old curtains. They hang the curtains from the stairs and top floor landing to protect it and the dust they are about to create from the rest of the house.

And it starts again; the drilling and hammering. At least it is on the top floor with the door shut so the dust will stay contained. And at least we know we will have finished rooms when they are done, not like the last lot.

I forgot to tell Izzy that the workmen were starting this morning.

I'm in the far room telling Alex which light fittings I want in which rooms. He has already asked me aggressively 'Why you do this?' ten times after every decision I have told him about, when I hear stomps up the stairs and see Izzy in her mismatched over-sized PJs ready to tell me and Ronan off for making so much noise, but is faced with Ivor and the assistant. They take their caps off to her with a chorus of 'Buongiorno' as she flings open the door.

"Oh hmm hi, anyone want a coffee?" she says, covering her tracks.

"Is that the TV star?" I hear the assistant ask confused at the unsightly sight of Izzy in all her real-life glory of messy hair, mismatched PJs and Sudocreme dabbed on potential blemishes, walking back down the stairs.

Once I am done talking with Alex, I close the door keeping the dust behind me. As I go down the stairs, I see Luca walking down the hall with his mattress on his back like a tortoise, trying to find a place away from the hammer drill above the room he was in.

"Italians are very hardworking, aren't they? I think most Irish would still be on their Christmas break now," says Mam, drinking her morning tea after she has updated me on what the weather is like in Ireland.

"They are not Italian, Ma, they are Eastern European. Italians are still on their holidays."

"Oh, so is it true that Italians are lazy?"

"No, they just know how to live life. Also, you will see in the summer where their work ethic comes from, starting early in the morning and finishing at the midday sun to eat and rest in the afternoon. With the heat you can do nothing else. It's bureaucracy that stops them doing anything promptly, and well, they know the pleasure in the art of doing nothing. They call it 'Dolce far niente', something we probably need to learn to do Ma."

"You are after reminding me, I must get back to doing my Italian classes on that thing you downloaded onto my phone... you know the lingo thing."

"Duolingo, that's what it's called."

Later that afternoon, I find Luca has moved into my study with the new desk, to use as his bedroom and do his course work. I haven't yet got to use my desk with the wonky drawer.

Perhaps me ever having my own space is just never going to happen.

"Don't make yourself too comfortable in here, you will be moving up to your own room as soon as they are done."

Mam is pottering around the kitchen. "I've been making a list of things you need. You don't have a rolling pin do you, no?"

As soon as I answer 'no,' she bombards me with; "A slotted spoon no? Where do you keep your tupperware? How do you live without a rolling pin and a slotted spoon? ... I need a plastic basin, have you no plastic basin? I'll add them all on the list of things you need to get. You also need to get CIF, Bonjela, corn flour, and a plastic basin. Did I say a plastic basin already? I need it for washing up and for soaking my feet. Also, it's handy for peeling a lot of potatoes in."

Before I have a chance to answer she has moved on to the next command.

"Pull out that basket there that you keep the potatoes in."

We don't have a basket to keep potatoes in normally, but we have created one since Mam arrived. "Look at that," she says stooped down pointing with her stick. "There's one in there, no I tell a lie there are two in there gone to seed. Do you see? An awful waste. Now pull them out and go out and plant them. Make yourself useful."

"Ma, I have fifty million things to be doing other than planting rotten potatoes."

"Just go on and do it. I won't let a potato rot. Everything else can go to hell but every potato should be used."

I'm wondering is it part of the Irish DNA left over from the Famine, that we can't handle having a potato rot.

Grabbing the soft potatoes with the gangly witch-like finger roots protruding out of them, I stomp out to the garden like a bold child. I'm doing it to have a break from her. I need to breathe, to take the biggest breath possible to stop myself screaming.

Halfway down the garden, I spot the overgrown ridge where I had planted seed potatoes the year previous in anticipation of my dad coming to live with us in time for my fiftieth birthday.

"Bloody potatoes," I mutter and I chuck the two seeding potatoes as far as I can down the garden. It's freezing cold out, but there is no wind or breeze, just still cold air only disturbed by my warm, loud, angry exhales as I walk back to the house, to where a tonne of work waits for me and Mam has set herself up with a pot of potatoes to peel.

I take a deep breath, open my laptop and begin to answer emails with my legs stretched out in front of me on the chaise.

"Does it really get very hot in the summer, it worries me," Mam asks, peeling another potato.

"Don't worry, Mam, it hasn't happened yet. It will be gradual and we can look at getting air con into your rooms if needed."

It's not the heat that has me concerned for Mam for the summer, it's the mosquitoes. She always says that if there is anything around to bite, it will bite her and she can't tolerate being bit. A fear that developed from growing up with flea-infested beds.

Before duvets or quilts were a thing, we had layers of wool blankets on our beds to keep us warm. They were the perfect nesting grounds for fleas. It wasn't as bad for us as it was for Mam's generation growing up, we just had the odd infestation.

And the only solution to the itch, beside regularly catching the hopping bastards and squashing them between your thumb nails was a paste made with bread soda lathered on. Egg cups full of the stuff were regular sights beside our beds. It must have been worse in Italy as fleas were how the plagues spread. We wouldn't have had a chance in Ireland.

13

NEW YEAR ESCAPE

I t's New Year's Eve and a beautiful crisp bright winter day. I'm joining in the Italian tradition of having a dinner involving lentils–an Irish stew with lentils involved. The tiny disks are to symbolise money and eating them on New Year's Eve should bring you good fortune in the coming year.

"While the stew is stewing away as stews do, will we all go out for a walk along the lake, to wave goodbye to the last year and wish it good riddance?" I say to the room of everyone bored with sorting through my jigsaw pieces, looking for the edges.

Our timing is perfect for joining yet another Italian cultural event; the 'la passeggiata' or evening stroll before dinner–a tradition seen in every Italian village or town. Italians out walking dressed up, groomed to perfection as la bella figura expects, strolling through the piazza or main street. For us, it is the lakefront. They stop and chat with neighbours and friends and discuss gossip, politics, news or show off their children, new babies or new dogs. La passeggiata usually starts or ends with an aperitivo or a gelato.

As it is New Year's Eve and there isn't a lockdown, it's busier than ever.

Ronan walks ahead with Paddy on the lead and Izzy has Looney, while Luca and I take turns pushing Mam along in her wheelchair. Looney is getting old, so she appreciates Mam's mobile lap to sit on halfway through the walk.

The last sunset of the year over the lake does not disappoint. Deep shades of cerise and turmeric, with dashes of pistachio and strawberry melt together like gelato five minutes after being served on a hot day.

I am just taking another photo when suddenly I hear Ronan roar "PADDY!" and I see the dog dash towards me and then past me faster than any greyhound. His tongue flaps out the side of his mouth and his long extension lead bounces off the ground every ten sprints before the aerodynamics of his speed make it take flight again.

His eyes seem happy not wild. Luca and Izzy had dropped behind chatting, and I shout at them 'Grab him!' as he shoots past them. They are on the case and run after him along the lakefront path, the Italians dressed in all their New Year's Eve finery making way.

Izzy is the fastest, screeching after Paddy all the way but he's not slowing down, he's heading towards the path that leads to the main road.

Luckily, one bounce sends the handle of his lead into the air and by some miracle it twirls around a lamp post Paddy has dodged, and with a casual pounce on top of the lead of a perfectly timed foot of a well-dressed man, Paddy grinds to a halt.

Several Italians jump on the lead to secure it being undone as they laugh at Izzy and Luca's comical puffed faces from their unexpected sprint in their winter coats.

It takes me a while to catch up with them, pushing Mam and Looney along, but as I make my way, I see Italians greeting their friends and neighbours along the path and I can tell by the few overheard words and the very excited waving arms and dramatic facial expressions, huffs and puffs and bursts of laughter that they are recounting the sight of the fast escaped Disney-looking dog with the long tongue and the two crazy Irish screeching after it.

"I just dropped his lead for a second to take a photo of the sunset," says Ronan ten minutes later as he reaches us. "He's so bloody fast!"

Since we adopted Paddy from the kennels, we have imagined several scenarios of what Paddy's past could have been. He was definitely trained and kept outside, I'm still banking on him being a truffle dog but diverse greyhound has now been added to the list of possibilities.

It was quite miraculous that Paddy got stopped before he got to the busy road but then again according to Italian folklore we are currently in the most magical time of the year—the twelve days between Christmas and the Epiphany.

It was believed witches were most present at this time, especially on the twelfth night (remember your Shakespeare?). The eve of the Epiphany, the fifth of January, was considered the most magical night of the year, when wishes could be made and the future could be predicted through 'signs' and games.

In some parts of Italy, an olive tree leaf thrown into the fire could tell you if your wish would come true or not. If it took long to burn, your wish would be fulfilled. However, if instead it burned too quickly, it was hard luck, try again next year and a sign to adjust your wishes.

It was the date girls placed three broad beans in various stages of being peeled, under their pillow and believed they would see their future husbands in their dreams.

In the morning, they would reach under their pillow and pull out a bean. If it was the fully peeled one, it meant the groom would be rich, if it was the unpeeled one, he would be poor and the half-peeled one indicated he'd be something in the middle.

It is also the favourite night for kids, as it is the night the Befana comes.

I was first told about La Befana a few years ago by a baker.

"What the hell is that?" I said pointing at the pile of dark grey lumps piled in the basket on the counter of the bakery.

"It is carbone, made from sugar." The baker smiled as he packed up my cream cakes. "If you are bad, La Befana leaves them for you."

"La Befana?"

"I think you call her a witch?"

He pointed to the smiling puppet witch sitting on her broomstick hanging from the shelf.

It turns out that La Befana is a happy smiling old lady, who rides around on her broomstick, comes down the chimney and leaves candy and presents for good children and a lump of coal if they are bad. A glass of wine and some food is left out for La Befana.

It all sounds familiar, doesn't it? As with so many pagan traditions and idols, when Christian gaslighting became all the rage, La Befana's action were absorbed into Santa and the lady herself absorbed into a biblical story.

The legend now stands that the three wise men stopped at her home overnight on their way to finding the infant Jesus. She was known to be the best housekeeper in the village, so the choice of house was natural. They all got on so well that the lads invited her along on their adventure, but naturally, after having three men stay in her house, she felt she had too much housework to do.

However, later in the day she said "feck it, life is too short to miss out on such an invitation," so she jumped on her broomstick and tried to catch up with them to see the baby they were so excited about. To this day, La Befana is searching for three men and the baby on the eve of the sixth.

While searching, she leaves all the good children toys and sweets, while the bad children get coal ('carbone'), onions or garlic. Anyone who sees La Befana will receive a thump from her broomstick—a rumour created to keep children in their beds. This scare tactic was not absorbed by Santa Claus, which is unfortunate as it's one of my favourites of the legend.

The ancient Italians seemed keen to scare their kids into sleeping, as this 'lullaby' tells:

Questo bimbo a chi lo do?

Se lo do alla Befana

Se lo tiene una settimana

Se lo do all'Uomo Nero

Se lo tiene un anno intero

Ma se il bimbo fa la nanna

Se lo tiene la sua mamma."

(English) Who will I give this child to? If I give it to the Befana, she will keep him one whole week. If I give it to the Bogey Man, he will keep him one whole year. But if the child goes to sleep, then his mother will keep him.

Of course, the early Italian Christians tried to get rid of the idea of a loved 'witch'. So on the morning of sixth January, sacristans would go from house to house leaving the 'Bboffe water', which was to be sprinkled around the house to keep witches away.

So on the fifth of January I got my beans, coal and olive leaves ready for the last Christmas celebration of the year Italian style, but skipped the Bboffe water. The world could do with the help of a few good witches at the moment.

Mam packs away the crib figures including the pizza-carrying shepherd and his wine carrying girlfriend. Who knows what will have passed before we see them again next Christmas.

Irish Stew
Serves: 4

There are oodles of Irish stew recipe varieties. This is how our family makes it. Stew is best when it is allowed to stew, so leave on a low heat for as long as you like to let the taste develop. Leftovers can be frozen and reheated.

We would often have stew from the same pot two days in a row. The reheated stew on the second day always tastes better than the first!

The amount of vegetables can vary to taste but here's a rough guide:

8 Medium potatoes peeled and quartered

3-4 Carrots peeled and sliced

2-3 Sticks of celery, sliced

1 Medium parsnip peeled and sliced

1 Medium onion, chopped to bite-size pieces

3-5 Sprigs of fresh thyme

A small bunch of fresh parsley

2-3 OXO cubes

Beef (cubed) or chicken (cubed) and/or a mug of lentils as a non-meat option. The quantity of meat is up to you but about the same amount two people would eat for dinner is a guide amount to add.

Method:

Put the potatoes, meat and all the vegetables into a large pot with a thick bottom. Add enough water until all the vegetables are submerged.

Add the fresh thyme and fresh parsley, these can be removed before serving if you prefer.

Crumble in the OXO cubes.

Bring to boil and then cover and simmer, stirring occasionally to stop the lentils or other ingredients sticking to the bottom. Cook until the potatoes are soft and have absorbed enough of the liquid to turn a light shade of brown. Season to taste.

Serve into bowls. I like to mash the potatoes and vegetables together in my bowl to make a thick mush! Others in my family like to leave the vegetables whole in the soup and some stir in a tsp of Bovril for a stronger taste.

14

POST & PERSIMMIONS

Walking away from the airport sliding doors, Ronan put his arm around my shoulders.

Every step felt heavier as I walked away from my ray of sunshine and returned to a home tinged with Luca's depression from not being around his friends and mounting coursework, and my Mam's method of keeping her sadness at bay by constantly giving me orders and telling me how I should be doing things. Tears pricked at my eyes, fighting me to be released.

Patrizia our postwoman is away. Postman Pat we aptly call her. A lot of the postal delivery people seem to be women. Our garbage collection is done by a few good-looking young women too. It's not difficult, as practically everyone in Italy has an air of beauty, the majority make the most of their potential let's say.

Patrizia has been wonderful since we moved in. We discovered we are the same age and we both have two children, hers fifteen years younger than mine, though. She lived in the UK for a stint as a student so she tries all her English on me as she wants to improve it. With each delivery, she stands at the gate and spends at least twenty minutes explaining why she is running late and in a hurry.

The previous summer she told me she is the older mum at the school gates and finds it difficult to make friends with women her own age since she moved here from the coast. So I suggested we meet up for conversation classes. I will help her with her English and she can help me with my Italian.

The first time we met for conversation classes was at a lakeside bar and I bought her a beer. She chatted to me in English and I tried to say some things in Italian, and we helped each other along. It worked well. Her husband Marco joined us. He has no English at all but I figured out that he is a funny guy, who I know Ronan will get on well with and have long conversations with in his usual Ronan magical way without being able to speak Italian. We committed to meeting again for pizza but never get around to it, but every time we see each other we say we must do it soon.

I remember Lucia telling me that it is important to make friends with your postman-woman, when you move to Italy. People buy them gifts of Panettone and prosecco at Christmas. It ensures your post gets delivered as priority.

I seem to have done the friends thing to the extreme as Patrizia texts me a little mailbox emoji whenever there is post left in my postbox. She'll call me to see if I am at home for a parcel delivery, and if I am not home, she will come into the garden and put it in a hidden place and send me a photo. She apologises when she has to deliver a bill.

While Patrizia is away on her holiday, there is a replacement postman. He calls with his mask on and hands me the letter through the gate, "Scusì, the fruit on the tree, may I take some, three or four?" he asks with admiring eyes pointing at my persimmon tree in the back garden.

"Yes, of course, help yourself," I reply.

He comes into the back garden, his post van outside. I get him a bag and help him pack the five pieces of ripe, plump, orange vitamin bombs of fruit he chooses and thanks me continuously. I'm happy for him to take them as that is five fewer splatters of orange slime to stain our courtyard flagstones.

I bump into Postwoman Pat the following day. She is rushing through town with a bundle of letters and she stops to tell me how late she is, and also about her recent holiday in the mountains, which takes half an hour while her double-parked van causes a backup of traffic.

I try to pull myself away and she says, "ah wait I just have this police fine to deliver to Signora Rossi, she is always getting fines, I will be back in a moment as I have a delivery for you, which I will give you now if okay, since you will not be home."

I wait, and she arrives back and takes a small parcel for me out of the van. "I am sorry there is a customs charge on this delivery for you, but I will pay it as you bought the beers when we met up."

I try to protest but she is having none of it. She thinks fair is fair; I bought her a beer six months ago, so she will pay the three-euro customs due on my package.

When I mention to Karen about my postwoman's amazing service, she says, "sure my postman arrived one morning all smiles, he said he had good news, my Pap test had come back clear. He said he knew as they use a different envelop for the negative ones. There is no such thing as privacy in Italy, they literally don't have a word in their vocabulary for it."

Now Christmas is over, things seem more like normal with mortar dust landing everywhere with Alex the Albanian is back working on the house again. As usual, and as expected at this time of year, my email is flooded with newly engaged couples keen to get married in Italy.

Not only that, but my clients who have had to postpone their weddings for two years due to Covid are keen to feel that this will be their year to finally tie the knot and want to catch up on their plans, arrange menu tastings and make-up trials. But this is what I am good at, or used to be good at; organising and planning all the logistics of making fifteen three-day events for fifty to one hundred and fifty people with twenty different service providers run like clockwork.

Ben, who has his own wedding planning business, has been my right-hand man since I started doing weddings in Italy twelve years ago. We both work in a similar way.

We create and sell packages with all the basics: The venue, the catering, the ceremony, the celebrant, the legal fees, on the day co-ordination and the planning fees.

This price doesn't change and so couples know exactly what that part of their wedding plans is going to cost. We then give them lists of services such as photographers, bands, hair and make-up artists, florists, transport.

Couples loved it, and by the third year of working like this I was getting booked out over a year in advance. I take on fewer weddings than Ben, so I pass all my surplus enquiries to him.

Also, for bigger weddings, I would pay him a fee to share the responsibility with me.

I got into wedding planning because I loved the logistics. It was like playing a big chess game; move one hundred people from one country to another, get them to a venue in a country where they don't speak the language, feed them, entertain them and keep them under control while simultaneously making sure a couple look fabulous, relax and stop anything that might cause them stress getting close to them so that they have one of the most amazing weekends of their life.

Usually on top of this there is the task of turning an empty field or courtyard into something that could be in a movie set, while dealing with twenty different service providers, their timetables, needs and payments. You have x amount in cash to do it, now go!

But this was only the end result. For eighteen months before I would deal with each couple once per week, helping them mould the dream wedding they had in their mind into something achievable within their budget.

I wasn't a stylist or into finding pink swans to match the bridesmaids' dresses; I was the queen of logistics. I left the fluffy stuff to decorators and florists.

However, the eighteen months only started after a couple booked. Getting the bookings in was a whole other part of the job. One out of every ten enquiries turned into a booking.

There was no way of knowing which one it would be, so I needed to give equal attention to all their important questions to help them make a decision, arrange visits to view venues or do virtual tours by video link. So, the one hundred and eighty enquiries that didn't book each year still took up hours of time and head space.

Most of my clients have been great. Their main concern is that their guests have a great time after travelling all this way to share their big day. Over the years, I've got to visit and stay at amazing venues, eat amazing food, drink fabulous wine and overall have a very special career that I proudly built myself.

As a result, Ronan focused on wedding photography, a service I included in some packages so we often got two business bookings at once. I enjoyed assisting Ronan so much that I did a two-year course in photography and became his assistant.

My business also meant I could give my niece and daughter a summer job helping set up weddings in Ireland when they were in their early teens. But, the benefit of my business that I was most grateful for was that it got us to Italy, that was the ultimate goal.

Now that we had achieved the goal and we are here living in Italy, weddings have fulfilled their need and the novelty and excitement has worn off.

After a two-year Covid lockdown hiatus, I'm finding returning to planning weddings is like trying to learn to write with my left hand. I am struggling and I recognise I am close to burnout.

15

MONSTERS

I have slipped into a new routine since Mam has arrived.

I get up in the mornings, make Mam her cup of tea and breakfast and bring it in to her. Mam listens to the Irish news on the radio and gives me a daily weather report for Ireland before I go out and get my own mug of tea.

Confident in my knowledge of the weather in Ireland for the day—which is usually, rain, wind, maybe some snow, cold and dull with a splattering of sun—I perch myself on the sofa.

Between 7.30am and 10.30am I write my one thousand words for the day, before starting on my emails from wedding clients and wedding enquiries.

At about 10.30am, Mam will come out to sit in her electric chair beside me and ask what I'm planning for dinner. I'll say I'm still trying to digest my breakfast and she'll scoff at me for being so disorganised. I then go back to planning every minute detail of twenty weddings.

Ma sitting beside me makes me anxious. I am conscious she is there and in need of something to do, even though she has my Kindle loaded with books and she is knitting jumpers for rescued battery hens.

She is using my Kindle account to the max, reading three or four Catherine Cookson books per week. Sometimes I'll convince her to try another author and she will inevitably finish the book in a day and tell me how crap it was and ask me why I recommended it.

I get a flashback to one of the Covid Lockdown calls I had with Dad. He talked about Mam with desperation in his voice, "She never shuts up talking, she goes on and on and on." I now see exactly what he meant. Mam doesn't seem to really like silence so she'll constantly ask me questions and tell me what I should be doing. As soon as I stand up and walk around to take a break from my computer, "Sit down and relax, will you?" And as soon as I sit down with a cup of tea for a break from work, "Do you see under that table? You need to sweep it, it's annoying the hell out of me. If I could get down on my knees, I would scrub that floor. Go get a brush and do it."

Or "I want to buy a frying pan/ a big pot /a different mat for my bedroom /a nightie / a tube of cobalt blue paint/ bread soda/ lamb chops. So when you get a chance today we'll go to the shops." There's always an endless list of random things she has thought about buying during the night.

She doesn't find it reasonable that the shops close at 12.30pm until 4pm. It doesn't suit her morning routine to be up and ready to go out by 11am. It doesn't suit mine either as that is when I work best. So we will often aim to go to a shop for 4pm. She finds it ridiculous that all the shops are so spread out and standalone.

"Let's go to the place we can buy the electric blanket and look around outside it before it opens." She means browse other shops, but when I drive her to it at 4pm she understands why I said that was not a good idea as it is a warehouse facing onto a busy road, it's not in a shopping mall.

To buy something electrical, we have to go to one shop, to get something like paint we have to travel to a different town to an art shop, to get a mat, well that would be the household goods shop which stands on its own in a town in a different direction altogether. There are shopping malls, yes, but they mostly comprise clothes and shoe boutiques, a big grocery chain, sometimes an electrical shop and lots of gelaterias and cafes. It's not like Ireland.

Today is a particularly busy day for me as I need to get some invoices done and it takes concentration. So to try to stop her thinking of things for me to do, I make Mam soup for lunch and turn on the TV to see if there is a movie she'd like in the afternoon.

I find myself not doing my emails but watching Doris Day play a housewife who finds herself in a job promoting Happy Soap. And even though she has been offered $80k per year for one day of work per week plus bonuses such as a free swimming pool being built overnight in her backyard, she decides she'd prefer to do her husband's bidding and be just the wife of a doctor and have another baby.

"Now that was a nice wholesome movie," Mam says, satisfied. "So what's for dinner tonight?"

"You've just finished lunch, do you never stop thinking of food?"

"It's what my life revolved around for the last sixty-five years, feeding your Da and you lot."

Dad. I leave the room with the excuse of checking for ingredients. I could feel the fizzing sensation in the back of my nose, rims of my eyes burning, ready for another losing battle with the hot angry tears that wanted to show everyone exactly how I feel. My mouth contorts, and the dull tightened band of pain of suppressed emotion takes over my crown.

It has been following me around, I can feel it so close sometimes that its breath makes the hairs on the back of my neck stand up and the muscles across my shoulders tighten even more than they already are. My body is developing natural armour–a solid shell of hard, tense muscle. It frightens me from time to time when it just appears unexpectedly; it whispers it will be gentle, but it has a smirk that you can't trust. Give it an inch and it will take a mile. It has a physical shape, a mass of dark grey blobbiness, like a giant turd.

It has stayed distant for weeks, sitting patiently on the other side of the room pretending to read a newspaper, even though it has no eyes, just dark voids. I had got comfortable with it there, but my acceptance of it staying distant seems to have given it privileges to follow me around and get closer. Too close for comfort.

Grief.

I'd got to know it well when my sister Eileen died, it loitered around for years. I had developed tactics of ignoring it until times I'd least expect to bump into it. I'd be enjoying myself at a wedding or shopping or chatting with someone on a drive and then it would happen; her song 'Come on Eileen' would come on and Grief would leap on me and dance all over me, leave me spinning and breathless. I'd got better at beating it off in recent years. It had given up on me I thought, just sticking it's head around the corner now and then for a quick hello. But it had found me again and had arrived with a suitcase.

I catch my breath and tear up, push it away. No, not now. It accepts but stays that little bit closer each time. Each push makes it bigger and gives it a little more strength. It reminds me there's no getting away from it. It's apologetic, nearly friendly. "Just go to bed alone and let me take over your body for a few minutes, an hour. Then I'll go," it smirks. But that smirk can't be trusted. It won't be a few minutes, it won't be an hour. It will be hours, days, weeks, months. Maybe it will never leave once I let it in. I can't let it in.

 I'll just keep pushing it away by staying busy. Accepting its presence with positivity. Brushing it off. Diminishing its character. But the more I do it, the more it smirks. Waiting patiently to pounce when I am least expecting it. I need to stay on guard.

Rob has called Mam. "You dropped your phone down the toilet I heard? You're an awful gobshite," she says.

The playful insult pings my heart. I have been texting Rob daily, "Any news?"

"No results back, they have to send them to my doctor and I need an appointment to see him and he's out the door with appointments at the moment so it will probably take a while..."

This was the last brush off he gave me. I've told him and his adult daughter Jenny to phone the doctor and the hospital and tell them this isn't good enough. With this latest excuse I am trying to work out how I can get back to Ireland to help him sort this out, he's being too soft and I know Rob, he'd rather not know so won't push it.

Mam is glad to be back to her regular daily count of calls from each of my three brothers and Rob.

"I just walked up the thirty-two flights of stairs in the house," Mam gleefully tells my brother Peter who's in New York. Apparently, we now live in a skyscraper to match any on the skyline he looks out on. "She means thirty-two steps, just in case you think she has become bionic," I explain in the background to my miffed brother. Mam had tackled our series of four sets of eight stone steps to the top floor for the first time to inspect Alex's work.

"I feel my back and legs are much better here, I might even go for a jog at this rate, you never know," again she is joking, what she means is her shuffling is getting less shuffley.

My phone buzzes, it's Rob's daughter Jenny. I go upstairs to take it so I can talk without Mam interrupting me. "Look, I am going to tell you, Dad doesn't want you or your Mam to know, but I know you love him as much as I do and you need to know."

She takes a breath. "He did get his medical results before Christmas. It's cancer and not the good kind, they can't operate."

I push the rising emotions aside, try to control my suddenly pounding heart so I can still hear her over its din. "Okay, so what did the doctors say for him to do?"

"Nothing! They told him go on as he is. They can't believe he's walking around pain and symptom free all this time. So I brought him to my therapist, she's a healer of sorts and she has put him on a strict diet of no sugar, no carbs, no starch and lots of greens. Whereas the doctors in the hospital didn't even tell him to give up drinking. It's unbelievable."

"What treatment are they going to give him, have they given a... timeline?"

"Not yet. They'll probably do chemo, Dad doesn't want to know details but we are waiting to see a specialist consultant... however, there's something else they said..."

A huge vicious monster comes into the room and towers over my cowering grief monster as she says the words, "it's incurable, so all we can do is pray for a miracle."

I say something like, "let's wait until he sees the specialist," and got off the phone quick. I am soaked in sadness. Drowning. The new vicious monster in the room is licking his lips, having gobbled up the grief guy in one bite. The grief monster was a pussy cat in comparison, so much more friendly and manageable. He has completely disappeared and I don't know how to play this new guy.

I had always imagined Rob and I growing old together. We were two peas in a pod; he was always there for all my decisions, to share my happiness and lift me out of my sadness. He was the one who hugged me. He was the one who congratulated me and told me how proud I should be of myself for doing whatever I wanted to do. He gave me the spirit of adventure and love of travel. I had thought of him whenever we did anything to the house.

"Rob is going to love this when he comes over ... I can't wait for Rob to see this." It was like I was doing everything for him. For him to enjoy as much as me, because no one deserved it more, and no one appreciated the little things in life as much as he did.

"Rosie, will you ever come down and fix the telly for me? Tipping Point is starting and the TV is gone off. Rosie, do you hear me?" My mother calls up the stairs.

I needed to be robotic, I couldn't show her I was emotional. And there is no way I want to be the one to tell her this, on my own, here in Italy. She might just die in front of me. I had been there before. No, she was not to know for as long as possible.

The tsunami of emotion got sucked back out to sea, leaving my ugly robotic underbelly.

Spooky moves from Mam's lap to mine, her neck arches up, her eyes seductively squinting 'pet me, pet me, how can you resist.' Or maybe I have it all wrong maybe she's saying 'pet me I'm here to help to sooth you.' Her soft, slick hair and the motion of stroking relaxes my throat. I take a deep breath.

For the coming days she goes from Mam's lap to mine but spends more on mine. "Have you abandoned me, cat? Cats are really quite a selfish animal, aren't they?" Mam tuts.

On the contrary, she is just going to the person who needs her most.

16

FOOD GLORIOUS FOOD

"What's for dinner today?" It's 11am but I don't protest.

"I'll have a look and see what there is." It gives me the opportunity to go out and blindly stare into the welcome cold air of the open fridge. I pretend to rummage as my face takes the opportunity to uncontrollably spasm again about Rob's news.

"I'll make pork with orange sauce. We can have potatoes with it if you like?" I announce, now under pressure to get through the mounting emails.

"Is there anything I can help you with getting the dinner ready?"

I give her two pots; one with water and one empty, and bring her in the bag of potatoes and the peeler. Peeling potatoes puts her in her happy place. Mam helping with any task means five tasks for me to prepare that one task.

I get two more emails done before Mam is finished peeling the potatoes and looking for another task to do.

"Is there anything I can do to help?"

"Do you want to iron or clean your bathroom?" I ask.

"Oh God no, I always hated cleaning and ironing, left them for my mother to do when yous were growing up, I'm not going to start now. Do you know most fatalities happen in the home, and a person dies from housework every three minutes?"

"I am sure that statistic is not correct, Ma."

"Well, I'm not taking any chances. Housework is dangerous I tell you. Is there anything else I can do?"

She asks me this at least ten times per day. And I get it, she is not in her own house, she doesn't want to be a burden and she is bored. But it is exasperating for me to try to find ways of keeping her amused all day.

I finally break. "Ma, like what?" I say. "Answer the fifty emails I've received already today or tile a bathroom? I mean what do you want to do that you can do? You are really going to have to help me figure this out."

She laughs, "I don't know. I am very happy sitting here doing nothing and being served on for a change."

"Yes Ma, you need to unwind and learn to relax, you don't have to be doing something all the time, and that includes talking." I snap and instantly feel mean. I don't like the person I am becoming, I shouldn't feel like this towards my mother.

She goes back to knitting, making random comments and in between her constant stream of words she'll fill the spaces with "Bibbilty bopity boo." Or other such meaningless phrases.

"Can you not get those stick-on tiles?" She is now trying to think of solutions to what I have offered her to do. "I got them and haven't seen them since. It's like if anything is too easy, they get rid of it."

I'm wondering who she thinks the evil 'they' are who have the authority to get rid of anything people find easy.

Mam watches the six o'clock Irish news in the evening. Every day it starts with reporting the Covid numbers that have tested positive and how many people are hospitalised with it. It continues in that vein, with some sector complaining how the restrictions are affecting them or the government talking about a meeting they are going to have next Tuesday about possible new measures. It's always on a Tuesday.

"Will you put on the short news, the one before the news? Cheerful Charlie will be on saying 'well a million people have it today but there might be another million. They are all grand but they might all die so don't get to happy about it'." Her mock impression of the guy who is looking after the Covid reports is really good and eases the tension I am feeling.

The food boxes have been the best thing ever for getting me through the last month. They not only provide me with gorgeous meals I don't have to think about finding the ingredients for, but they have also been instrumental in helping me improve my cooking skills and my Italian as I no longer need the translation app to read the instructions. I now know the words for different herbs, vegetables and tasks like mix and add.

I am now more adventurous when shopping too, seeking out pecorino rather than parmigiano, strozzapreti rather than spaghetti, tortiglioni rather than fusilli.

I know how to use pancetta, guanciale and zucca, salvia and zenzero for flavours. I can taste the difference for the better of using a mix of beef and pork mince rather than just manzo. The Italian names of spices are familiar to me.

I know not to add the salt to the boiling water until immediately before putting in the pasta.

I know I can coat chicken with flour seasoned with smoked paprika, sear in the pan and then coat with BBQ sauce or sweet chilli and bake in the oven to make a quick, easy, tasty dinner. And to add peanuts or chopped almonds to meats and veg to add another element of flavour and texture.

I can make a dressing of mayonnaise, mustard, spring onion for new potatoes. A balsamic and olive oil dressing for salad and how to caramelise onions using a small bit of sugar.

So I don't need the box deliveries anymore, I just mix and match my knowledge to produce a delicious meal every night, and enjoy my new hobby of cooking.

I've overheard Mam talking to cousins and relatives on the phone and besides telling them we live near 'Lake Tiramisu' I have heard her continue the rhetoric that Rosie can't cook. "The chips she makes are disgusting," she says, referring to that one incident of viagra-needing oven chips I made six weeks ago.

"They eat a lot of pasta and mince. And they use so much olive oil! The only place we could buy olive oil years ago were small bottles in the pharmacy. You'd warm it and use it for earache to dissolve earwax. They even put it on salad here for goodness sake. And hardly ever a potato and never a piece of liver or a lamb chop."

It will be a dark day in my kitchen if internal organs hit my hob. And it's not spring yet, so there is no lamb. Although it is something I am not fond of eating either. I am not into eating babies of any type.

The following day, I am still picking breakfast cereal out of my teeth and Mam is again out asking what I am making for dinner that day.

"You have to have a plan of what you are going to eat every day, this is a ridiculous way of living. You should have stuff in your freezer to pull out the night before to defrost. I'll organise you."

"We really don't need to be organised. We are happy the way we are."

She tuts and ignores me. "The first thing you need to do is make a list of all the dinners for the week."

She sits down and opens one of her many notebooks.

"So, I've made a list; we'll have stew on a Monday. Chicken and potatoes on Tuesdays. Pork chops and potatoes on a Wednesday. Coddle on a Thursday. Chips and fish on a Friday. Saturday you could do something like potatoes and liver and then Sunday a roast with roast potatoes. "

She's jotting all this down while my chest tightens at the idea of knowing what I'm going to eat every day for the rest of my life. Never mind the idea of the main staple in every dish being starchy potatoes.

"It's not really how we operate here, Ma."

"Well, you have to have some sort of plan. We'll go to the supermarket, leave it to me. We need to make a list of all the things you usually buy and then each week you go through it and mark off the things you need that week. I wrote a list down for you this morning."

I haven't been at the supermarket as much in my complete pre-Ma time in Italy as I have been in the last few weeks. I usually leave grocery shopping to Ronan while I work full-time dealing with wedding stuff. But, of course, I can't expect Ronan to be running Mam to the supermarket every day.

"What's that?" she says, pointing to the containers of clear liquid on the bottom shelf of the baking aisle in the supermarket.

"That's pure alcohol, Ma."

"What? What's that for?"

"It's for making limoncello and other digestifs the Italians like to make."

"Good God! That couldn't be sold in Ireland, could you imagine? Everyone would be downing it straight... get me a container of it."

"Why? What do you want that for?"

"It would be great for making poteen."

"Mother of God, you are not setting up an illegal poteen still in my house!"

"It's probably not illegal here."

"No Ma, you are not getting it. Stick to the whiskey."

I'm starting to wonder how the Italians do it; live with their parents in harmony.

Although the average number of children Italians have is two, the family living in one house or apartment are larger than you might assume. Ageing family members in Italy are usually taken care of by younger generations, with sometimes three generations living together in the same house—Nonna and Nonno, Mamma and Papà, i bambini and sometimes even an aunt or uncle or two.

There is not an Italian word for the emotion of being lonely, like there is not one for privacy either. Perhaps the two go hand in hand as families have always lived together.

Italy has nearly twenty-thousand people over one hundred years old and has held the world record for the oldest living human nearly every year for the last couple of decades. Italy also has the second highest life expectancy in the world.

The Mediterranean diet, hills and steps keep people in general good health. People retire earlier, giving a more relaxed, stress-free lifestyle to the elderly. The midday riposo offers a way for the oldest family members to still share in a meal and visits from their children and play with and hug their grandchildren—if they are not already living with them, that is.

On weekends, extended families get together for pranzo di Domenica (Sunday lunch), either at a relative's home or a local agriturismo. They gather at long, family-style tables, often seating fifteen to twenty people.

"How was it living with Nanny all those years?" I ask my mother, about living with her own mother, on the drive home from the supermarket. I'm hoping to glean some insight into how to make this new living arrangement work better for us.

"Oh, sure it was great. She lived with us from the time my father died at sixty-three so she was there from the time Eileen and Peter were just babies. So she cleaned and cooked. I never cleaned in my life. She helped rear the five of you... Well except you. She was old by the time you came along, so Eileen reared you."

Thinking back, Nanny was like an Italian Nonna, always in the kitchen cooking up a pot of preservatives, marmalade, chutney or a stew or casserole. Or cleaning. While my memories of my mother are of her wallpapering, painting pictures or gardening. Or getting glammed up to go on the twice-a-week date nights with my dad as they had an in-house baby sitter. When Nanny got old, Eileen took over.

Any memory I have of Mam in the kitchen, Nanny is there alongside her. I realise I had three mothers of different generations bring me up. The same way as old-style Italy.

So maybe that is the trick for your parents to live in harmony with you. They need to be there from the start, to help with the children at the time when they are needed most, and by the time the children are grown and the parents are older, everyone has their routines, their own friends and independent lifestyle that crosses over and intermingles with each family member's lives.

This hasn't been the case with us... I'm quickly learning that flying your 85-year-old mother into a new setting and expecting everything to be rosy is not the way to do it.

17

CAR COCK UPS

The issue of a car is still hanging over us like sour grapes on a vine. We haven't heard from the woman with the bouffant hairstyle and silver blue eyeliner, who had trouble finding Ronan's cock several times before.

When we visit the place again to re-register our car, we take Sherwin with us as he managed to successfully re-register through them previously.

Because of Covid restrictions, only two people are allowed into the office at any one time. So I stand there in front of the desk with Sherwin and the woman stares at me blankly as if she has never seen me before. "I'm the woman with the Irish car?" I say in Italian to remind her.

"Ah, sì sì."

She takes my thick faded denim-blue cardboard file from beside her computer and signals for us to come around to the side table. There is a sticky note on the front of the file.

"Ah, we are waiting on your cock," she says satisfactorily as if solving the clue as to why she hasn't done the job expected of her.

"Seriously?" I say in disbelief as she opens the file and skips past the first two pages which are the COC document and a photocopy of it.

"Aspetti," I say remembering the correct ending for 'you wait' rather than saying 'I wait' or 'he waits' or 'they all wait'.

I lean over the counter and flick back the two pages.

"There is my cock!"

"Ahhh sìììì."

I quickly close the file and peel off the Post-it note with COC written on it, crumple it and say "for the trash." That sticky note has cost us three months delay already.

"Ahh sìììì sìììì," she says with a little laugh and dramatically throws it in the bin.

She then opens the file and turns over each page one at a time and puts them face down while muttering words like "sì, sì, sì. Allora...Va bene... ok" as if verifying each page, and then when she reaches the end of the pile, she turns it back to the start and does the same thing again. There are a lot of pages. At least three photocopies of each requested document.

I could feel one of those laughs rising, the type that happens in a situation where laughing is completely inappropriate, usually when it's very quiet and everyone else is serious.

It hasn't happened to me in a long time but this one is rising fast and when she gets to the end of the file and starts to do the exact same thing again, and Sherwin looks down in dismay at me and says, in his strong London accent, "What the hell is she doing?" I couldn't hold it back any longer.

Luckily I can do silent laughing. My body just shakes, my face scrunches and tears well. It's not a pretty sight and I can usually disguise it with a cough or pretend sneeze but that is definitely not an appropriate thing to do at the moment with everyone aware of Covid. The mask I'm wearing disguises most of my contorted facial features, except my eyes which tears flood out of. She looks up, thinks I am crying and shuts the file.

"Okay, we move on to the next stage."

"The next stage is getting the new plates?" Sherwin asks.

"Have you had a meeting with the auto office?" she asks.

"What is that?" I say.

"I make you an appointment."

Sherwin asks her what this appointment is for, I sort of understand her reply but I feel I must have it wrong. Sherwin translates. "They will go through your paperwork and check it."

That's what I thought she had said.

"Is that not what she is being paid to do for the last three months?" I say, although she hasn't asked for money yet, nor have we paid her a cent.

She sits down at her computer and goes onto an appointment page. Together, between Sherwin's and my understanding of Italian we have the following conversation:

"The nearest office is Perugia or you can choose one further away."

"Why would we choose an office further away?"

"The offices are very busy, the nearest appointment is in three weeks' time."

"Oh, so the offices further away are less busy and we would get an appointment sooner?"

"No, they are busy too. It would be about the same timing."

So I choose the nearest office and agree to an appointed time. The laughter is well gone; confusion has replaced it and I feel annoyance rising.

I tentatively ask, "how long will it take to get the plates after the meeting?"

"About a month or two," is her smiling-eyed reply.

I feel a Veronica bank moment coming on, where I might lose my cool and ask her why she is smiling and not apologising for not doing her job, which has already cost us a lot of money and problems.

Now, between the waiting time for this mysterious meeting that we didn't know we had to have, and the waiting time afterwards, we are talking about another three months of car rental. This process, which was to take one month, has now turned into a six-month time suck, because Bouffant Head Woman didn't bother to open the file. I break the news to Ronan. His words are not repeatable.

On the drive home, we calm ourselves and think through our options.

"We'll just have to continue renting this car for another month or two," I say.

It seems the easiest but most costly solution.

"I've already looked into it, just in case there was a delay," says Ronan. "And it's not possible to extend the rental for another month. Car companies are not permitted to do short-term rentals beyond two months or something. And anyway, renting is bloody expensive, it's an expense we just don't need. Long-term leasing is expensive too and what I have read and understand it isn't possible as we are self-employed by a company in a different country."

I go through all the options in my head, if we didn't have Mam here, we could use the van while we get sorted, but she needs to get out and about and can't get in and out of the van. She can only get into cars with a certain seat height.

"Other than attaching a motor to Mam's wheelchair and a trailer for us all to sit in, I think there is only one option for us..."

"Buy a secondhand car and leave the idea of changing the plates of our old, but perfectly good car, aside for now?"

"That's the one. But we need to do it fast, the rental on this runs out next week and we can't drive the other car now that it is in limbo between countries."

Urgh.

18

TWO RONANS

Ronan likes car shopping. I hate it. Sherwin offers to take us around car dealerships he knows on Saturday. Himself and Shelly pick us up after lunch and we head off. But each one we go to is closed.

Car dealers may have the broker name of big car companies above their shops, but they are usually local independent dealers with a staff of only two or three people. And they all seem to close for the afternoon riposo.

"You'd think car dealers would cop on and open on a Saturday afternoon when people have time to browse for a new car?" I grumble, thinking of all the work time I am wasting looking at the locked gates of car lots.

"Well, it's also to do with how the working week works in Italy," explains Shelly. "In Italy, the average work week is about thirty-six hours with the maximum hours set at forty hours."

"Overtime isn't permitted to go over forty-eight hours," Sherwin chips in. "They definitely go with the concept of work to live rather than live to work. And it's recognised as a right, considering the government standard is that every worker gets four weeks paid holiday around the August Ferragosto vacation period, as well as twelve national holidays."

We look through the locked fences into the yards like we are looking at exhibits in a zoo trying to spot the illusive bargain. But many of the cars look quite battered or are out of our price range. There is a shortage of new cars because of Covid, which has had a knock-on effect on the secondhand trade-in market.

While their offices are closed, we find one with an ungated yard, so we pull in and take a look around. The area is small enough to walk around and see all the cars within twenty minutes. The ones with prices in the windows seem high for what's on offer. All the cars have scrapes and dents from the tight narrow streets and the Italian way of driving.

"How about this one," I shout to Ronan who comes over, elated that I am actually interested in a car. We are both looking in the windows of the Fiat, trying to see the milage on the clock, Ronan is checking for rust.

"Yeah, it would depend on the price. This one looks okay too," he says about the car next to it. Again, there is no price in the window, but we can see inside and it looks in good condition.

"What are you guys doing?" says Sherwin coming over to us across the grass verge running through the car lot.

"These two look good but it would depend on the price, milage is okay for the year and–" says Ronan trying the doors to pop the bonnet.

"Guys," interrupts Sherwin. "This side is the car dealership, that side of the verge is the car park for the shops over there. You are just looking in the windows of people's cars, not cars for sale. Get back over to this side before you are caught on CCTV and arrested."

As we scuttle back across the grass verge that creates the invisible line and Ronan is saying, "they really should be more clear about which cars are for sale and which cars are to rob."

My phone buzzes with a text message.

"Speak of the devil," I say. "It's from Rob."

"I've my chemo starting date. Valentine's day. How nice!"

My heart hurts a bit. I want to see him, hug him make things better for him. And then I get an idea and I text back as we walk to Sherwin's car.

"Why don't you come over for a quick holiday before you start? You could fly into Rome with Jenny. We could do some sightseeing and then you can come up here the following day, see Ma and have a nice time."

"I can't see why not. I've always wanted to see Rome. Let's do it."

"Leave it to me, I'll arrange everything." I'm excited. Rob loves history and even though he has travelled extensively, he has overlooked Italy—the land of visible history. I want to make this a really special trip; something he can think and talk about while getting his chemo over the coming months. Also, Alex will have finished the top floor by then so the house will look complete and I can't wait for Rob to see it.

But there's something I need to do to make it happen. I need to get my booster Covid shot so I may travel on the train to Rome, as they have announced that everyone needs the Super Green Pass to go on public transport from next week.

I still can't make my appointment online without the elusive Tessera Sanitaria health card, so I go to a pharmacy, queue at the desk with my Green Pass and code fiscale and make an appointment for a few days' time without a problem. Ronan isn't so successful.

It turns out his first vaccine appointments were made with him registered without his middle name, but his middle name is on his passport and included in his code fiscale, so now there are two Ronans on the Italian system that are competing to be the right one. One has been vaccinated, and the other has not. The pharmacist throws her hands in the air, she can't do anything about it. So again, Ronan can't get the required vaccine to function in Italy.

To solve the problem, we go back to the Sunflower pharmacist who originally gave Ronan the vaccine. He has a soft spot for us as he honeymooned in Ireland. He also has a team of young pharmacists working with him who are computer whizzes, and can find their way around the complicated Italian healthcare software.

After forty-five minutes and four pharmacists' time around the computer, they finally make an appointment for Ronan. If we didn't have anyone else to think about, Ronan and I would have stopped off to eat somewhere on the way home to save ourselves the trouble of having to make dinner.

But instead, I have to plan and think of something creative. So while Ronan is in the pharmacy, I nip into the butcher next door and buy some loins of pork to do in an orange and apricot glaze for dinner.

I know Mam will have a pot of potatoes ready to go and she has been hinting at pork chops for the last week. Pale bland pork chops served with bland boiled potatoes does nothing for my saliva glands, but a tasty orange glaze makes the idea of pork a lot more attractive. She can have the bland stuff the following evening when I am in Rome.

As Luca was late getting his vaccine, due to bureaucracy and his age group, his Green Pass is still valid for another month. So Luca will come to Rome with me, and Ronan will stay at home to keep Mam company and look after our pets.

Orange & Apricot Glazed Pork
Serves: 4

1 Orange

2 Cloves garlic cut in half

2 Tbls of apricot jam

1 Tbls of soy sauce

2 Loins of pork

Olive oil

2 Tbls of flour

Salt and pepper

Method:

Grate the orange peel (not the pith) then cut the orange in two and squeeze the juice. Squash the garlic.

In a saucepan add the jam, orange juice, half the grated peel, garlic and soy sauce. Add pinch of salt and pepper and about 40mls of water.

Bring to boil and then reduce to minimum heat for about 7 minutes.

Remove the garlic from the sauce.

Cut the pork into slices (about 1cm wide). Coat the pork slices in the flour.

Heat the oil in a pan and fry the slices of pork until cooked (about 2 minutes each side).

Add the orange sauce to the pan with the pork and on a low heat stir them together for just a couple of minutes, until the meat is coated, and the liquid is reduced to a glaze.

Plate the glazed pork, and garnish with the remaining orange peel.

Serve with rice or potatoes and green beans.

19

PRESSURE COOKING

B y the time we get back, Rob has called Mam and told her he'd be over. I think he might also have had a word with her about the pressure I am under with work, and that perhaps she can make her own breakfasts in the mornings.

"Don't bother making me breakfast in the morning, I can do my own when I get up. I know you are busy with work."

She is delighted that Rob is coming over.

I have a sense of relief. The next morning feels like a real indulgence; it's the first time I can sit in bed and write since my bedroom was finished. However, the dogs need to be let out and me tapping away on the keyboard is disturbing Ronan.

Ronan is a night owl, and I am a morning person. We spend about three hours in the same bed each night, Ronan tries to be as quiet as a ballerina waiting to go on stage when getting ready for bed, but he's more like an elephant in a glass house and two out of three nights he will wake me.

I race to get back to sleep before his head hits the pillow, if I don't, my sleep is finished as his thunderous snoring starts within minutes.

Even if I do get back to sleep, we now have Paddy sleeping beside our bed who, having possibly been a hunting dog in his previous life, is eager to get outside by 5am.

He starts a type of tap-dancing routine at 4.30am psyching himself up for the impending release. Ronan is not woken by Paddy's morning dance routine but considering a spider making its web from two rooms away would probably wake me, Paddy's tap-dancing sounds like thunder to me in the early hours.

Between me not being able to go to bed until after Mam has everything she needs to retire after 10pm, and being disturbed by Ronan at 2am and woken by Paddy at 4.30am, I am feeling slightly sleep deprived.

I don't want to wake Ronan, so I throw on my dressing gown, gather my stuff and head down to our luxurious blue velvet sofa with chaise, so I can sit with my feet up while working on my day job wedding stuff.

However, Mam has loaded the chaise, which runs alongside her electric chair, with things she just might need at any given moment of the day ... a pair of binoculars, ribbons on a stick to play with the cat, two balls of wool and knitting needles, an Italian-English dictionary, several notebooks of assorted sizes, a long shopping list and a plate with left over cracker crumbs.

It's eight in the morning and I can hear the Irish news blasting from Mam's room, so I pop my head in and offer a cup of tea.

"No, No, I'll get it myself when I'm ready."

The advantage of Ronan being a night owl is that he usually cleans the kitchen before bed. And I am glad to see last night was one of those nights; the kitchen is sparkling.

So, with the kitchen clean and no breakfast duties, I can get a head start on a difficult workday. I open my spreadsheet of 'to dos' that I have been avoiding as it is littered with potential headaches waiting to happen.

There's an email from the cash bar supplier for my weddings to say he went bankrupt during Covid and he is no longer in business. This is a massive problem as I have sold a lot of my weddings with a bar available for the three days their guests are at a venue and he was the only one that provides such a service in this part of Italy.

If I can't find a bar provider, I'll have to set up and run a bar myself, along with coordinating the wedding and being Ronan's second-in-command photographer for some of the weddings too. That's three full-time jobs running simultaneously.

I am googling Dolly the Sheep to see if there has been any progress in cloning humans that I have missed, when I hear Mam's loud slipper shuffle into the kitchen. She never gets up early, my three hours of alone time in the morning are precious, when I can work in silence without interruption.

"I'm making an omelette do you want one?" she calls to me.

"No, thanks."

"Have you no cheese, no?"

"Yes, there is cheese."

"I don't think you have any."

I briskly put down my laptop, march to the fridge where she stands blocking the door.

"Stand back."

"I'm looking for the cheese."

"I know but if you get out of my way, I'll find it for you. It's there," I say pointing in front of her.

"There I've found it..." she says simultaneously. "Why do you push everything to the back of the fridge?"

"I don't."

"I can never find anything when you do that."

"I'll put on the kettle for you," I say, walking away.

"Thanks, do you want a cup?"

"No, I'm fine I just made one."

She gets busy and I march back into the sitting room and recommence trying to piece together a wedding booked in 2018 that has been postponed three times because of Covid. They can't understand why things have gone up in price four years later.

"Why do they make these bloody packets so difficult to open," I hear from the kitchen.

I take this as a cry for help, so I put back down the laptop and go out to the kitchen, where she has the package of cheese now successfully opened.

Back to my computer.

"Have you no onions, no?" She calls out.

"Yes."

"Where?"

"In the vegetable drawer."

"That's a stupid place to put them, I can't open that."

"I'll get them." Down with the laptop again and out to the kitchen.

"Ah, you sit down, I know you have work to do," she says opening the fridge for me so I can get at the vegetable drawer.

"It's not that drawer, it's the one here in the cupboard so that you can get to them," I say, retrieving the onions.

I'm back at my makeshift office on the sofa skipping on to the next thing that might be easier to tick as done off my to do list.

Does Deirdre Henry want a flower arch or not? I'm trying to remember what was decided as it's not on her final order and yet we went through twenty different flower arch options. I'm searching through a load of different emails to find the final decision. Mam shuffles in carrying her mug and plate of omelette.

"I think I made green tea instead of black. I used the bags in the yellow tin."

"Yes, that's green tea."

"Yeah, I think I made green tea," She tuts unsatisfied. She sits down into her chair like a bag of spuds being dropped from a height.

"Do you want me to make you black tea? The one you like?"

"No, this will do," she says with a look of distaste on her face. "Are you sure you don't want some omelette?"

The whiff of cooked egg and onion fills the room, making me feel nauseous.

"No, thanks I'm fine, I don't eat first thing in the morning."

"But you've been up hours? Fasting is not good for you. Do you have one of those eating disorder things?" She's not meaning what she says, she is just filling the silence, but I'm not entertaining this conversation. There's silence. She knows I am working. Spooky comes in and meows.

"Pussy cat are you starving, is no one feeding you?" she says loudly to the cat sitting washing herself on the arm of the chair. "Aww, you poor pussy cat. Did you not have your breakfast? Did Rosie not give you any breakfast either?"

Bloody hell, I haven't sent out the invoices for two weddings I realise, trying not to get riled by her words.

She finishes her omelette, leaves her plate down on the chaise and announces, "I think I'll make a quiche," before launching herself out of her chair and back into the kitchen.

I can't stop thinking of the catchy chapter I want to write in my new series. But I have to stop myself. I have all this wedding stuff to get through before I can indulge and lose myself in a forest of words.

"Did Ronan not get the roll-out pastry I asked him to get yesterday, no?" she calls out from the kitchen.

"Yes," I shout back.

"Where?"

"In the fridge."

"I can't see it. He mustn't have got any, I asked him to. I'll kill him."

I take a deep breath, "I'll find it."

"There it is," I say, pointing to the packet behind where the cheese was, but has been left on the counter.

The previous sparkling kitchen looks like there has been an explosion. There is onion, empty eggshells and grease everywhere.

"Maybe I'll make the quiche tomorrow, my back is at me today and I have been standing too long already. I have decided I am going to cook more in this lovely kitchen of yours, it's such a shame not to use it."

"What are you talking about? We do use it."

"It doesn't look used."

"That's because we keep it clean."

But she's out of the kitchen and heading into the garden.

I need a break and to do something physical as I'm too agitated to concentrate. I just finish cleaning the kitchen, putting it back to its tidy self and I'm about to wipe the island counter top when she's back again.

"There's no need to go out for dinner so much, when you have a lovely kitchen like this."

"Twice per week is hardly a lot and with Covid we haven't been out much for a year."

"Where's your food mixer?"

"Why?"

"I'm going to make breadcrumbs."

"For what?"

"To make stuffing." She has handfuls of herbs.

"Why don't you sit down and rest your back for a while, we don't have a need for stuffing at the moment."

"You could have it for next Christmas, it will last in the freezer."

"Well, how about reading instead for a while? We have a whole eleven months to make next Christmas's stuffing."

I make myself and herself a cup of tea and sit back down to work, while Mam scrolls through the books I've downloaded through my account for her ferocious reading appetite onto the Kindle reading app on her tablet.

I'm focusing on my bar dilemma. Where am I going to find two-hundred bottles of beer, two-hundred plastic glasses and all the bar supplies I need?

"There's one book there, and it's disgusting," she says, interrupting my thoughts. "Don't read that. I'll delete it."

"It's not yours to delete, so don't."

"I'm just telling you, it is disgusting, started off okay and then what she didn't do to him. Up against the wall, in the back of the car, it's absolutely disgusting, pure filth. I'll delete it."

"Mam that is my account, don't delete it! And don't start telling me which books I can or can't read. I am reading books in different genres to learn the romance market... I'm fifty years old Ma, I can handle reading a bit of sex... Which one is it anyway?"

She shows me. I don't tell her it was one I wrote under a pen name years ago, which I uploaded to share with a few writer friends to see if it hit the right beats. It didn't, but the sex scenes were good. I make a mental note to delete it as my romance writing has 'matured' and gone a completely different direction with the Hero-scoping series I am working on and my first novella 'The Cosmo Club'. Although Mam will not be allowed read these, as there is still some sex in them, although a lot milder than the ones she has just got hot under the collar about.

"Just read the books I have downloaded for you. Not the ones I have downloaded for myself, okay?"

She huffs.

I am calculating how many measures in a bottle of gin and how many drinks a group of eighty guests would drink per night. And then working out how much I'd need to buy and how much I should charge per drink to cover costs... Eighty by three drinks is—

The silence is suddenly filled with a loud instructional voice.

"Il Ragazzo."

The 'you got it right' chime bings on Mam's Duolingo app.

Eighty by three is two hundred and forty drinks, and the number of measures per bottle is—

'La Ragazza' Mam repeats the word loudly. There's that chime again.

My agitation is rising. I can't concentrate, there's no point.

"I'm going up to have a shower," I say, hoping a break will lower my blood pressure.

"You only had one three days ago, why bother? You are fine. Sit down and relax."

Alex better finish upstairs fast and get Luca out of my office, otherwise he might be given the job of digging a second grave beside Asha's.

20

GET OUT

I t's important to learn the difference between the words for external and internal.

Alex has brought his cousin the carpenter back who did such a good job restoring some of the interior doors already. Alex seems to have an extended family here.

I think it is in the same way Lucia has a whole range of adopted parents from different countries. We are her Irish family, but I have been introduced to other returning international guests and several Italian women who are; "like my family, they are my Swedish/Russian/Finnish/second Mamma and Papa." They smile warmly, thrilled that Lucia makes them feel so special, like we once did.

I am beginning to think Alex's cousins are the same—adopted tradesmen he has worked with for years, who are now blessed with the honour of being considered his family as he trusts them so much. Like Ivor, his cousin Ettore is from somewhere other than Italy but they use Italian as their communication language and in his case as with AlmerRoberto before, he has adopted an Italian name as his real name is too complicated to pronounce.

I had expressed an interest in getting a quote for some of the windows to be fixed with new latches so that Mam can open them with ease and they would close more securely. Not against burglary, but because every time there was a storm, some windows on every floor blow open and we run around the house barricading them shut with whatever is lying near them like a scene out of a horror film.

To add to the effect, a small gap is inevitable which acts as the perfect musical reed for howling winds to whistle eerily through. Paired with Italy's fabulous thunder and lightning, and voila, welcome to the set of the next Adams Family movie. At least we have gotten rid of the mould and cobwebs set design.

Alex seems to have adopted the Italian way of accepting the job as booked if you ever casually say the words 'I might like to get X done at some point.'

"Alex, I need a quote first."

"Ah it is not much, don't worry, you can pay us whenever you have the money."

"No, Alex I need to budget for this."

"It is €200 per window and door and €400 for the French doors, okay?" he says as if I have pestered him into telling me a state secret. He hates discussing money.

"Well, that seems reasonable. Okay, we will move ahead with getting four of the windows done downstairs and six doors upstairs."

I had not been specific with Alex which doors I was referring to.

So when the carpenter arrives and asks if it is the internal doors to be done or the external ones, I say the word I am sure is correct for internal, while rushing out to a meeting.

The temperature has dropped to minus two Celsius. I have heating but when I get back, I can feel the 'freshness' of the morning frost very well with a clear uninterrupted view from each of our three balconies.

My wordage mess-up has landed us without the three upstairs balcony doors on the coldest weekend of the year. They needed to be done too at some point, so I don't say anything.

It's like freddo and caldo; the words for hot and cold. It took my brain ages to stop using caldo for cold. It means hot by the way, freddo is cold.

I always got funny looks when discussing weather with strangers while waiting for a train or something and they would be wrapped up to the nines, their breath showing and saying something like "Mamma mia the temperature," and I would respond, "Sì molto caldo."

However, I put my foot down when Alex suggests the carpenter take the sitting room and kitchen window away to be fixed.

"No, he needs to do them onsite and have them back in the same day," I say to Alex. I cannot have no windows downstairs for a few days, especially not with my mother here.

"Does your mother go somewhere else?"

"What no, like where?"

"A cousin perhaps?"

"I don't have cousins in Italy. I don't have any family here."

"Ah come on you do, we are like family now. You and Roman you are good people I trust you and that makes you family. Lucia considers you family and I now consider you family."

"Okay, so do you want to take my mother?"

He laughs, "I have to work. But it is better she is not here when there is work to be done."

"Well, we don't have a choice, so they do the windows on site same day, or we wait until the summer," I say.

"Okay, okay, he will do the windows here starting tomorrow, one at a time so it will be slower. "

Alex continues, "One more week and we are finished upstairs and then we start the big bathroom and then we are done. I move on to another job. You will never see me here again, except when you invite me for dinner. We must all have dinner together."

The pressure is on, "I still haven't found tiles I want for that bathroom, nor bought the fittings."

"Why not? You better hurry if you want me to do something nice in your toilet."

That really doesn't sound good.

The work crew arrives early which is good as Mam is still in bed. The carpenters remove the sitting room windows and start working on them, while Alex and Ivor are upstairs plasterboarding the ceiling in what will be Luca's bedroom.

They plane the windows, make adjustments and paint the frames grey before skipping off for a coffee.

Alex comes trundling down the stairs at high speed.

"Your friend Mick Kelly has called me. It is not good. He says we need to get off site, we cannot work here as we do not have the permissions. He is on his way." Alex is already winding up an extension cable and packing up. "I told you that you need to get rid of these guys, I do not trust them, they will report everything, why is he still involved? We need to leave I am sorry."

I'm looking at our very open windows in both the sitting room and kitchen and think about Luca sitting at the desk that I wanted for myself in my own office space.

"Alex you are not going anywhere, you have to finish the work here, Mick Kelly does not dictate who comes into my house."

But Alex is not listening he is looking over my shoulder and sees Mick Kelly coming in the gate, so shoots up the stairs two steps at a time.

Mick Kelly knows his way around to the back of the house.

I meet him at the back door.

"Rosie, they need to leave, they cannot work here. They do not have the permissions," Mick Kelly says.

"What the hell?" I say as I watch Ivor climb over the balcony behind Mick Kelly's back and drop to the roof of the shed. Mick Kelly is about to turn around, so not wanting him to spot Ivor climbing down the wall to the side passageway of the house, I throw my hands up in the air and raise my voice in over the top aggression to him.

"What the hell? Are you saying we cannot have someone in to paint the place? Come in and explain yourself," I usher him loudly to cover the sound of Ivor jogging away.

"I need the permissions for the plumbing and electrician," Mick Kelly says explaining, taken aback by my burst of anger.

"But they are not doing that."

This is not really a lie as they are not working on the plumbing yet and the electrician is not due for another week. "And Mick Kelly neither you nor Tomo have responded to calls or texts since November, so how are we supposed to know what is happening or what is needed from us to continue the work?"

"Rosie, they are not permitted to work here, it is still under Antonio's licence so he is responsible for any workers in the house. These are not his workers."

Now I was getting irritated for real.

"This is our house and they have our permission. You are working for us and you should have sorted this."

Ronan chips in, "They even have their own tools."

Mick Kelly persists, "They cannot continue. They must leave the premises now," he says with great urgency as if he has heard there is a bomb planted under the house.

My redhead blood is being ignited, "Eh... no you are working for us and I tell you what, you can get off our premises, how about that?"

Mick Kelly just stands there not knowing what to say or do, while I am staring him down. There's no way he is moving anyone out of our house when there is minus two air wafting into our living area and a teenager to be moved from my space as quickly as possible before he gets too comfortable.

"What permissions do they need for painting and decorating?" says Ronan in an exasperated voice, that is nearly only audible to bats.

"You don't understand, Antonio is the contractor for this project and we need to close the project first before you take on a new contractor."

"The bloody project was closed months ago. Antonio has been fully paid for his...efforts."

"No, the project is not closed."

"Why not?"

"To close the project, I need to a final inspection."

"Okay, so do a final inspection," Ronan says.

"You want me to do the final inspection and close the project?"

"Yes! That should have been done when Antonio pulled out surely, and when the invoices were handed in for the 50/50," I say.

"You want me to submit the invoices I have for the 50/50?"

"YES! Please tell me you have submitted them? We are relying on that final payment."

"I will submit them."

"You haven't submitted them?"

"I will submit them. And I come for the final inspection."

"Bloody hell."

Mick Kelly goes out and talks to Alex outside, who is looking coy after taking the backdoor rather than the balcony exit.

Micko comes back in to us and Alex heads back upstairs two steps at a time again.

"Okay, so Alex needs to get me the certificate from the electrician before I can close the project."

"But we haven't had an electrician work here yet?"

"But he needs to do the work and then we close the electrics on the house as it needs to have the correct certificates."

"Okay, I get that. And we of course want all the electrical work certified. But they won't be leaving midway through decorating or getting the windows done."

"No, there is no need for them to leave. I will be back next week to do the final inspection." And with that, he was gone.

"Did he actually think he could get workers out of our house?" I say in wonderment to Ronan.

"Che palle!" exclaims Ronan, meaning 'what balls', a crude Italian version of 'what a nerve'.

I need a cup of tea. Or possibly a drink. I might be an alcoholic before this house is finished or just to get over the shock of Ronan speaking two words of Italian after four years.

21

AFRICAN GARDEN

Ronan is unpacking the shopping he just returned with, including a small packet of wipes with a pink tree on the front; 'Femina Intima'.

"Ronan what did you buy these for?"

"For cleaning Paddy's ears. The vet said his floppy ears need to be cleaned often to stop infections."

"But Ronan these are for cleaning your arse with."

"Are they?" he says casually, not caring really.

"Anything with 'Intima' written on it, is usually to do with bidets or arse cleaning of some sort in Italy, and more so, 'Femina' probably means it's for female arses."

"So they'll be more sensitive for his flappy ears, perfect," Ronan responds, munching on a cracker.

The packet is forgotten about but pops up on the kitchen counter every now and again when Ronan has finished cleaning

Paddy's ears and then just doesn't have a place to store them so leaves them out.

Mick Kelly has arrived to do the final report to close the project under Antonio's name. Alex and Ivor did an exit stage left as soon as they heard he was coming. They have just about finished upstairs but I haven't been up there as I didn't want them to feel I was inspecting their work. Besides, I was so busy with work I just wanted to leave them to it.

Mick Kelly accepts my offer of a coffee in the kitchen as he needs my signature on several forms that I don't understand, as usual.

I spot the Femina hygiene intimate wipes on the kitchen island close to where he is sitting, with one half of a wipe hanging out. He is probably wondering what the hell I am doing in the kitchen. I quickly say, "They are not for my arse, they are for Paddy's ears."

"Che?"

"I wasn't cleaning my arse in the kitchen, if that is what you are thinking," I say, handing him his coffee as I feel my neck reddening.

"I have forgotten my pen. Can I use this one?" he asks politely. I then realise he was looking at the pen lying beside the packet and not the wipes themselves.

I decide not to say anything other than "yes".

"Shall we go upstairs?"

I'm now getting redder. From having discussed the hygiene of my intimate areas, to hearing a line from a movie said in an

Italian accent. I know he means to go up and do the measurements for the final report, but it still makes me blush.

"Yes, let's get this done," I say a bit too enthusiastically as I speed towards the stairs, hoping the swift movement will cool off my burning face.

"Wow, it is very nice... Alex did all this?"

Mick Kelly is genuinely impressed by the standard of work done. So am I as I walk around the finished top floor for the first time.

They have left the place perfectly clean after re-plastering and painting all five rooms and hallway.

The bathroom, branded as Luca's, has been tiled with the black, rust-tinted tiles we chose and had delivered months ago, after the mix up with quantities. They go perfectly with the square rain shower I bought when bathroom shopping with Luca and Izzy over a year ago. At last, all the supplies that have been lying around are being used.

Subtle shades of grey and cream were the perfect choice for the bedroom walls and the Turkish light fitting with cracked glass light bowls hanging on five pendular different length chains from a dark metal central crown, looks amazing above the stairwell.

I wished I had viewed it first with Alex so I could hug him. Instead, I am trying not to act over-awed with Mick Kelly here. THIS is what I expected from the guys he recommended, not the clown show of Antonio's and Tomo's crew.

"This window is beautiful," he says looking at the large statement double-glazed window I have had fitted instead of the cobweb-strewn double wooden windows that were at the top of the stairwell previously. It has the best view of evening sunsets in the entire house and perfectly frames the pendular lights from outside looking in. "But I think you will need to cover it in summer because of the heat it will generate, like a glass house."

I hadn't thought about that, but I'm guessing the open three floor hallway is big enough to handle the heat.

He's measuring the radiators. "I don't know if they will be big enough to pass the energy inspection, but we can say you changed them afterwards."

I don't know why we have to have an energy inspection that is going to cost €800, it's not like we are applying for any grants related to raising the energy level of the house. This floor is the warmest floor of the house now, thanks to all the insulation. Any radiators bigger than that would have been too much.

"It is important that we apply for the 'Habitable certificate'. Without this you are not supposed to live in the house."

This certificate, to certify that the house is fit enough to be lived in, even though we have been living here for over a year now, will be another €800, he informs me.

"These costs are mounting up again Mick Kelly, but I know they are covered under the 50/50 bonus scheme, so at least we'll get that money back soon to cover costs."

"It is very difficult to apply for the 50/50. They have changed the rules since December," he says, a look of concern on his face.

I find it hard to swallow; this money was to be back to us by now. Forty percent of 70k is a lot of money to us, especially as we borrowed the amount on a short-term loan that needs to be paid off soon.

My first thought as I stand there looking at him, hoping this isn't his way of breaking the news the scheme is finished, is that if he had done his job and applied for the bonus when I gave him all the paperwork, then we wouldn't be in this situation that is potentially going to cost us dearly. Just like the bouffant woman in the car place and Veronica in the bank.

"They have stalled the scheme because some people abused it. Owners of a palazzo claimed one million in restoration and then used the same paperwork to apply for palazzo number two for ten million," he says.

"So, the government have changed the rules to make it more difficult for everyone, rather than checking the paperwork in the system that works perfectly fine if the paperwork is checked properly?" I say, exasperated.

Like the car change over. This is the second time this week I hear Italians use the excuse 'the regulations have changed' for not doing their jobs in a timely manner.

I'm also miffed at how the bonus renovation system can be abused. For one, the maximum claim is 97k, so how did someone claim one million? Secondly, historical buildings and luxury villas are excluded from the scheme, so how did an owner of two palazzos put in a claim? And three, the amount of stamps, cross checks, invoices, receipts and paperwork that had to be done to get our first 26k back makes me believe the application process is pretty difficult to abuse. I am not going to challenge Mick Kelly over it, although his words ' I don't know how long this application will take and how long it will take for the bank to pay out', makes me extremely worried.

His concerned face does not ease. "There is also another problem with the registration of the property as one house. They have come back twice saying it can't be done."

"What is the problem with the house now, I thought we sorted this?"

"It is not the house but the land... As there were nine owners the land is divided differently. So this," he says, pointing to a patch of outlined ground, about big enough to park a car, beside the derelict garage on the plans he has taken out of his bag.

"And this part," he points to another patch beside the other shed twice the length and half the width.

"And this part," he says, pointing to a central part of the garden, outlined roughly the size of the area we just burned the Christmas tree on.

"They are having difficulty with these three plots. So they have said we need to get a typographer to do a new aerial map of the land."

I'm feeling some of these problems are being created just to keep people in jobs. I have too much going on in my head to figure out why they have a problem with these particular small patches of land around the house which is just a biggish garden, it's not like a field.

The garden had been carved up like a mini-Africa when taken over by colonisers, random borders drawn and passed on like twenty jigsaw pieces. We own all the jigsaw pieces and even though they fit perfectly together, some authority could not accept that they formed one picture, they need a typographer to come out to verify it.

"I will need my fees or part of my fees paid, is that ok?" Mick Kelly asks as we walk back down to the kitchen.

Considering we haven't paid him a cent since he started working with us on this house over twenty months ago, I think it is fair to pay him something, even though he communicates at the pace of a sloth taking at least two weeks to respond to texts or emails, after several attempts to contact him and strong threats or pleadings.

His management fees are 4k, the rest of the 15k owed to him, is comprised of various town hall fees and different certificates for different stages of the planning.

"How about I pay you fifty percent of your fee and 2k towards some of the certificate fees and then the rest when the 50/50 comes through?"

I'm hoping this will keep him on the case with the bank.

"Remember the authorities from the commune can come at any time within the next twelve months and say 'no we think it is a luxury villa'. And then you would have to pay more taxes.

"Even though Marco has sent them the photos to say this is not a luxury residence, it is up to them to decide if it is luxury or not... How many kitchens do you have?"

"One, well two if you consider the room with the sink for my mother."

"If they see that, then they will say it is two separate living places."

"But it isn't a full kitchen."

"Do you need it for the next year? Could you wait for another year before making it into a kitchen?" I glance toward the small kitchen and notice Mam has left her dinner plate from two nights ago with some leftovers of my peanut chicken. I bet she was saving it for the dogs and forgot about it. The waft of chipper oil hangs in the air around the hallway outside the room from one chip making episode to the next.

"I don't think my Mam can resist making chips for that long. How about we move the washing machine in there and we call it a utility room?"

"Perhaps that could work."

Considering the woman from the commune passes by the house every day on her way to work and is watching closely enough to have noted we were in it on Christmas Day, my feeling is that the commune will come. If they are all from the area, I think nosiness disguised as official business will have them all out as soon as they get a chance.

Peanut Chicken

Serves: 4

4 Chicken breasts

Finger of fresh ginger

1 Lime

2 Handfuls of peanuts

Olive oil for cooking

1 Clove of garlic

1 Carrot

Broccoli florets (enough for 4 servings)

Sweet chilli sauce

Mixed oriental spice

Flour (to coat the chicken)

Basmati Rice (enough for 4 people)

Method:

Heat oven to 220°C.

Cook the rice according to instructions.

Mix a couple of tablespoons of flour with the two teaspoons of mixed spice. Add some salt and pepper.

Dry the chicken with kitchen paper. And then coat the chicken with the seasoned flour. Finely cut the garlic and ginger.

On a pan, heat the olive oil and brown the chicken on each side for two minutes.

On a baking sheet, spread baking paper and place the chicken breasts on the paper.

Coat each chicken piece with sweet chilli sauce and cook in the oven for about 12 minutes.

While that's cooking, cut the carrot into half-moons.

Divide the broccoli into small pieces. Fry the garlic and ginger in a pan with some olive oil, add the broccoli and carrots and a small amount of water. Stir fry until the vegetables are tender. Season with salt and pepper and the juice of the lime.

Chop up the peanuts. Cut the cooked chicken into slices.

Make a bed of rice on each plate. Place the chicken on the rice, sprinkle generously with the chopped peanuts and place the cooked veg by its side.

22

BOOSTER DANCE

There is a constant dripping noise. The last few mornings it has woken me up and I follow the sound only for it to move. It's early February and the first signs of spring are popping up.

The mid-morning is warm enough to sit outside for the first time since Mam's arrival. For her birthday we got her a luxury sun chair. Wide, solid and with a thick padded cushion for comfort and a glass holder on either side—one for water, one for whiskey—along with a slot to hold a mobile phone.

It's Ronan's birthday week too. His new age of sixty-six is retirement age in Ireland, which entitles him to his Irish State pension.

I can't wait to give him his present. He opens the large box and inside is a cuckoo clock made in the Bavarian Forest. "Now that you are retiring, you should get a clock and I thought this would be an apt one to give you."

It will forever remind me of the time Luca, Ronan and I were sitting outside appreciating living in Italy and we heard a cuckoo for the first time. And Ronan asked if cuckoos were actual birds. He thought they were only fictional creatures that lived in clocks.

"Don't waste a nice morning. Hang out your washing," Mam calls into me from her new sun chair as she sees me carrying out another basket of washing. She likes telling me to do things when I'm in the process of doing them.

As the weather is turning, drying washing only takes a couple of hours outside. It's this time of year I take all my summer clothes out of storage and freshen them up. During the summer, laundry is dry and ready for folding in less than an hour. There is no need for dryers in Italy.

As she has given me an order which I am already doing, she changes her tactic. "Are you doing more washing? Do you ever stop? You are like a laundry woman... I've laundry behind my door if you are putting any more on.... Aww isn't it just gorgeous today. Sure, what more would I want?"

With that there is a loud bang and a flash from the transformer on the train tracks that sits on the embankment beyond the end of our garden.

I immediately think of hearing from a friend that the dead show themselves present through electricity. Dad being new to this game, hasn't learnt to be subtle yet, he goes all out and blows a transformer.

Later in the day, while I'm cutting the pampas grass, there is another explosive bang and a puff of dirty yellow smoke rises from the transformer box.

"Hi Dad," I say low. I take it as a sign of his approval of us all enjoying the garden together for the first time. It was what he was looking forward to most about moving here; sitting in the garden with Mam watching different birds than the ones he knew from Ireland and helping us develop the garden.

"I wonder what will happen when a train goes by?" says Mam anxiously.

"We'll soon find out," I say, hearing the low hiss of a train approaching.

"Sacred heart," Mam blesses herself.

The train passes without incident.

The next day, two guys in bright yellow jumpsuits are walking along the train line. I am trying to think of the words for "yesterday, there was an explosion". "Bomba," I am thinking might be an appropriate word. But then I decide to just watch them from the distance. I am sure they know what they are doing and don't need my assistance by causing a bomb alert.

Late that night I awake to the sound of voices coming from the garden. They are loud and jovial and calling to each other over hammering.

I look out the window and see a weird-looking vehicle, like something out of a sci-fi movie, sitting on the tracks behind our garden. It's about twice the size of a large van with bright yellow piping running all over it, throwing beams of light in every direction. A gang of workers pile out of it and join others standing on the line, their florescent suits luminous in the large bright white orb of light on our section of train track.

Their loud chatter carries through the stillness of the night and keeps me awake until 4am as they work on replacing the transformer box. They are gone without a trace before the first train passes slowly and quietly at 5.30am.

I am trying to sleep, as I have my booster vaccine appointment that morning and I've heard it can make you tired and ill. But of course, like any time I try to force myself to get some sleep, my brain resists all the more. And then I hear the dripping noise again. I spend an hour walking from room to room, trying to find the leak but then it stops and starts again. Drip, drip, drip.

By 7am I resign myself to the fact that I am going to go twenty-four hours without sleep. I hear Mam's radio on, so I make us both our morning tea.

"You're awake early," I say.

"A bloody blackbird woke me up tapping on my window," says Mam crossly. "Do you hear him? He must be at the kitchen window."

I sneak into the small kitchen next door and spot the feisty blackbird preparing for spring, attacking his reflection in the window, getting rid of his stubborn opponent who is always where he is. His window tapping creates the perfect dripping sound effect.

Spooky is sitting on the table, paws tucked under her, watching the entertainment as it if was a theatre show put on especially for cats.

Later that day, blurry eyed from lack of sleep, I arrive at the vaccine clinic that is set up in the community centre of a nearby town. It's eight degrees, the covered walkway where I join the queue is heated with infra-red heaters and divided in two by a barrier.

The tougher FFP2 masks are obligatory. Marquee pergolas have been erected to cover the interior grass courtyard. When I was here for my first and second vaccines, wild boar had ploughed this courtyard up the night before. The grass is now protected by what I recognise as a dance floor I have previously hired for weddings. But I don't think they intend us to dance.

On the other side of the barrier, an elderly Red Cross volunteer leads six 'processed' people, all about sixteen to eighteen years old, back down the other side of the barrier from the top. They are expressionless, bored and zombie-like. I feel like I'm in a sci-fi movie.

I have filled out the form as requested. However, putting my first name first and my last name second has completely messed up the guy's head. He is searching for me on the list under Rs and eventually figures out, with relief, I am under M.

"Ah in Ireland you put your first name first, here we put our second name first and first name second."

I get that it's better that way for filing systems but when he says it; it makes as much sense as when I try to explain Italian wedding menu choices to couples.

"You need to pick two first courses. Two primi piatti."

"Oh, so guests will have a choice?"

"No, they get both."

"At the same time?"

"No, one after another... It's their first and second course but they are both called first courses."

"We don't quite understand."

"Your guests will get their first course and then they get their second first course."

"And then they get the second course and a main course?"

"No, then they get their main course which they call the second course. But really the second first course is their second course."

"Why don't they call it the first and second course then?"

"Because it's Italy?" Is the only answer I can usually give to this.

I have got used to it by now, the same way I have got used to calling the first floor of my house the ground floor, the second floor the first and the third floor the second. And yet, when officials ask me how many floors my house has, I need to answer three.

Everyone dealing with me in the vaccine centre seems baffled about the pronunciation of my second name. It's not Italian. They pronounce it 'mele - D', 'mele' means apple in Italian. And, as I have filled out the form ass-ways, it becomes my first name. So now they are calling out 'Apple' in Italian which I have to get used to answering to. Maybe they will think I am Gwyneth Paltrow's daughter.

A second woman checks my paperwork. I have forgotten to put my code fiscale. She fills in the long code of letters and numbers, in the two places it is needed.

I am given the waiting number of thirty-seven, and I take a seat in the adjoining room where numbers fourteen to nineteen are being led away across the dance floor.

It's only when I am sitting waiting I realise my name, the way they are pronouncing it, translates to Rosie Apple-D.

After about thirty minutes it is mine and five others turn to 'take to the floor' and we are briskly led to another large room with five chairs, two against each facing wall and my chair beside the door. Its coldness isn't helped by the open doors on either end of the room. One waiting woman is asking what the point is in this, why not leave us in the warm room, but there is no one there to answer.

The jolly leader is back ten minutes later in her shiny, newly designed Red Cross gear that looks like a high-fashion ski suit. I wonder if a fashion designer has created them to give the workers a boost during this difficult time. Armani designed the Italian police uniforms after all. And let's not forget Hugo Boss designed the Nazi uniforms in WWII, so designer Red Cross uniforms are not a farfetched idea.

She leads us through the labyrinth to the smaller waiting room of five green chairs; it's the same room I sat in six months ago for my first and second vaccine.

I go in when Mele is called. I am paranoid that people are staring at the woman whose mother called her Apple.

"Second dose," The nurse states rather than asks from behind the counter.

"No, I am here for my booster."

There is a kerfuffle and some keyboard tapping by the two nurses at the computer while the third tells me to sit and jabs me. They print out my record showing all three vaccines.

"So, will my Green Pass be updated automatically?"

"No, you bring this to the pharmacy and they will print it for you."

I go out and wait the mandatory fifteen minutes and then go home. It's too late for the pharmacy. It's 12.30 and they have all gone home for their 3.5 hour lunch break.

I won't have time the following day to get the Green Pass as Ronan has found a possible suitable car for sale online that we need to go and see. We don't have much choice, and have already decided we'll take it. If we don't sort out a car before I go to Rome, we won't have any car after Friday when the rental expires. Ronan has arranged a 1pm meeting with the guy to view the car, which is surprising, as that's lunchtime.

The Green Pass update will have to wait until the following day. I think, I am in the system now so getting my Green Pass updated shouldn't be a problem like it was the last time. But that would be too logical.

How stupid of me to suppose something like that would be straightforward in Italy.

23

CARS & TRAINS

W e take Mam along with us to the car dealer, to ensure the seat is the right height for her to get in and out of okay.

I'm under pressure. I have accounts to file. Tiles and a bathroom suite to source and buy online, a contract to send out, flights to book for Rob and Jenny coming over, Colosseum tickets to book and accommodation to find.

We arrive at the car dealers at 1pm. And sure enough, it was too good to be true, there is a big lock on the gates of the car courtyard.

It transpires, Ronan had suggested 1pm, but had not got a response. To anyone else this would be unconfirmed, but to Ronan his suggestion means the meeting is happening. I am fuming with Ronan as I have so much to get done today. I call the guy; he is at lunch, he'll be back at 3pm. He then texts that he can make it back for 2.30pm.

So, we go for pizza. The waitress scans our Green Passes and Mam's comes up as invalid. So I quickly hand her the QR code of Luca's and it's fine. Mam is now an 18-year-old boy, should an authority come to check.

I take deep breaths and persuade myself to be like an Italian and take the riposo time to enjoy lunch with my family and forget about all the stressful things waiting for my attention. It works. We have a pleasant lunch and Mam proclaims the pizza she has at the truck stop is the best pizza she has had since arriving in Italy. Other attempts have not impressed her.

We view the car. Mam approves of the seat height and Ronan takes it on a satisfactory test run.

Albert, the car dealer guy, is a nice guy. He doesn't speak a word of English, but his wife does and she is dealing with the paperwork.

I fill out the requested forms for the change of ownership and she takes a photocopy of my passport as I don't have an ID card yet. I've also given her proof of my insurance back in Ireland.

She asks for my Tessera Sanitaria, which I don't have, but we have done our homework and we know from government sites that you only need to be resident to buy a car in Italy—a Tessera Sanitaria is not needed, although a lot of car dealers might ask for it.

Once they check the facts, they will realise it is not a requirement. That is what we have read on one of the ex-pat social media sites.

We have come prepared and have printed out the document from the internet stating this. "Ahh," she says, accepting it.

However, there is a problem; the proof of previous insurance needs to be for six years and the cert I have is only proof of three years. It's bizarre that we have to show we were previously insured on our old car, to buy a car that will need a completely different insurance policy.

We go home and call the Irish insurance office; "Three years is the maximum amount of time we issue them for."

There is no getting around it, but let's say a three can become a six quite easily with a bit of Photoshop. Italy's bureaucracy is turning us into criminals.

We return to the office that afternoon but the woman isn't there, there's a different girl sitting in her chair. We saw her walk across the yard as we arrived, behind the car dealer guy who has gone into the back offices of the building.

Ronan is busy talking into his phone as he still lives in hope that using Google voice translate works. It doesn't. His slight stutter seems to become more pronounced as he tries to figure out what he wants to say while saying it.

He doesn't pause before correcting himself which leads to long rambles of senseless English sentences, repeated back robotically in Italian while he looks hopeful that it is understandable.

Ronan directs it towards the girl and starts talking over it in broken English, trying to get answers from her. The girl looks up from what she is doing. "Ronan, Ronan," I say, trying to stop him.

"Rosie, stop I want her to tell us when the bloody car will be ready."

He hasn't noticed that while the girl is tall and looks like an office worker with her glasses, she's doing her homework.

I ask in Italian where the other woman is, and she answers in English. "My Mamma is not working this afternoon, she has an appointment, but my father will be back in a moment as he needs to bring me to gymnastics."

Ronan has just been asking an 11-year-old girl demanding questions about when the car will be ready.

Albert returns and apologises. His daughter acts as translator. He takes the document from us and tells us to come back tomorrow.

The following day, his lovely friendly wife is back. She calls the government office to start the changeover. They take all my details and ask for my Tessera Sanitaria.

She explains I don't have one and tells the official we don't need one to buy a car.

"But you must have one to buy a car."

"No, apparently they don't," and she reads from the document we have supplied, explaining we just need to be resident.

The woman on the other end is giving long-winded monologues of how she believes it is necessary to have Tessera Sanitaria and eventually agrees that she will have to check with her supervisor. Their supervisor will not be in the office until afternoon. Meaning after 4pm.

We are not going to wait around for three hours so we leave carless again to travel the forty minutes home.

The tightness between my shoulders feels like if I move it, it might snap like a brittle piece of ice. Once again, Italian bureaucracy is breaking me. Every time I straighten, I can feel some bones crack. I desperately need a massage.

Back home, I work through the rest of my To-Do list. I book an apartment in a palazzo in the centre of Rome within walking distance of the Colosseum. Shelly has a friend in Rome who I have met, who is a tour guide so I book her for an afternoon to show us around the Colosseum.

Now that I have Rob and Jenny's flights booked for three weeks' time, and the day exploring Rome planned within an inch of its life, we just need to finalise the car.

At 4.30pm we get a call; good news, you don't need a Tessera Sanitaria to buy the car. So you can come in and finish the paperwork.

"There's more paperwork?"

"Yes, and to make the payment."

So we race back to the dealership before the rush hour traffic hits, we do the signatures and then I go to make a payment only to discover my bank has a 3k max transfer limit per day. I transfer the first 3k but it's going to take another two days of payments before we can take the car. That leads to Sunday and we have to return the rental tomorrow.

Luckily, good friends come to the rescue. Shelly is going back to the UK for a week and offers us her car. Sherwin drives Ronan to the airport car hire so he can return the car hire and then leaves Shelly's car with us.

Ronan, in the meantime, has found an ex-pat insurance broker online who will insure the car for €380 per year, rather than the total of €700 by the Italian insurer.

At last, on Monday, the last payment goes through and Ronan texts the dealer using Google Translate.

"We will come in the morning to collect the car, okay?"

"I am sorry, I won't be there tomorrow," texts back Albert.

"Will no one be there?"

Ronan reads his reply, "My colleague will be, but he doesn't speak English."

"Neither do you!" Ronan texts back.

"Oh yes," he texts back followed by the laughing emoji. "But it would be better if I was there."

I persuade Ronan to wait until Wednesday, after all we have Shelly's car until the weekend if necessary, and I really could do with a day without having to fight my way through Italian forms and potential problems. Just one day.

That evening I go on the Irish government website for updating Green Passes. I fill in Mam's details and her government number and submit. I get an instant automated message saying she will have it in one to ten days.

I also order a shower door and tiles for the bathroom. More things ticked off my list, but dealing with clients is taking up most of my time. I start working at 7am and don't finish until 10pm each day to get things up to date so that I can fully enjoy the Rome experience with Rob and Jen.

Ronan and I collect the car. It's our first left-hand drive car and seems wider than our last car. I insist on driving part of the way back, to get used to it and clip a parked car's mirror going through town while Ronan grips the dashboard with white knuckles. This is going to take getting used to. But at least our car issue is now sorted.

The day I am going to Rome, I remember I need to get my Green Pass updated 'shit, crap, bloody hell, I forgot'.

Off to the pharmacy and my phone has decided to quit service. My Google Translate app won't work and I am mute again, fumbling in my dusty brain cells for some words to combine to make myself understood.

It's the same woman who whacked my passport off the desk shouting on the phone to the commune when I was trying to sort out my Tessera Sanitaria previously. She understands I need to update my Green Pass.

"Can I have your Tessera Sanitaria?"

"I don't have one."

She looks at me blankly.

"I have a code fiscale."

"Ah yes, that will do." We are both relieved.

She inputs my details, and the computer says no.

She goes off to get advice.

"How did you get a Green Pass before?"

"My friend did the necessary work for it," I reply, thinking of the two women in Puglia, without whom we would still not be able to travel by plane or train.

She takes my passport, then asks to look at my phone messages. As she scrolls through my messages, I'm thinking she will not get any tips there as we had given Karen's number as our contact number.

She tries the computer again. She doesn't like to admit defeat so folds up my documents and says she is sorry but the portal is down. I presume she is talking about the non-existent portal that takes you beyond Italian bureaucracy, that only a few are allowed through for each thing, in case someone with two palazzos or a stolen Eastern European car tries to get through. Italians are very reluctant to admit something is their fault.

"But I need to get a train today to Rome."

"I am sorry, but the regulations have changed."

She writes the names of two doctors down on a Post-it and hands it to me saying I can go see these doctors at the clinic on the hill—they deal with foreigners. I look blankly; I am not sure how this is supposed to help. Maybe the stress on my face is showing, and she knows I will need psychiatric care by the time I've finished trying to get my Green Pass.

There's nothing for it. I am not missing Rome. I will use my mother's QR code. Surely, I can pass as eighty-five by now with the amount of stress I have been through in the last few months.

On the off chance, I text the two ladies in Puglia; "I need to get a train today can you help get my pass updated."

Within ten minutes I get a call from one of them, out of breath running back to her office computer to help me. She is not sure if she can, but she will try.

24

CIVILISATION?

With an hour to spare, the women in Puglia have done it. They queued at the administration office and got my Green Pass. With a racing heart, and a lot of relief, I am on a train, with Luca, for the first time in two years.

Ronan offered to drive us to Rome, but the car has started to beep a loud warning alarm, like someone has not fastened their seatbelt. And the oil light is glowing, so he's going to bring it to the mechanic to get a check-up. Anyway, I love travelling by train.

I am enjoying watching the scenery trundle by; ancient ochre towns melting into hilltops, tilled hills showing the first greens of life. A flock of sheep outside Rome with three huge black dogs walking amongst them, ready to protect the woolies from wolves. I've missed absorbing Italy.

It will be another eight hours before Rob and Jenny arrive, so we go for a stroll around Rome, traversing by the Trevi Fountain.

"Do you know over €3000 per day is thrown into the Trevi Fountain?" says Luca, who, as always, is a mine of information. "They vacuum up the coins every night and then give it to a charity, helping to feed the homeless of the city. It's looking much better than the last time we saw it."

He's right, the fountain has been beautifully restored to its travertine calcium white and aquamarine waters with the restoration funded by the fashion house Fendi. Not a brand I like, since an ex-girlfriend of my brother's boasted of her Fendi handbag made from 40 different types of frog skins.

But I liked what the big designer brands were doing—taking the amazing landmarks of Rome under their wings and funding the restoration of them to their former glory.

I booked tickets for Luca and I to see a visiting Klimt exhibition, an exhibition I have been dying to see. He's one of my favourite artists since school and I've seen none of his work in the 'flesh'. I've even written a murder mystery around one of Klimt's paintings in the book I dedicated to my dad called, 'A Brush With Death', which he ironically read the week before he died.

The exhibition was planned and advertised before Covid started, and I didn't think I would get to Rome before it was due to end in a couple of weeks. Our ticket was for a specific entry time.

With an hour to spare, we go for dinner at a restaurant beside the gallery. It's nice to have some time away with Luca to chat uninterrupted, especially as he has been quite down recently.

"Mam, I want to defer my art course, I have fallen behind and missed too much because of the trip back to Ireland for the funeral and all that. Not being able to attend in person and it being all online... well, I am just on my own. I have no friends here."

"Yet..." I say. "No friends yet." I still live in hope he will feel Italy as home and I understand having friends here would play a big part in that.

Four of his friends from Ireland are coming over for a week in April which will lift his spirits, but I hate seeing him under pressure.

"I'd just like to take a year out, earn some money and hang around with people who I can speak to without having to over think about what words to use."

I get it. He has a dry sense of humour and humour is a difficult thing to translate into a different language and culture. I too find it difficult to joke in Italian, I feel people cannot get to know me when they can't understand my humour. So part of my personality gets lost in Italy.

"How about if one of your friends comes to stay for the summer and you can run the bar for the weddings?"

Over dinner we work out a plan for creating a summer job for him and a friend running the pop-up bar from May to July. It will give Luca an income and me the bar I need to keep my clients happy.

For a couple of hours Luca and I get lost in the golden spirals, swirls and colourful geometric shapes of Gustav Klimt's masterpieces. It feels so good to be at a gallery again. A form of happiness that has been dormant in me since Covid restrictions started comes alive again.

We get a taxi to the apartment I have booked for the night through an online booking site. Laura, a young woman from the hosting management company arrives to let us in and show us to our apartment in the fifteenth century palace with a grand marble hall entrance. Each floor around the huge inner stairwell is divided into several private apartments.

As she shows us the knack to opening the tricky lock with the huge key she tells us, "This palace belonged to a very important woman called Beatrice Cenci."

"Oh, what did she do?"

"I don't know, as this is the first time for me showing this property, but the street is named after her also. I will look her up on Google while you complete the payment through the link my colleague is sending you now by email."

As I scroll through my phone waiting to see the email arrive, Laura googles Beatrice Cenci.

"Oh, she died," states Laura, sitting at the table reading the Wikipedia description.

"Well, I hope so, otherwise she would be about 400-years-old."

"No I mean she was killed," says Laura continuing to read. "She murdered her abusive father who beat her mother and brothers and raped Beatrice. She was beheaded on the bridge for killing him..."

"Jezuz."

Laura keeps her head down, reading selective sentences about our ghost hostess.

"The Pope showed no mercy as he did not want copycat murders. She was not the only one involved, they tortured her lover to death... and her brothers, except the youngest, were also killed for the murder. The youngest was made to watch and then made a slave and they divided all his inheritance between the Pope's family.

There was an outcry about her sentence and people begged the Pope to show mercy as they all knew what a cruel and horrible man her father was.

She became a legend and a symbol of standing up to the aristocracy... Legend has it that on the eve of the anniversary of her death she can be seen on the bridge with her head under her arm."

This is just not getting any better. I'm thinking of asking if they have any other accommodation available.

"Please don't tell me that her anniversary is tonight?"

"No, it is in a few days. I think I will go to the bridge that night and see if I can see her," says Laura with some excitement.

"I hope she is not concerned about how she looks for the day and comes back tonight looking for her hairbrush for her underarm head," I am genuinely a little concerned this could be a possibility.

Once we have the keys and have had a tour of the apartment, I go down to the road just as Rob and Jenny arrive by taxi. It's the first time I've seen Rob since his diagnosis but in Rob's way, as always, he is upbeat.

The following day, we meet the lovely Anna for our guided Rome tour. Two students in their late teens are trying to get into the Colosseum with the tickets they have bought. Their

Green Passes are three days expired and they are being refused entry.

It's outdoors.

This green pass thing has gone beyond a joke. I don't see the point. Anna intervenes to try and help, depriving them of an education because of bureaucracy she argues, but the security guy is not having any of it.

I had been to the Colosseum before, but with a good guide it was a whole other experience.

"There were eighty entrances, or vomitoria as they were called, to Flavian's Amphitheatre, the proper name for the Colosseum. One solely for the Protagonists such as the Gladiators, one just for the Emperor and, the one on the opposite end to the gladiators' entrance, was not an entrance but an exit. The gate the dead were brought out from," Anna explains as we walk towards the Protagonist's entrance.

"As a result of such efficient design, experts believe the Colosseum could fill with fifty thousand people in just fifteen minutes and empty in as little as five."

"You can imagine walking out into the arena through the Protagonist's entrance... the crowd of seventy or eighty thousand people cheering, the travertine stone gleaming blindingly white in the sun."

Walking through the arch I can just imagine the screaming crowd gradually coming into view. Anna has the skill of building the atmosphere so much that the hairs stand up on the back of my neck as she guides us through the entrance the Gladiators took into the massive arena.

"Below where we are standing was where the props and animals were kept; such as crocodiles and elephants. They had these hatch doors they were brought up from. And you can imagine how scared the animals would be. For three days they would not be fed, completely in the dark and then brought out into the bright sun and the noise of the crowd and facing death."

This made me sadder than thinking of all the people that were killed here. But then Anna lifted our mood by incorporating a few fun facts.

"Gladiators were celebrities. Women would bottle gladiator sweat and sell it as perfume. They even had a special tool to collect it with. And although this was built and designed over two-thousand years ago, the designs of modern stadiums are still based on ancient Roman arenas. The efficient design with the vomitorium, meant the Colosseum could fill with 50,000 people in just 15 minutes and empty in as little as five."

Anna continued the comparison of Roman and current times in her quirky way:

"The games and food were free, it was the Emperor's way of keeping the people happy. Propaganda. Now they give us free Wi-Fi."

Across the walkway, we walk through The Forum. Layers of history, where what we call civilisation developed. And the best we could do with it was men killing animals and each other for the enjoyment of others. But it gets worse.

At The Forum we see where the Temple of the Twelve Vestal Virgins was. Picked at the age of seven, they were trained in baking and keeping the eternal fire going. At forty years of age, they could retire and get married or whatever. If they fell in love and broke the virginal deal before the age of forty, their punishment was to be buried alive with a loaf of bread and a torch. The guy was flogged to death.

We walk around past the Victor Emanuel Monument and through the grounds of another amphitheatre, which was there before the Colosseum and used as a theatre. There are apartments built above the top layer now, including an apartment once owned by Sophia Loren.

We enter the Old Jewish Ghetto. It was here in 1555 the horrible Pope Paul IV declared that Jews and Christians should not mix nor speak to each other and the Jews were banished to this small area, their land and property taken. Put in lockdown for three-hundred years. Told to wear a yellow star or yellow hat or scarf to identify themselves as Jewish and not allowed past the ghetto walls during daylight. Victor Emanuele united Italy and knocked down the walls of the ghetto, giving Jewish people their freedom back.

At one of Anna's favourite restaurants in the old quarter, we feast on falafel and hummus, kosher lamb, baccala cod done in a tomato and raisin sauce, peppered chicken and gnocchi in meat sauce. But we all agree our favourite dish is the double deep-fried artichoke, while we look out at The Forum; The centre of the civilised world.

On our left we have the Colosseum where Christians were fed to lions and people clapped as competitors fought to the death. On our right we have the Jewish ghetto where the Jews were degraded and treated abominably by Christians for three hundred years. And in front, we have the Vestal Virgin Temple, to keep the flames of hope burning by virgins who, if they performed an act of love would be buried alive as punishment. Civilisation indeed.

The day in Rome was a huge success. We walk back along Circus Maximus to where I'd arranged for a chauffeur van to meet us and drive us back to Trasimeno. It works out not much more expensive than us all buying train tickets and will be more comfortable and less tiring for Rob, although he seems to be the one with more energy than any of us. We discussed telling Mam his new life challenge while he is here but she is so happy when he arrives we don't want to spoil the moment, and as Rob says "Why tell her?"

Mam is perplexed at why Rob won't eat the buckets of chips she makes for him every day and, that he is not on for partying with her, has her even more miffed. At least he is on for a few games of poker and a cigar so she stops questioning his new fascination with health which she thinks is very unhealthy. "Jenny is putting too many stupid ideas in his head; no drink and no potatoes, it's taking this heathy thing all too far."

They stay for a week and return to Ireland refreshed and ready to face the challenge ahead.

The following day after they leave, I get a message from the Irish HSE app to say I had been in touch with someone who has Covid. The only Irish people I have been in touch with are Rob and Jenny, and neither of them have Covid and I am not even in Ireland. I delete the app. I am losing my patience with the layers and hoops that have been added to the Covid crisis.

At a time when the region of Umbria is considered a white zone with the numbers dropping hugely and talk of the Green Pass being eliminated at the end of March for under fifties, Green Passes are still required for customers to be served in the bank, but not to go into it. It's needed to go into some DIY shops but not supermarkets.

My brother's kids in Ireland have all had Covid twice within three months, including his partner who has been fully vaccinated.

People's patience with restrictions is definitely waning. It feels as though we're all going to stop considering this a 'crisis' soon.

25

BEDS & VIOLENT DINOSAURS

Furnishing a twenty-two-roomed house with a low budget is not an easy task. Yes, we've got our sofa and dining table and chairs, but there are still all the bedrooms to be done.

I also have two sofas and two armchairs which I have stripped down to their frames, cleaned and prepped for re-upholstering last summer.

But I still don't know where they will fit in. At the moment we don't need additional sofas and chairs but I want to give upholstery a go. I've watched two or three YouTube videos on how to do it and it seems fairly easy with a staple gun as your principal weapon. Ronan and Alex moved all the frames out to the garden while I was in Rome to free up space in the house.

We have too many rooms acting as storage rooms; we need to figure out what to keep and what to throw away. I've never had a house where everything had its place—the secret to tidiness, I believe—but we were far from that stage.

However, now that the top floor was finished it was coming closer to being possible. Things were starting to get moved, boxes and bags were being unpacked without fear of being embedded with mortar dust. But I knew the bulky suite of furniture I wanted to upholster was something Ronan was dying to dump. Alex was his wingman. When my plans for upholstering the chairs would come up, Alex would say, "Why you want to do that? Just buy something nice. I bring you to a furniture shop."

It was the same when he would have to move the boxes of books we had shipped over from Ireland along with the encyclopaedias from the 1940s that were left in the house. "Why you keep these? Throw them out and buy a Kindle."

That was not going to happen. I couldn't wait to have a wall-to-wall bookcase to display them all in. But that is a long time away.

While carefully stripping the first armchair, I made mental notes of how it was done. Working backwards, I figure out which fabric pieces were layered on top of others. Removing the thousands of tacks they used in the 20s and 30s is time-consuming but strangely enjoyable. I note the materials used—straw for stuffing, horsehair, and mismatched fabric patches for places hidden from view.

I make several trips to a large fabric shop in a town twenty minutes away with Ronan driving. I am still getting used to the steering wheel being on the other side.

Ronan hates haberdashery stores, which are like Aladdin's cave to me, so he stays outside. There's a guy with a German Shepherd pup waiting outside too, so that keeps Ronan happy.

It has taken several visits for me to decide and figure out what I need. This is our third visit to the shop so I don't expect to have to give Ronan directions; we go off the motorway, straight down the road and come to the roundabout where we take the first right off it and...Ronan drives past the massive shop.

"Seriously Ronan have you got a memory of a goldfish? "

"What? Was that it? How was I supposed to recognise it without the German Shepherd pup outside it?"

That was last October. I got as far as one armchair finished in a royal blue velvet and covering the spring bases of the sofa and second armchair with sack cloth before being called away to say goodbye to Dad.

The six-foot-long roll of fifteen meters of velvet has been making its way around the house, waiting to be used. As well as the waist-high layers of foam I got in a car upholstery section of a DIY shop that will substitute the straw. I'll do it in the summer when I have finished my weddings and have time to think. We are not in any hurry for more seating so I need to prioritise. Time to get some bedrooms started.

I have a thing about brass beds, and the great thing is they are out of fashion in Italy, so I watch out on Market Place for them and can pick them up for €100 per double bed.

I see two single brass beds on marketplace; they are proper antique beds. I see they are in Umbria and better still, the location indicated, is our town.

"Are these still available?" I text.

"Yes."

"Okay if you will do both for €70, I would like to take them. I live on the Main Street where are you?"

"Okay. I am in the Piazza."

"Okay when can I collect them?"

"On Saturday."

"Okay where will I meet you?"

"In the town square, I will be drinking there."

"Okay. My husband will meet you."

"Whereabout will he meet you?"

"Outside the Coop."

Now I've never paid much attention to the names of supermarkets and I just presume the supermarket in the town square is a Coop.

So off Ronan goes with Luca to collect the beds in the town centre. But there is no one waiting outside the busy supermarket.

"He is there now in a red van can you see him?" I text the guy.

"No. I am here."

"My husband is in the van, he says there is no parking available."

"There is lots of parking available. I can't see him."

Of course, it's not this easy, as I am using Google Translate to translate everything I need to send and un-translate everything he sends to me. In the meantime, Ronan is constantly buzzing my phone with; "Where the hell is he? There's a cop car here, I can't stop. He's looking at me suspiciously."

"Are you at the supermarket beside the piazza?" I text the guy.

" I am at the Coop."

"Is that in the town centre?"

"No."

"Okay, he is at the wrong supermarket, he'll be with you in five minutes."

I text Ronan; "He's at the Coop."

"The supermarket practically opposite our house?"

"I think so."

I am aware there are two supermarkets of the same name on our street. One big one and one small one. Both Coops.

Five minutes later I am standing in the kitchen and I see Ronan drive by. "Bloody hell I must have told him the wrong super-market again." I'm feeling guilty but his van has slowed, he's indicating, he must have forgotten something. He has hardly driven past our driveway by mistake, has he?

But no, he is driving across the road and... into the next-door neighbour's garden?

I am trying to figure out what the hell he's doing. So I go out the front door and there is Ronan's van, but no Ronan. Next of all a guy comes out of the house, wearing a mask of course, carrying the top part of a brass bed.

He is waiting at the van. Ronan follows him out with the bottom part of the bed and Luca has the two joining rods.

Ronan passes by the guy and throws the bed section over the green fence. The guy is looking at him bewildered as Ronan takes the other part of the bed from his hands and throws that over the fence too.

Ronan is shouting over to me, "The seller of the beds is our bloody next-door neighbour."

"Lui e mio marito. Abitiamo qui." (He is my husband. We live here). I say to the guy who is probably thinking the man throwing the beds over the fence into his new neighbour's garden, has lost his mind.

"Ahhhh," he says.

"Ronan did you not explain that you lived here?" I say as he throws the other two parts across the fence.

"I tried."

"But in English? "

"Yes, of course!"

"But he doesn't speak English."

"Yes, obviously."

Ronan really doesn't understand this need to learn the language of the country we are living in.

A few weeks later, the same house next door has pink organza bows tied to its gate posts. Her son, who sold us the beds, has welcomed a new baby daughter. It is why he was selling the beds, to make way for the crib for the new baby when they visit the nonna.

Often you will see organza bows in blue or pink tied onto house gates or balconies, signalling the baby has been born and its gender. The Italians are very over the top with pinks and blues and bows for babies. There are very few gender-neutral baby clothes, except in the bigger city stores in the north of Italy that house the designer brands.

We bump into the brass bed guy during the evening passeggiata along the lake. He introduces us first to his three-year-old, her name is Louisa, and then to his new born very beautiful, cute baby, her name is Eloisa. In Gaelic Irish 'eile' means 'the other'. So effectively, he has called his two kids Louise and the Other Louise. But, of course, it doesn't translate to that here, it might just be weird if he moves to Ireland.

This happens in reverse too. I know an Irish woman here whose kids are called Sull and Annie. Sull in Italian means 'On the' and 'Anni', depending how quickly you say the 'N's, means 'Year' or 'Anus'. So when she is shouting after both her kids in Italy, or calling them in from the garden for their dinner, she is shouting 'On the year' or usually, 'On the Anus'.

I ask what Louisa got for Christmas and her mother responds in English, "The violent dinosaur, you know him?"

"The Violent Dinosaur? Really? There is such a thing? I haven't heard of this but then again I am a bit out of touch with current TV shows for kids."

"He has been around for many years. He is big and violent... Barney?"

"Barney, the violent dinosaur?... Oh Barney! The violet dinosaur!"

"Yez, that is the one."

26

EAGLES & TURNIPS

S helly calls and asks if she can take Mam out for an afternoon. She knows it's the day Rob is seeing the consultant and I am anxiously waiting and unable to control my random sobbing. Mam still doesn't know of Rob's illness.

So Shelly offers to bring Mam out so I can talk to Rob after his consultation and digest the prognosis.

"Are you not coming?" says Mam as I walk her to Shelly's car.

"No, it's just you and Shelly."

I can see she's trying to adjust to this idea. "I don't think I have gone on an outing with someone else by myself before. Not without your father. And we'd always drive... I do miss..." I bite my lip at the surge of emotion for my Mam having to adjust to so many new ways of life since Dad died, but then hold back a laugh when she finishes the 'I miss' sentence with 'my car' instead of my dad's name.

The consultation goes well. The doctor said Rob will be a long-term patient of hers which is good; it means he's not going to another dimension anytime soon. While it is a cancer that can't be cured, it is one he can live with. I had a chance to talk to Rob and Jenny who are both upbeat and optimistic having spoken to the consultant.

So by the time Shelly gets back with Mam I am feeling ready to face life again, rather than feeling I could break into a thousand pieces at any moment.

"Did you have a nice time?" I ask, giving my Mam a hug and a genuine smile. I feel I have been so hard on her in my robotic 'just get through this' state.

"Shelly is very good, she brought me all the way to the top of the mountain and back down again. The roads are very windy up the hills, so many treacherous bends. I don't know how they drive on them. I never want to do that again, my heart was in my mouth."

"I brought your mum to the restaurant up the hill for lunch but it's closed until April, so we came back down to the lake to the fishing marina near San Feliciano," says Shelly.

"There were grey birds down at the lake, I thought they were seagulls, but your mum said they most definitely weren't." I cringe at the idea of my mum telling Shelly she was wrong in her dogged 'I'm right you are definitely wrong' way.

"Oh, we are all bird lovers in our family and know-it-alls, so we like to know the names of birds. Don't we, Rosie?" She holds on to me tight as we make our way into the house and she gladly sits back in her electric chair.

"I think they're in some of the photos we took of the boats, your mum was saying she likes to paint, so she said she might paint them."

"The birds?" I ask shouting in at them while putting on the kettle.

"No, the boats," Shelly says and then thoughtfully suggests to Mam, "I have an easel in the shed you can have if you like?"

"Ooh that's nice of you. I'm not sure if it would last here with the cat and dogs but I'll give it a go. What do you feed it?"

"What?"

"The eagle. What do you feed it?"

After some speedy clarification, Mam graciously accepts the easel and asks Shelly; "Do you have any binoculars?"

"Hmm... I think we do actually."

"I'll take them as well. Rosie's binoculars are crap and there are lots of little birds hopping around that fruit tree and I'm trying to figure out what they are."

"I've already told her which birds they are, but she doesn't believe me," I say, handing out the cups of tea.

"If you want me to come over any time you need to go out Rosie, I'd be happy to hang out here with your mum," says Shelly thoughtfully.

"Will you all stop fussin'," says Mam. "I'm perfectly capable by myself. Sure, they're off in a few days on a trip to Florence. Well for them."

She says this as if we are going on a holiday, when in fact it's the first day I'm back working with clients. This couple are arriving over for their wedding menu tasting with the caterer in Florence. We have a meeting with their venue manager and the florist. They booked Ronan for the photography, so he needs to come too.

Although he would be coming anyway, even if he wasn't their photographer. The thought of trying to find my way around an Italian city or small town I am not familiar with while driving, makes me break out into a cold sweat.

We'll be leaving early and arriving back late. Even though Luca will be in the house, I'm still anxious.

"Can you bring me to the shop, I want to get a few things before you go?" she asks the day before our Florence appointments.

She buys yet another mop bucket.

"Mam, you already bought a mop bucket and several mops."

"But this bucket is different, it has the squeeze clamp thing for squeezing."

"But you don't mop or squeeze. The other one hasn't even been used yet."

"Leave me alone, it's my money and I'll spend it how I wish...Blast, they don't have what I am looking for here."

"What is it you can't live without until I come back in twelve hours?"

"Turnips. Can you get me some turnips before you go?"

"Turnips?"

"Yes, I want to make a recipe when you are gone. Parsnips will do if you can't get turnips."

I get a flashback of the explanation of why there was a hammer and a knife on my parent's bedroom windowsill the day of my father's death. "To cut me turnips in bed."

"Turnips?" asks Ronan when I get home and tell him Mam's requirement while he's making the dogs' dinners. "Come on, you are supposed to be getting ready to meet this couple not hunting down turnips."

"I know, but I just want her to be happy, to feel at home here."

After five different shops I give up. "I'm sorry Ma, I couldn't find any turnips."

"What about parsnips?"

"They are even more difficult to find in Italy."

She tuts. "Does this country have anything? I'll just have to use up the potatoes so. It's better with potatoes anyway, I don't really need turnips."

27

ITALIAN POTEEN

I n Florence it feels odd to be around people again and discussing weddings face to face after two years of recess.

It feels very civilised to be trying out fresh pastas, risottos and cuts of meat all done to perfection. Followed by a visit to the florist where a profusion of gorgeous perfumes greets us as we walk in the door. Fresh flower scents always remind me of visiting Mary Street flower market in Dublin at dawn with my mother during her stint at doing wedding floristry.

She started by taking a class to learn how to do the bouquets for my sister Eileen's wedding, then neighbours and cousins asked her to do theirs. This was in the days of tear drop bouquets and when all guests got a carnation buttonhole. Each carnation needed a wire pushed up through the stem, through the heart centre of the flower, then bent into a loop and pulled back down, securing the wire to the flower-head before it was twirled between your fingers with green, slightly sticky floristry tape. I became the fastest flower-wirer in the house.

She also made my sister's wedding cake; three tiers with the most delicately petalled roses all made from sugar icing. Eileen had seen a picture in a magazine, Mam researched it and found she needed liquid glycerin to make the pliable icing to mould into the flowers.

I was nine at the time and remember my Mam trying to find someone who was travelling back from the UK to buy her some as it was not something you could get in Ireland.

I was put to work helping to make the ninety tiny roses needed. I still automatically make them when left with plasticine, window putty or anything soft and pliable.

Maybe it was these years of wedding flowers and cakes that originally put the idea of wedding planning in my head as a good business option.

Doing the catering tasting and being at the florists with an excited couple has me nearly forgetting why I hate weddings. And for a few beautiful moments I forget Covid ever existed.

"How was your day with your granny?" I ask Luca, returning late to a surprisingly clean kitchen. Mam was already asleep.

"Ehh, different. She got me to walk over to the shop with her to buy frozen pizzas, tins of pineapple and two bottles of whiskey at eleven o'clock this morning. She pushed the wheelchair across and then piled all her shopping on it."

"Oh, that was good of you to go with her."

"The only thing was, she forgot her PIN number for her bank card. And I was getting into a sweat. The cashier was looking at me like I was some sort of criminal."

"Oh gosh, I can imagine it looked like you dragged this poor little old lady in off the street to buy you booze and pizzas."

"I hadn't thought of that..."

"Then why did you think she was looking at you criminally?"

"Because she knew we were going to put pineapple on pizza," he exclaimed.

"I think you have turned Italian."

"My only saving grace were the bags of barley she bought. It took ages to find. The word for barley is orzo by the way... in case you ever need it."

"I thought that was the word for bear?" I say.

"No, that is orso. A completely different sound."

I can't imagine myself ever really been in a situation where I would confuse reading the word for orzo with orso. Unless it was on a menu or ingredients, and I think I'd know they meant bear rather than barley.

"What did she do in the afternoon?"

"She said she was going to cook some stuff and would call me if she needed me."

That's weird, the kitchen is clean.

"And did she need you?"

"Only once, to open the tin of pineapples for her pizza... actually twice, the second time was to squeeze the mop bucket thing."

"Wow, maybe she's turning over a new leaf and has caught the cleaning bug."

"Here's hoping," says Ronan.

For the rest of the week, I'm practically tied to the computer with the amount of work I need to get through. The last of the rotten persimmons are falling and splattering all over our courtyard like big sticky water balloons. They smell of fermentation and are attracting the first of the springtime insects.

The fermentation aroma has seeped into the house and seems to be getting stronger, even though the fruit is getting less. Ronan has noticed it too and I don't want to make a big deal of it as he might take a chainsaw to the tree. He is always cursing the splattering fruit, since one landed directly on his head last year covering him in orange slime.

"I've been watching the birds and all that fruit falling off the tree. It's such a waste of food, can you not do something with them, make something?" Mam says, sitting in the garden looking through binoculars at the tree two meters away.

"Like what?"

"Wine."

"I don't think you can make wine from persimmon fruit."

"Don't be ridiculous you can make delicious wine from all sorts of stuff, including turnips."

It then dawns on me.

"Is that why you had me running around searching for turnips?"

"Perhaps."

"We live in the land of grapes and wine. In September you can make wine from the bunches hanging in our garden. Or you can buy a decent local bottle of wine for the price of a turnip."

"Well, maybe not to make wine. You know an uncle of mine used to have a poteen still in the country and the police would come raid him regularly, take all his poteen and break up his still. They never arrested him or charged him, they would just confiscate his booze a couple of times a year... probably until their supply ran out and then they would do it again."

"Is that what you are thinking? Poteen?"

"That's always a possibility."

"Oh my God Ma, is that... is that the smell?"

I don't wait for an answer I am marching through the house, my nose in the air following the ever-strengthening whiff to her little not-yet-functioning kitchen. Except it is functioning. On the table there's a variety of glass jars and bottles saved from passata sauce, honey, olive oil and whiskey.

I cough and splutter, and cover my nose with my sleeve at the strong whiff that hits me from the mop bucket.

"God what's that smell?" says Luca, walking down the stairs.

There's a mouldy mound of potato mash and cooked grain in a squashed up pillowcase, sitting in the mop bucket. My good silk pillowcase.

"Is this what she had you squeezing the other day when we were out?" I ask Luca as I hold my breath.

"Yeah, she didn't really explain, I thought it was laundry she was trying to wring out in a weird way using the contraption on the mop bucket. What is it?"

"Poteen. Your 85-year-old granny is making moonshine in Italy."

"Oh, is that what she wanted the pure alcohol for?"

"What?"

"Yeah, she asked me not to tell you but she bought a gallon of that pure alcohol we see in the supermarkets."

I fling open the cupboard under the sink and there it is; a five litre plastic container of alcohol half full of ... chopped raw potato.

"Don't touch that!" Mam calls as she approaches the door.

"It's an experiment. An experiment in poteen, Italian-Irish moonshine. The Italians use lemons, we use potatoes, it's an old Irish recipe."

"Poteen is hardly an old Irish recipe we should be proud of. And Ma, poteen makers don't use potatoes to add flavour to alcohol, they are added to create the chemical reaction to make the alcohol."

"Oh... well it might be nice. Can't go wrong with anything involving potatoes."

"Ma this is not happening, this is going to attract flies never mind the fact the commune could call in to inspect the house at any time to see if we are a bloody luxury villa. Brewing your own alcohol might be illegal here, I don't know."

"Don't be ridiculous every house brews wine. They even have a room for it, a can't something or other."

"Cantina mother, a cantina." She has a point but I don't know if nearly one hundred percent alcohol would be acceptable. I know that vineyards have to get a licensed company to take their grape must away after the skins have been removed from wine making so that they won't be tempted to make grappa. Grappa making needs a specific licence.

"Ma, booze is as cheap as chips here, I'm sorry, I'm not risking being arrested for moonshine production at this level. It has to go," I say, already pouring the offending smelling liquid down the sink.

"Don't mention chips. Yours are disgusting."

Italian Lemon Moonshine (Limoncello)

In Ireland, poteen was made from potatoes, turnips or even tree bark. It is illegal for good reason, as the first alcohol from the distillation is methyl alcohol and is deadly even in small quantities. So please don't follow my mother's example!

Ingredients:

8 Big organic lemons (unwaxed or treated)

1 Litre (4 cups) of pure alcohol (95°)

600g (3 cups) of granulated sugar

1 Litre (4 cups) of water

Equipment:

A Vegetable peeler

A 3 litre large glass jar with an airtight lid

Glass bottles with airtight lids

A Sieve

A Funnel

Bottles with airtight caps or corks

Method:

Wash the lemons and pat dry with kitchen paper.

Grate the lemons. But only the yellow not the white pith as this will make the drink bitter.

Put the lemon zest in the glass jar and pour in the alcohol. Seal with the lid and store in a cool place out of direct sunlight. Shake the jar every day for two weeks.

After two weeks, filter the liquid with a sieve to remove the lemon peel.

Put the water (not the liquid you have just strained) and sugar in a saucepan and bring to boil. Stir continuously until the sugar is dissolved. Leave to cool.

You will end up with about 2 litres of limoncello, so sterilise enough bottles for storing the limoncello in. You can do this by boiling them in a pot of water for at least twenty minutes then draining them upside down. Do not towel dry.

Once the syrup is cold, add it to the infusion of lemon alcohol and mix well. Now pour the limoncello into glass bottles with hermetic closure or cork stopper. Store the bottles in a cool, dark place for one week.

Chill for three hours in the freezer compartment of your fridge before drinking. Limoncello can be kept in the freezer as the high alcohol content and sugar stop it from freezing.

Enjoy!

28

EASY SOLUTIONS

There's a man following me around the supermarket. He keeps on trying to talk to me so I walk faster. Finally, I can't ignore it any longer and I abruptly stop and face the cheeky bugger.

"Scusi Signora. É mio carrello."

I've taken his trolley and left mine two aisles away.

I always have a fondness for this particular supermarket as it is where we were buying bananas when our non-offer for the house was accepted.

I'm back buying bananas again, along with a big bag of spinach and coconut milk. Since Rob's visit, this has been my breakfast.

"It's a great way of getting your daily greens in, the first thing in the morning," Rob said, filling the liquidiser three quarters full of washed spinach leaves, a half glass of non-dairy milk and a banana. Rob mixes his spinach with water or oat milk and uses berries instead of bananas.

My head is in speed mode, I rarely get out without Mam anymore. But I am expecting Alex and Ivor to arrive and wanted to have breakfast before they started, so I could hide in my room and not be asked five hundred 'why' questions by Alex.

Mam also had an encounter with a man while I was out.

"A little man from the Amazon called while you were out," says Mam, smiling like a Cheshire cat when I get back. "I practiced my Italian on him. I said 'Non ho Italiano. Non capisco'. He smiled and nodded. Then I said 'Grazie' when he left the package. Amn't I great?"

She's nearly doing better than me at Italian. She's making more of an effort at least. I really need to give it some time every day, but even though I don't have a minute to myself to spare at the moment, she has reminded me it is something I have to give some priority to. What if she got sick, or I got sick and needed to go to the hospital? Or even to get by doing day-to-day stuff, which is happening more often now that Covid restrictions have been lifted.

Having Mam here is making me get out and making me interact more. I can't hide behind the helping hands of my Italian friend Lucia or of Karen much longer. So I find a seven week Italian class online that has a free bootcamp running over the next five evenings. I sign up. They are starting at the basics but they cover conversation, writing and listening. I am hoping it will loosen my tongue tied-ness.

It will also help stop me morphing into an old Irish woman. Being around Mam all day every day for the last four months, is getting me into the habit of doing small talk. In Ireland the weather takes centre stage of every casual conversation. I am also finding myself using phases such as;

- 'Ah sure, why not?'

-'These days.'

-'It's not like it used to be.'

I am just short of saying, 'those were the days'.

All the old Irish woman phrases that erupt from my mouth make me cringe, when really I want Italian words seductively rolling off my clunky Dublin tongue. It would not happen by itself, I needed to work on it and stop telling myself I can't do it.

Alex is back to start on the big bathroom.

"I will do something nice in your toilet," he exclaims or threatens yet again. He loves working with us as we keep on top of payments.

"You are good people, I have never had people pay me so quick. People in Italy don't do this. I am still chasing money for jobs I did four years ago."

I text Mick Kelly to see if there is any word from the bank about the 50/50 money. But no, they have stalled the programme for the foreseeable future.

"When is the topographer coming?" I ask him, grabbing the rare opportunity of him responding to my texts immediately.

"He has already done the documents necessary."

"But he hasn't been here?"

"Yes, it is a fusion of plots. With the software he didn't need to come."

"So we have to pay him €400 for rubbing out some lines?"

I don't get a response nor do we get a bill or an invoice from the mysterious topographer, maybe Mick Kelly will add it to his final bill and we can discuss the cost of line erasing again then.

Ronan goes to get the car fixed. The beeping alarm is doing our heads in. He was already at the mechanic with it weeks ago when it first started but the mechanic reassured him, having researched the warning lights and checking the oil levels, that it was just a broken sensor in need of replacing. The car was not going to blow up or stop functioning. He gave Ronan a quote and told him to come back in a month's time when he was less busy.

So for a month we have driven around with the loud incessant beeping until the date arrives for Ronan to go to the mechanic.

The mechanic spends twenty minutes looking up the sensor problem online again.

"It is not important," the guy states.

"I know, but when can you fix it?"

"It is not important."

"Yes, but you said to come to you in a month to fix it, so here I am."

"No. When did I say this?"

"Last month?"

"No, I don't know how much it would cost even."

"€153 plus labour, you printed it out for me."

The secretary is nodding. She remembers and is looking apologetic about her boss.

"But I don't know how long it will take to fix. It could take hours! It is not important you can drive with it, it is just a sensor."

"But I want it done. The beep beep is driving us nuts. We drive with the radio on very high to drown out the noise."

"Aw bene, bene," He says satisfactorily. "You have found a solution without mechanical interference. That is good because I cannot do it."

Ronan storms back to the car to where I am waiting, "I've come to the conclusion that all Italians are bloody crazy. I need to find another mechanic."

29

WELL OILED

I t's March, my birthday month but I don't want to celebrate. It's not because I don't want to be fifty, I am glad to have got to this age.

The plans I had for a big party to celebrate my fiftieth were to go hand in hand with celebrating Mam and Dad's arrival to live in Italy. Rob and my brother Jim were to bring them over, so it meant all my favourite people would have been here.

But with Dad having passed and Rob unable to travel, the idea of having a big party like I had originally planned makes me feel sad rather than happy.

"We have to get together this month to celebrate your birthday," says Karen. "How about you come along to the vineyard visit I am arranging next week for some journalists? I am sure Ronan and Luca can manage your mum for a day."

"I don't know."

"There's wine tasting involved."

"Right so, I am sure they can cope. Where will I meet you?"

Karen meets me at Siena train station.

We weave our way up to a large, modern-style fortress with an inner courtyard near Volterra. The owners are not Italian, but have spent millions creating a state-of-the-art cantina with organic wines made from the surrounding rolling vineyards as far as the eye can see, planting new vines and caring for the old with the best techniques and equipment available. No expense has been spared on the massive high-tech building.

We are taken on a tour starting at the collection and sorting room where grapes are checked by hand and leaves removed. They then gently travel to the ultra-modern cellars beneath. Giant, tulip-shaped concrete vats line the cellar walls. Above the vats, a large silver tube runs on a computer-controlled track around the cantina, feeding the vats with grapes from the sorting room above.

"The tulip shape helps to improve the circulation and fermentation process of the wines. The fermentation happens completely naturally with the natural yeast in the environment," our guide explains. They are like fat bellied, giant, glutinous kings, being fed grapes into their big open gobs.

The second cantina has the more traditional style massive wooden barrels where the oak-aging process happens.

It's comforting to see how sterile and clean professional cantinas are, having had our first wine making experience in Guliano's dusty basement, serving us a claret with earwig and ant undertones.

Karen and I take a circular glass elevator up to the tasting room. The room's focus is a huge glass table lit from underneath to help show the colours of the wines like beautiful liquid lamps.

A glass wall overlooks the space-age cantinas below. Trying seven wines before lunch, from crisp new whites to aged reds, goes to your head pretty quickly. By the time I get to number seven I am lapping up being told about the hints of liquorice and notes of blackberries. I nod and take a slurp of what tastes like a great red wine which on a normal day, and without the previous six tastes, I would have described as nothing special.

We're invited to the cantina's wine shop for more tasting.

"The wine here is expensive don't be tempted to buy any," says Karen, knowing my tendency to be a sucker for supporting local businesses, even if they are millionaires.

At the cantina's shop I see a sign with the wines listed, my favourite red is €9, and the white is €12.

"Karen, you have gone so bottom shelf for your wines," I laugh. "These prices aren't expensive." But she's not listening, she is distracted answering a journalist's question.

"I'll have two of the last red we tried and two of the first white."

The owner, who has shown us around tots up the price on the till and bags my wine.

"That will be €122," he smiles.

I gulp. I look at the sign again on the counter and see the heading on the top; 'Price Per Glass'.

I don't want to seem like the gobshite that didn't know, so I just grin and hand him my bank card. That's nearly a whole window refurbishment down the drain.

Back home, I stick the bottles of wine in the back of the cupboard, they will be for Christmas or several special occasions. And I will ensure all who sample it appreciate the blackberries and liquorice undertones within.

For my birthday, Shelly has surprised me with a visit from a masseuse to the house. Such a thoughtful gift, but then again I have been moaning at her about how stiff and tense across my shoulders is and we had spent a night exchanging our worst massage stories.

Mine being in Central Park in New York where the pop-up masseuse was having an argument with the masseuse beside him, and took his aggression out on my back, leaving me bruised and winded for a week. Shelly's was a massage where she was asked to turn over and the masseuse started massaging her breasts.

"This guy is very good. Helga get's him to do a home visit every month," assures Shelly.

A good looking thirty-something year old Italian arrives wearing a bright orange tracksuit top and light blue runners. I'm thinking he needs to head off to referee a match somewhere afterwards.

I have a chair in the room, but he has brought his own massage table which he sets up. Oh nice, it seems I am getting a back massage too perhaps or shoulders lying down.

"So you can get under the towels with just underwear and I will be back soon."

"For a shoulder massage?"

"No, Shelly has booked you a full body massage." I hear Shelly's car pull into the driveway, she's late arriving, but she has booked a massage after me so I'll get to talk to her then.

I'm thankful for shaving my winter coat off my legs that morning. I strip off and then suddenly remember my choice of underwear, silky mini knickers and no bra. Well, the no bra was intentional, I didn't want the straps getting in the way of my shoulder rub. I jump under the towel just before he comes back into the room.

I'm consoling myself thinking the knickers shouldn't matter either, it's not like ... oh it is like... bloody hell the towel is up around my waist as his hands slither up and down the backs of my calves.

He's got skilled hands and great technique, but I'm very conscious of my cheek-revealing silkies giving him an eyeful. He's now working on the back of my upper legs. Oh, that's a move I haven't experienced before... a wiggle rub, that sends waves of wobbles across my cellulite. Hello, the glutes are getting it too.

Seriously, I can't relax. I can't remember the last time I even looked at my bikini line. He pulls my legs from my hips by my feet; I feel I might end up two inches taller by the end of this.

He has moved on to my lower back; the towel has been pulled back down to cover my wobbly bits, thank God.

Okay relax, he's a professional... that's very low on the lower back... relax, relax.... Just think Rosie, here you are in Italy, in your house... which could be a luxury villa if the tax man gets his way... having a young Italian man rubbing baby-oiled hands all over your body... oh why did I think of it like that? I snort, trying to dismiss the thought that, if left unchecked, will rattle my funny bone.

Okay, and relax. Great work on the shoulders ... really getting in there to all the tension spots. Back of the neck, he must be nearly done now, and I survived, didn't quite relax but I'm sure I'll feel the benefits.

"Okay so turn over please..."

Oh okay. I obey and rotate under the two towels. He's working on my legs again, he goes as far as my thighs touch, for once I'm so glad they touch. Relax, relax, relax, relax, he's a professional. Although I wish it was over... I shouldn't have drank that vitamin drink just before he arrived along with the second cup of tea, my bladder is filling up.

Now my arms.

"Are you warm enough?" he asks.

"Yep"... that came out a bit high pitched.

Now the front of the shoulders.

Okay nearly over now.... my stomach is making funny noises.

That was good. I tell myself, focus on how good your shoulders are going to feel aft... OH MY GOD what just happened?

The towel has been thrown off my front ... my very bare front ... I am lying on a plinth, face up, naked from the waist up, in front of a man who is not my husband for the first time in thirty years. I don't think I was even this naked giving birth and my birthing team were all women come to think of it. He's massaging my stomach gently. I hope he doesn't get any firmer that bladder isn't doing too well.

I suddenly remember Shelly's weird massage story about the unexpected breast massage she got, was this that guy? I'm sure she said it was a Thai woman. Maybe she thought my reaction was pleasant excitement and not shock. I'm biting my lip it seems to help keep my eyelids, that are now straining to open because of my ever-rising eyebrows, shut.

His hands slide up between my breasts and up to my collarbone, no breast check or wobbles, thankfully.

He covers me again with the towel and moves back to my collarbones and neck.

"Okay, Rosie relax there for a few minutes," he says and steps out to wash his hands. I can't get off the high table quick enough and pull my clothes on before he gets back in.

"That was great thanks, I'll get Shelly for you," I say a bit breathlessly.

"That was lovely," I smile at Shelly who is having a coffee in the kitchen. I'm not lying, it was great, I just didn't know what to expect next.

"Your turn." I can see her looking at my face. I realise my eyebrows are still so high they are nearly reaching my hairline.

Shelly goes up to the room, and an hour later leads the masseuse to the door with equally raised eyebrows.

"He did a few things differently this time. I think I only got a back massage the last time, when he flicked me to the front I was thinking of you thinking of my Thai massage experience."

"That is exactly what I was thinking!"

It would normally be too early for a glass of wine but we both need it after our Italian man handling experience. So I crack open one of the special bottles I was to save for Christmas and we both enjoy a glass with lots of laughing. "For zero ending birthdays, you get to celebrate all year long," Shelly informs me. "So here's to the start of many strange, but great experiences this year."

30

NOT MY PARTY

On the day of my actual birthday, I work as usual, answering emails and just getting on with things. I've told Izzy not to come over. I just want the day to pass.

"Well, we'll have to do something to mark the occasion," says Ronan.

"I don't really want to. I'd rather ignore it. Maybe we will do something in the summer, when I'm more on form and Izzy is here and Rob can travel again."

Rob has had two chemo sessions so far and both have gone well with no major reactions. He's sticking to the Keto style diet of lots of greens, vegetables, organic meats, fish and no sugars, starch or carbohydrates. He's also still working out and working his day job.

"How about we at least go out for pizza? Your Mam likes pizza and there's that pizzeria on the corner in town that we are always saying we should try."

"There is a pizzeria I'm always saying we should try?"

"Yes, yes, the one on the corner near the bank?"

I vaguely know where he is talking about but I have no recollection of having an urge to try it out. But hey why not, I don't feel like cooking and Mam does likes pizza so we can't go wrong, which we seemed to have done every other time we have brought her out to eat so far.

"Have they no potatoes and a lamb chop with gravy, no?" Is usually the first question she asks when we look at a menu in a restaurant.

I've convinced her to try some other things but risotto was described as baby food, meat with a side plate of grilled thinly sliced vegetables tasted good but why wasn't it served on the one plate? And why were the vegetables so hard? She preferred a bigger pile of boiled-to-mush vegetables and potatoes. Even the burgers weren't right, they were too big to get her false teeth around. The tea was like dishwater and never offer her an espresso again, "a spit of coffee".

Although she managed and cleared her plate every time and said it was delicious once the complaining was done.

Mam painted me a picture as a gift. "It's a donkey's face." I love donkeys, so I am touched. "It's for when you make an ass of things, you can look at this picture and smile."

"Oh, hmm thanks."

"But I also got you this. Ronan went and got it for me."

She hands me a bag. An Apple bag. Inside is a brand new iBook Air. I'm speechless.

"I've been watching you struggle with that big machine and a few nights ago I heard your Da say to me; 'Buy Rosie the best computer you can get, she deserves it.' Okay, granted I had drank a few more drinks more than my usual but I am sure I heard his voice."

"Mam you shouldn't have, you really shouldn't have. These are bloody expensive. You need to keep that nest egg Dad left in case of emergency."

"Oh, look I might as well spend it. Sure how long do I have? A year or two? Might as well enjoy it."

"Ma, you are eighty-five and in good health. Here in Italy people often live to be one hundred and more. You could have another twenty years to go."

"Waaa," she screams and laughs. I laugh too but, it's true she could live for another twenty years, which would see me at seventy still looking after and living with my mother. The truth of the possibility dawns on both of us and our laughter turns into more of a panicked hysterical laugh. "While it's nice to be generous Ma, at the rate you are spending money and dishing it out to everyone, you won't have any left within two years."

"Maybe I should move back to Ireland and cut my life expectancy to a more reasonable level. There is no way I want to live another bloody twenty years.

"Your Dad and I always said we have seen too much already, been through too many changes. I can't keep up. It's all alien to how we loved life... Going out for a few drinks, dancing... We didn't have much, but we had enough to be happy. There was none of this climate change or killing or hatred. Even knowing when you turned on the TV, you were going to see something nice. Not blood and violence or mad sex."

"There was hatred and ugly stuff happening when you were growing up. Sure you lived through World War II and pre the Civil Rights movement. Can't get much uglier than that.

"We just hear about more stuff now, we have access to what's happening all over the world, on every street and we are fed it twenty-four hours a day. But there are also good things happening in the world, it's just that they don't make shock headlines."

I think back to when I started a good news section in a magazine in the 90s and they scrapped it because of lack of interest from sponsors. Readers enjoyed it though.

"Aye, indeed. But I still have lived through too much. Another year or two will do me."

"But we don't get to decide. You need to preserve your nest egg Ma. Okay?"

"I'm not giving the computer back. I'm sick of you cursing at that other machine every day. If you are going to get those books written then you need it, your Dad told me and that's all there is to it."

"Tell you what, when I have a bestseller, I'll pay you back."

"I think I'll have to hang around the twenty years for that. Talking of nest eggs, I was going to boil some eggs for a salad but there's only two eggs, so I left them in case someone else wants them."

That's my Mam; generous to a fault, giving a compliment and taking it back as quick, and depriving herself for others.

"You need to go buy more eggs. And when you are at the shop, I need—"

"Mam, it's my birthday, I am not going anywhere today. I am doing exactly what I want to do."

"You are right too. Go lock yourself away in a room with your new computer and write your book. I know that's what you really want to do."

So she does know me.

I'm sitting in my bedroom, under the attic where Alex and Ivor are working. There are things being dropped on the ceiling and I'm worried my lovely, smooth-plastered ceiling I wake up to and appreciate every morning, is going to fall down in slabs on top of me, my dogs, my bath and my new computer.

Even though it's my birthday, I don't get dressed up to go out. We're going to walk to the restaurant. It's chilly but dry and Mam is dying to take her wheelchair for a walk.

At the restaurant, there is a long centre table with enough seating for thirty people and two shiny gold helium balloons in the centre. A giant five and a giant zero.

"What the?" I say, feeling a little sick.

"That's not our table. Don't worry. I mean I didn't plan anything. That's our table over there." Ronan points to the corner where Shelly and Sherwin, Blodwyn and Welsh Ivan are sitting waving with a half deflated 'Good luck' Pikachu balloon, trying to stay upright.

"Surprise," says Shelly. "Surprise that's not your birthday table, just a co-incidence. There's another group booked in for a fiftieth, sorry!"

"It's fine. It's such a relief... I was thinking, has he rented a crowd? I only know about five people in Italy."

"And sorry about the balloon," says Shelly. "But there's a story attached. Remind me to tell you it later."

Mam asks for a ham and pineapple pizza, we don't translate her request to the waitress in case she throws us out.

"You won't get pineapple on a pizza in Italy."

"But it's the only one I like."

"That's because it's the only type you have ever tried. How about this one?" I convince her to get the same as me. Tuna and red onion.

The guests are arriving for the big table. Just before the birthday 'girl' makes an entrance, a friend or possibly a sister rushes in and grabs the balloons off the table exclaiming quietly but loud enough for us to hear, that 'she' would be offended by them, she doesn't want anyone to know her age. They are pushed down behind a table across from us. "Shall I get them and put them on our table?"

"No, I like our balloon. And you need to tell me the story about it."

As Shelly starts her story, I can see the size of the beer they have brought her compared to Sherwin's does not impress Mam. I suppose they don't expect a little old lady to want a pint-sized glass of draught.

"I was late finishing work," starts Shelly. "And I rushed over to the next town as I knew the Chinese shop there had helium balloons. I chose a lovely happy birthday balloon and brought it to the counter and paid her €5 for it."

I could see our pizza is being taken out of the huge open-flamed pizza oven central in the restaurant. It's glow as warming as the love around the table from my friends and family.

"I stood there looking at her and she stood looking at me until I eventually said 'helium air'," continues Shelly. "She says 'ahhh you want it blown up?' I said 'yes of course I hardly just want a flat foil balloon'.

"And she says 'but it will be expensive'. And I said 'how much?' and she pauses and says '€5' and I said 'yeah okay lets do it'. And she says 'but it is expensive' and I said 'I don't care, give me the bloody air'. Well, I didn't say bloody but you can imagine I was in a hurry to get back and to get ready.

"So after ages, someone else comes over and they are both fiddling with this gas cylinder behind the counter and she eventually gets the balloon attached and it goes 'sssssss' and 'pop!'. And she tells me to get another balloon. So I go over and bring her another balloon and she attaches it and it goes 'ssssssss' and 'pop!' again. She tells me to get another balloon, and it happens again. I go get another one and at this point I'm late, so I just grabbed the balloon from what I thought was the same pile and she attaches it and it goes 'sss' and as soon as I saw it rise at all, I shouted 'enough, that's enough'.

"She sealed it and handed it to me without any string or weights attached. And then I noticed it wasn't a happy birthday balloon. So that is why you have a 'good luck' Pikachu balloon, with twine attached and a rock from our garden as a weight."

As more wine is consumed, Shelly attempts to get under the table and crawl over to steal the hidden balloons, but there are too many of our legs in the way.

We have lots of laughs and go our separate ways to our cars. Ours is parked directly outside in the disability parking space as Mam brought her blue disability badge over and supposedly they are accepted by the Italian authorities. We couldn't miss ours, as attached to our window wipers are the 'offensive' gold '5' and '0' balloons.

"She did it while you were at the bathroom," says Luca, laughing. "She had us all block the view of the other party while she and Blodwyn crawled under the table and then they ran outside with them."

————

I overhear Mam chatting with Rob the following day.

"Ah yeah, we went out for dinner at a restaurant. You know me, I never enjoy eating in restaurants. I ordered a beer, and they just presumed I wanted a small one. And then I had a pizza. It was crap. It's the third pizza I have had since I got here and all were awful, one crust was too thick around the edge and the other was like a wafer, too thin and they have no pineapple pizzas. I asked for one and they all laughed. It's the only type I like ham and pineapple.

"I had chips too. A basket of them, they were strange looking, but they tasted better than Rosie's. Did I tell you about the chips she made me? They were disgusting."

I can't believe she is still going on about my only cooking failure since she got here, four months later.

"The only good thing about the place was that we could see them cooking our food in the fire behind the counter. I think

Tony would have approved of it. At least you can see what is going on, and that there are no rats."

We don't find this type of statement about restaurant hygiene strange in our family. I never ate in a restaurant until I was about nineteen while on a date. Dad didn't believe in wasting money on eating out when there was perfectly good food at home.

That, and because he did a stint in the health inspection department in the 1970s, he was convinced all restaurant kitchens were overrun by rodents and poor hygiene standards, especially hotels.

So growing up, we never ate out nor stayed in a hotel. I've made up for it since, but it still makes Mam uncomfortable to think of the possible vermin running over her food in restaurant kitchens, like Dad had convinced her was happening. I think Dad just didn't like spending money.

"I don't know why they think pineapple is so strange on pizza when they have fruit for dinner. Well Rosie does anyway, she made this orange and apple and liquorice flavoured thing, I can't remember what it was called. Strange. I'm not complaining it was nice, just strange." She's talking about what has become one of my favourite dishes to make; Warm fennel and orange salad.

"There's no path outside her house, it's a disgrace." Mam continues on her rant forgetting Rob was only here recently and is familiar with where we live. "I don't know why people put up with it and don't insist on a path, but Rosie says they are used to avoiding mopeds and bicycles along the roads, so they will have no problem swerving around my wheelchair."

I'm laughing. I can't imagine what she would think of some of the hill towns where I've been. Even some of the most popular such as Positano, where there are winding busy roads with no paths and thousands of steps, there is not a wheelchair ramp anywhere in sight. You never see people in wheelchairs in these places, it just wouldn't be possible for them to get around.

Our town is one of the most wheelchair accessible towns I have found in Italy. It's the only place in Italy, other than cities, that I have seen people going around in motorised wheelchairs by themselves. It's something I always looked out for during visits, as I had hoped someday I would have my elderly parents here. But now that Mam is here, I'm not sure it is the best idea. Not because of the wheelchair but because we might drive each other nuts.

Warm Fennel and Orange Salad

Serves: 4

2 Fennel bulbs

3 Carrots

2 Oranges

1 Apple

2 Tins of cooked kidney beans

2 Tbls of soy sauce

1 Carton of Greek yogurt

Honey to taste

Two handfuls of hazelnuts

Sprinkle of salt

Olive oil

Method:

Preheat oven to 220°C (200°C in a fan oven).

Chop the carrots into batons and slice the fennel into biteable sizes.

Place the fennel, carrots and chopped hazelnuts on a sheet of parchment paper, sprinkle with salt and olive oil for 20 minutes.

Grate an orange and squeeze half of the orange into a bowl, mix in the Greek yogurt and add the honey to taste.

Rinse the cooked kidney beans. Add the soy sauce and a splash of olive oil and whizz until you have the consistency of hummus.

Slice up an orange and an apple.

Put the vegetables on a plate while still warm. Alongside them, put a dollop of the orange yogurt and a mound of kidney bean hummus.

Place the sliced fruit around and sprinkle the warm salad with remaining chopped hazelnuts.

31

HE LEFT ME

The problem with having a twenty-two roomed house is that when you mislay something it takes longer to find it.

So when you are looking for something, such as your husband, you walk from room to room on all three floors searching, and then inevitably, you find that said husband is in the car waiting for you all that time.

"I'm here!" is no longer a sufficient direction, when there are twenty-two 'here' options.

After finding the missing husband, it's then you realise that you have put your life-support machine, aka your phone, down somewhere during the search. You then have to retrace all your steps to find the phone. This usually takes twenty to thirty minutes. I do this at least twice a day. The way I look at it is that I perform the equivalent of a forty minute to an hour workout on a stair machine each day just looking for stuff.

Izzy has come over for a weekend.

"Mam, roll your shoulders back, you are starting to walk stooped... When are you giving up weddings? You have been talking about it for years and the stress is starting to show on your face... And why are you talking like Nanny?" Izzy is concerned about me.

This is never how I expected to be at fifty. I find I'm relying on the bannisters. I am not great at any heights and have a fear of escalators. It's the handrail moving at a slightly different speed, my body moving but other things staying stationary. But now I am finding the stairs a chore.

They say you become like those you spend the most time with, and I feel like I am rapidly turning into an 85-year-old woman.

Also, I have spent little time with Ronan. Yes, we see each other on and off all day every day, but between work and looking after Mam, I have become mechanical. It's like I'm living through an apocalypse, I'm just spouting orders at him for our survival; 'We need dog food' 'We need this bill paid', 'Mam needs whiskey'.

He has been very patient with both Mam and me. Having your mother-in-law move in with you can't be easy, especially when she wants things her way.

Mam's collection of things she needs around her daily has grown.

Each morning she brings her small clock, torch, whiskey glass, hand fan, various medications, large bottle of Gaviscon, diary, notebook, iPad, phone and reading glasses out of her bedroom to join her menagerie of other items including an English-Italian dictionary, fly swatter, pack of cards, binoculars, bag of knitting, crucifix, rosary beads and various photos.

Her collection of objects started on the windowsill and her side table but as her collection has slowly grown, it has now spilled onto the velvet chaise.

When I see she has cleared her finished dinner plate onto my velvet sofa, which she is feeding the dogs scraps from, I have had enough.

"Ma, if you can get up and get your glass of whiskey, you can bring your finished plate out to the kitchen."

"I only put it there for a minute."

"You are playing cards and I've asked you not to feed the dogs from your plate, I hate begging dogs and I don't want them in that habit."

"I wasn't."

"You are!"

I'm laughing, as she is holding out a ball of rice in her fingers which Paddy is happily nibbling on while she is denying it.

"It's only a bit for goodness' sake. Stop making such a fuss."

I hate feeling like I am being such a cranky nag all the time, giving her basic house rules to live by. Before they mark the velvet, I grab the plate and pick up all the bits of spilled rice. I take the plate to the kitchen and march upstairs to get something that is now much needed.

"Here," I say presenting her with a pretty wooden box I had bought for my office. "This is for you to put all your stuff in. I'm sure we can leave some of it inside, in your bedroom or your kitchen. You don't need all of it around you all the time."

"Ah no, I like having things near me."

"Okay then keep them in the box."

"Hmmp."

I don't give her a choice and start loading things into it.

Not everything will fit. So I focus on clearing the windowsill at least. I like clutter-free windowsills. Amongst all the stuff she has piled on it, I find a crust from a sandwich.

"Ma what the heck?" I say holding the offending object up before her. "Ah, I forgot about that, I was keeping it for the dog."

"Ma, no feeding the dogs scraps, if you do this, you are going to have ants."

She pretends she likes the box but I can see she isn't happy not having everything spaced out around her like a magpie sitting in a nest of shiny things she has collected.

The following afternoon I come down and see she has kept everything in the box, which she has put... on the windowsill.

"Mam are you getting enough sleep?" Izzy asks me. "You are not yourself." I'm guessing she's referring to my short temper and robotic motions of getting through the day, let alone my developing hunch and slower pace.

"No, it's awful. I used to get just about seven hours with your dad's snoring and clunking around when he comes in, but now with Paddy it's got shorter. He must have been a hunting dog, as he is full of life at 5am and wants to go out."

"That's ridiculous, Mam, you need your sleep. Paddy needs to get into a new routine, leave him down in the sitting room."

"But he's so sad when he's not near us."

"Mam, that is ridiculous."

"You are right. I need him out of the room. I can't function like this on four hours sleep especially as I'll be starting weddings soon."

With that Ronan comes into the sitting room. "Ronan I have made a decision. I need more sleep, so Paddy has to get used to sleeping in the sitting room."

"We can't leave Paddy sleeping on his own, you know how he howls."

"We can. He'll get used to it."

"No, we can't."

"Yes, we can."

"Right, you move out to another room."

"No, I won't move out of my bedroom so you can sleep with the dog, you move out," I say.

"Okay, I will."

And with that he gets up and leaves the room.

Izzy and I stare at each other.

There is a whole lot of banging around in the room above.

"Has your father just left me for the dog?" I ask.

"I think so..."

I didn't feel that bothered, but I felt I should.

"Actually, I think a stint of living on my own would be a good thing," I say to Izzy, swinging it into a positive action. "I see how your granny is struggling to adapt to be on her own without constantly having someone to order around. I need to learn to enjoy my own company again... So right, that's decided then. I'm living on my own."

"You're hardly on your own with Nanny, Dad and Luca in the house?"

"The house is big enough for us all to live separately but together. Nanny downstairs, Luca on the top floor, Dad in the west wing and me in the east wing of the first floor. ... I think this means your Dad and I are separating?"

"You're separating? Shouldn't he be in on this decision?"

"He was, he just left me for the dog."

"Do you not think this is all very... sudden?" Izzy says.

"Oh you know us, We don't wait around. That's the way we are."

"But you and Dad... I was basing mine and Dave's relationship on the same bond you two have. Now you are cracking my illusion of the perfect relationship."

"Oh, it's no big deal, the person you choose to have kids with is not always the best person to spend your later in life years with. I could do with something different, a change."

"Mam!"

"I don't mean a different partner, I just mean a change, some time to myself."

"Eh, you may have not noticed, but your mother moved in with you about six months ago, that sort of eliminates that idea."

"Anyway, he's just making a statement. He'll be back in the bedroom tonight, I am sure he won't sacrifice our relationship for the dog."

But he didn't come back into the bedroom.

A week later and he was still sleeping on the futon he'd set up in the room next to me, with Paddy happily sleeping beside him.

I got angry, then sad then angry again.

But I didn't show it. Instead, I enjoyed Izzy's company before we took her to the airport and said goodbye.

Driving back from the airport towards the golden hills with newly greened streaks of vines, I take the opportunity of me and Ronan having a rare thirty minutes on our own.

"The evenings are getting longer and a bit more sun." Of course I start the conversation with the weather, I was becoming an old woman after all. Time to get to the crunch, we had no time to waste.

"So what's with us? You've actually left me for the dog?"

"We can't leave Paddy on his own yet, you know how he howled the first few nights."

"I know, but I need to sleep and you don't wake up when he needs to go out, I do."

"I do now."

"That's because he is sleeping beside you."

"But it's not just Paddy is it?" He says apprehensively. "I feel I haven't been able to have a conversation with you since you got back from Ireland."

"Hold on, you spend all your time upstairs on your computer, we don't eat together as we don't have a dining room, and I am just spending every moment of the day either working or making sure my Mam is okay."

"I know... everything just feels different. You have a lot to deal with at the moment. Grief for your father, Rob, your mother, work, the house ... Something had got to give, and at the moment it's us."

"I know... I feel I am spread too thin. I can't divide myself into so many parts anymore like I used to, I just might crack."

"And I get it. You need your sleep.... Have you slept better the last couple of nights?"

"Actually, yes, like a log," I say, realising I have been having a solid eight hours of sleep for the first time in a long time. Not only that, but I had been waking at seven and got my writing done while the rest of the house was still sleeping. It was actually really nice having my own space. I even had time to meditate one morning.

"I have been sleeping really well too. It's nice going to bed and reading for a while. I haven't done that in ages as I didn't want to wake you."

"Well, if you came to bed earlier... without Paddy."

"He'll just wake us all howling. Anyway, the house is big enough for us to have our own space, it feels quite ... civilised."

"... It is actually nice," I say taking a view of it from a different angle.

"You can come into my boudoir anytime you like," he says. "As long as you don't disturb Paddy."

"Eh how about we use my room for our meet ups? No dogs involved."

"Deal."

My room... I never had a proper bedroom to myself. Life was definitely taking a different turn.

32

DOCTOR CHICKEN

S pring has sprung in Italy. The persimmon tree has stopped pooping on top of our courtyard, Mam now comes out every day to watch the birds and tells me what I should be doing, and Ronan has started working on clearing the sheds.

Shelly drives with me to a garden nursery she knows that sells hedging. Seeing the excitement I get from rows of bare branches stuck in pots she says, "There's a much bigger centre I must bring you to, you will love it."

"Bigger than this? This is as big as they get in Ireland I think."

I'm loving it. I still have too much to do in the house before I can start focusing on the garden, but I want to get a hedge started to divide the garden and give us privacy from the surrounding neighbours in years to come.

Every year counts, so the sooner I get the shrubs planted in the garden, the sooner the garden will have some structure to work with. Ronan has followed us in the van and we pile in twenty Red Robin shrubs that are four foot high.

I am so tempted to buy lavender, rosemary and trailing roses, jasmine and wisteria to create the fragrant walkway I envisage down to the vines, but there is so much prep to be done first that I hold myself back. Piano, piano (slowly, slowly).

The following morning I am up early. I throw Mam's breakfast into her and avoid conversation as she will inevitably tell me how I should and shouldn't do what I am about to do. My emails can wait, it's the weekend, it's weather is good and I can't wait to get out into the garden.

The ground is soft and easy to dig. One plant after the next spaced out about a meter apart, I get the hedge planted within a couple of hours. Just as I hear the clanking of Mam's aluminium walking stick.

She's smiling. We're alike in that sense; being outside in a garden is our happy place.

"You've planted them already? I was sure they would be left to rot in their pots before you got around to doing it."

I take her arm and guide her down to the centre of the garden, avoiding the holes.

"You planted them across there? What did you do that for?" she says, pointing at the hedging three quarters of the way down the garden.

"It will divide the garden into secret spaces. I'll put an orchard beyond that or maybe a pool."

"It's such a shame, this beautiful lawn would have made a perfect place to play tennis," she sighs.

"TENNIS? When in my life or your life have you ever seen me hit a ball successfully with a tennis racket? Or even held a tennis racket for that matter?" I say in shocked amusement.

"When I was your age, I played tennis all the time."

"WHAT?" I burst out laughing. "Ma, when you were my age, I was sixteen and you and Dad ran off down to the countryside to live. You definitely were not playing tennis. You never played tennis or any sport in your life, neither of us did."

She laughed a little at what she had said. Caught out on her on illusions of the life she'd had. "Well, you need to do something physical rather than sitting around on that computer all day."

"That's my work, Ma!"

She ignores my protest. "You need to get yourself moving, you're getting fat. You can start by pushing me down to the lake."

"I've just spent three hours digging, that is physical enough. I'm now going to have a cup of tea, and if you continue like this, I will have no problem pushing you not just down, but also into the lake."

Ronan has arrived out and has been working on clearing the shed. He has his hoodie hanging on the tree and is lugging wood around on his shoulders just wearing a vest top. "Ronan you were told last year not to be lifting anything heavy."

"Well, this wood will not shift itself. I can't see your mother doing it, even though she might have been John McEnroe in her last life."

"It's warm, but the wind is still chilly when it picks up," says Ronan making conversation with Mam about one of her favourite subjects while putting back on his hoodie.

"Sit down and relax for God's sake," says Mam to Ronan even though he has only been out working for ten minutes.

As soon as I'm finished my tea, I procrastinate about facing my emails, "I'm going up to clean the bathroom."

"Why?" says Mam. "Is someone coming?"

"No... I just clean them regularly... Maybe you could clean your own bathroom Ma, if you are looking for something to do?"

"Sure no one goes into my bathroom. It's a long time since I cleaned a bathroom. I honestly can't remember when..."

"Is it hard on your back?" I say sympathetically.

"No, I just don't like cleaning... I prefer to be out here in the garden. While you were out yesterday with Shelly, I escaped. I went to the shop by myself with the wheelchair and bought me whiskey. I couldn't reach the shelf, so I went over to the woman at the deli and said 'Aiuto' and she came out and helped me get it down. I'm very proud of myself. I also saw the Westerians were out at the house down the road."

"The Westerians?" I am trying to figure out which nationality she is talking about.

"Yes, the purple ones. They are all over the house, hanging out of the balcony."

Now I am really confused.

"You should plant some in the garden. It grows well here."

"OHHH Wisteria! Yes, I'm going to plant it along the empty vine posts so we have a tunnel of... westerians."

"Oh, that will be beautiful."

"I was trying to find CIF and bread soda in the supermarket, but couldn't see them there, so when you are out get me CIF cream, not the liquid stuff and bread soda as I think something bit me in the garden yesterday. If there's anything around that bites it will get me you know."

This does not bode well for the summer, as the mosquitoes can be quite persistent here.

Later, at a bigger supermarket, I, at last, find CIF cream and buy it as instructed. It brings back memories of the cluttered shelf in my childhood home where a bottle of half used CIF, Mr Sheen and a rusty tin of Brasso sat for years gathering black dust, cobwebs and somehow grease.

Everything was always sticky with grease, which probably explains my detest for deep fat-fryers and used frying pans. I'm surprised that I am surprised that the bottle of CIF does not feel greasy as I tentatively take it from the shelf in the shop (the double surprise is not an editing error–cleaning products can double surprise you at times). But if it's what she wants and it keeps her busy cleaning for a while, I am happy to get it.

"There you go. I'll leave it in your kitchen," I say unpacking the CIF from the shopping.

"Oh, no that's not for me, it's for you to clean with."

Ronan has moved on to clearing off the patio and moving all the bricks I have spent days placing on the grass to visualise my star gazing platform, back into the pile they came from, much to my annoyance.

His neck looks swollen and by the late afternoon he looks like he has been doing body building on just one side of his body.

"I think I must have been bit by something," he says showing me his back. On his shoulder just below his neck there are three distinct mounds and streaks.

"I don't want to be an alarmist but that doesn't look good."

"Yeah, I'm finding it difficult to swallow."

"I think you need to get that seen to. I'll call Sherwin and get his doctor's name, he says he speaks very good English."

"His name is Fabrizio Gallo," says Sherwin sending me his contact details.

"Gallo? That means chicken doesn't it?"

"Yeah it's a common enough Italian surname," says Sherwin.

"So our doctor's name is Fabulous Chicken?"

"Well, not quite."

"It is now."

Doctor Fabulous Chicken can see Ronan in an hour, so off we go with his swelling neck. The doctor is young—in his late twenties—and already nearly bald. His father is a retired cardiologist, his mother a GP and his sister a neurologist. He is currently working in shifts at the hospital but when his mother retires, he will take over her GP practice.

In the meantime, he needs to rely on the goodwill of the other practitioners who rent rooms at the clinic, which I think is just a converted house. There's a small waiting room with a reception area, previously the original lounge and kitchen. Through a door into a small dark L-shaped hallway, there is a maze of doors into small consultation rooms. Each has a desk with a chair on either side, and an examination bed. Some are without windows, which is why I think they started off as bigger rooms divided up.

"Ah yes you have been bitten and stung by a scorpion. Three times it looks like. They are only like a bee sting but near the throat is probably not a good idea."

"I felt a bit of a sting, but I thought nothing of it. He must have been stuck in my hoody."

"Perhaps your family can be some of my first patients," says the young doctor, he's very enthusiastic. "I've got a new scanning machine. It is fantastic, you can see everything inside you. It is a small version of a big machine they only have in Milan," he says proudly. "Look watch I will show you." The machine is plugged in on his desk as he demonstrates on his own hand.

After hearing of Ronan's stay in hospital the previous year, Doctor Chicken insists Ronan comes back for a thorough scanning. An appointment is made for the following day at the same time before he starts his shift at the hospital.

"Nice guy, I really felt I got to know him inside and out," says Ronan back in the car, "especially his hand".

Ronan returns home from his appointment the following day after two hours, with a clean bill of health.

"He said I have the insides of a thirty-year-old."

"It took long enough."

"Oh, the consultation only lasted an hour, the other hour was him telling me about his split up with his girlfriend and asking my advice. Nice guy." Ronan has yet again made another friend, but at least this time it was through conversations in English.

Mam comes shuffling in.

"I told you not to do so much laundry. All that washing you hung out earlier now needs to be taken in from the damp night air," Mam says. Yet another instruction on how I am doing everything wrong in my life.

"Ah but that is the beauty of living here Ma, from now until October it doesn't get damp in the evenings, so you can leave your washing out all night and the morning sun will have it fresh and ready to take in by the time you get up."

"No dew? I'm not sure if a trust a country that has no dew."

Luca has just come down the stairs and passes Mam in the hallway.

"What's Nanny talking about?" he whispers, looking confused. "She doesn't trust a country that has no jews?"

33

VISITORS

A lex has finished the big bathroom. Black slate tiles on the floor and white metro tiles half-way up the wall, topped all the way around by beautiful mosaic tiles I found on sale. They are varied in shades of grey and black marble with an imprint of a gold emblem on some of them.

Alex is complaining, "Why did you not buy a sink for me to finish the bathroom with? I wanted it to be nice."

"It is nice and it will be even nicer. Don't worry, I have a plan."

With Ronan's help I pull out the Singer sewing machine stand I had sanded and painted nearly two years ago. It had been waiting patiently for this moment in the shed, along with the bowl-like ceramic hand basin.

Within an hour, Ronan and I have a wooden top screwed on to the stand, a hole cut central for the waste pipe, a hole for the water pipes for the tall black tap, and the surface tiled with the remaining mosaic tiles.

We slot the stand into place in the bathroom, silicon the ceramic basin into place and, after some cursing and maneuvering, Ronan has the waste and water connected.

With a modern circular mirror hanging from a black leather strap above, the bathroom looks picture perfect. Even Alex is impressed by our sink.

It's all done just in time for four of Luca's friends, arriving over from Ireland, including his girlfriend. It's so refreshing to have the sound of happy chatter and laughter ringing its ways around the house. Hearing Luca laughing out loud nearly continuously does my heart good.

Their visit is in perfect timing of a local sagra focused on craft beers of the area. Due to Covid it's the first sagra to happen locally in two years. So they enjoy hanging out in town watching the sunsets. At this time of year, the landscape during late afternoon starts to look like it is behind a peachy pink filter

.

Usually all through the year there are sagre popping up in towns across Italy. These are food festivals, where long, family-style catering tables are set up so that locals and strangers can dine together in the streets.

It is estimated that in a normal year there are over forty thousand sagre in Italy each year. Each sagra celebrates a particular food item. So it could be a type of cheese, meat, nut, fruit or berry –prosciutto, almonds, chocolate, fish, grappa, bread, spelt, oranges, chocolate, sheep. If you can eat it, Italy will celebrate it.

Having a bunch of 19-year-olds around for a week lightens my mood and makes be feel less like an old woman.

The day they had planned to go to Florence, it's raining and dark and dull, so instead they stay in. I suggest a cocktail-making class. It is something I have been meaning to do with Luca before he starts working as a bartender when wedding season kicks off in a few weeks.

We make Aperol Spritz, followed by a cookery demonstration of my growing in popularity version of carbonara.

Mam comes out and warns them against having my chips. Not that I was making any or have made any since that one time months ago when she first arrived.

"Her chips are disgusting. Awful."

"I only made them once and they weren't that bad."

"Oh, they were. They were terrible. Disgusting. I'll make you all some of my chips and give you a decent meal, how about that? You need more than just that pasta stuff she makes."

Luca's friends are laughing at the cook-off between mother and daughter unfolding in front of them.

I have to admit, Mam's chips are very good.

Having finished their final exams, Luca's friends are telling me about the colleges and courses they will be starting in the autumn. For some it means moving to Dublin, but there is a huge shortage of accommodation there, which means they will need to do a two hour commute each way if they can't find somewhere to live. I'm relieved that Luca is doing his studies in Italy.

Ireland is now the most expensive EU country for cost of living —it's a staggering forty percent higher than the EU average with accommodation costs nearly ninety percent higher than the rest of Europe, making it the second most expensive country to live in Western Europe. In fact, the cost of living in Ireland is more expensive than ninety-five percent of countries in the world.

The estimated costs for a single person per month without rent is around €2730 and for a family of four is around €4810. Whereas in Italy, a single person estimated monthly living costs are €763 without rent. And for a family of four average monthly costs are €2691 without rent.

So the cost of living for a family of four in Italy is less than the cost of living for a single person in Ireland, by quite some margin.

The cost of living in Italy fares well compared to other countries too. On average, it is fourteen percent lower than in United States. And rent in Italy is, on average, fifty-three percent lower than in United States.

Mam comes in with another heaped bowl of chips, on the end of the conversation when the girls are saying the price of a packet of cigarettes is €20 in Ireland. She is followed by the waft of frying oil which overpowers my burning incense.

"That's ridiculous, Ronan would never survive. Cigarettes are €4 here," says Mam. "I wouldn't survive living there any longer either, a bottle of Irish whiskey is €20 cheaper here, can you believe it?"

"Ireland is the most expensive in Europe for alcohol and tobacco, more than double the average," says one of the girls. "I studied the figures for an essay."

"What is Ireland doing to itself I don't know, driving us all away," says Mam tutting before saying. "Let's have a game of poker!"

So for dessert there is a game of poker led by Mam with the remaining half of her Christmas cigar. And as a thunder and lightning storm brews outside, the evening is finished with a tarot reading session for each of Luca's friends. I have not read cards since New Year's Eve of 2020 when Lucia and I predicted a disastrous year ahead for our businesses involving weddings. Covid shook everything so much that I didn't want to see what the future held.

The girls all enjoy my predictions of future love and career paths. By the time it comes to Luca's turn, I lay the cards but he has lost interest so he and his friends head into the sitting room to watch a horror movie while the storm is going on.

As I clear up the cards, to the background of the loudest clap of thunder I have ever heard, I can't help but glimpse at what his cards predict ...Walking away from an old life to a new life path, travel to distant lands. A new start... and love.

Aperol Spritz

Aperol is made from rhubarb, cinchona and the herb bitterwort, which gives it its bitter taste. The tannins in rhubarb stalks improve digestion and gut health. Cinchona is used for increasing appetite, digestion and treating bloating.

The root of bitterwort is used for loss of appetite, fullness and gas. It is also used for hysteria. So a good all-rounder to have in a cocktail; it helps you get an appetite and keeps your hysteria under control.

60ml Prosecco

40 ml Aperol

Soda or fizzy water

Orange slices and ice

Method:

Fill a large wine glass with ice. Add 3 parts prosecco to 2 parts Aperol. Top with a splash of soda water. Garnish with a slice of orange. (11% alcohol)

34

SOMETHING NICE

The weather is warming up and Mam is already finding the breezeless warm air in the sitting room uncomfortable.

"How about we turn the art room into a sitting room? The current sitting room can then become the much-needed dining room as it is attached to the kitchen?" I suggest to Ronan.

We walk back and forth between the two rooms figuring out layouts and within five minutes we are starting to clear the 'art' room to turn it into 'la stanza tranquilla' – The quiet room.

It is on the opposite northwest-facing corner of the house, so it doesn't get direct sun and remains cool during summer. It's also quieter, away from the thoroughfare of the back door and kitchen. This will mean when sitting in there I won't have to get up fifteen times an hour to let the dogs in and out.

We call in Alex, as I want the ceiling re-plastered in the room that will become a dining room. It's the ceiling that we put six coats of different paint on before we moved in, and all coats peeled and fell like bad dandruff within a week.

Of course, Alex does not just focus on the ceiling.

"Why you do this? We need to move this," he says, pointing to the stove we proudly installed the week before Christmas eighteen months ago.

"We are not moving that," I say, shocked at his suggestion.

"Why? You think it's nice there? It is stupid there, these stoves are made to free stand in a room not in a fire place. But if you want the room to be ugly then that's okay. I don't care."

"Ugly?"

"Yes, if you move this into the front sitting room, where you need heat, then we build an open fireplace here—something nice like it should be. A house like this needs a big open fire.

"And you need a stove in the front room. It's warm now but what are you going to do in the winter, freeze to death? Come on Rosie, this could be a very nice room but if you don't care and want to keep it ugly, it's okay with me." He shrugs like a lover just dumped.

"But we don't have a chimney in the front room."

"You don't need a chimney we will just put the pipe out through the wall. Come, we look where we put it."

I find myself following him to what will be the new sitting room.

"We can put it here or here," he says, pointing to the two outer corners.

"Well not that wall, as that is where I want to put a ceiling to floor bookshelf."

"You have that many books?"

"We have boxes of books that have never been emptied since we moved from Ireland and crates of books that were left in this house."

"You would need encyclopedias to fill so many shelves."

"Well, we do! From the 1940s, they are in Italian but I can't wait to have them out on display."

He looks at me oddly. "I have books at home I bring them to you, to fill up your shelves."

"No, I don't need books to just fill up the shelves. We will probably have enough ourselves, ones that mean something to us. They were gifts or signed copies."

He's looking at me weird again. "I do not want them, they will be gifts don't worry."

I give up. I'm imagining my beautiful shelves full of thrillers in Albanian, along with his kid's old schoolbooks.

We walk around the outside of the house and view the points the pipe from the stove could come out. The front, as suggested, was out of question. It would need to be on the side wall, not so visible. So the stove location was agreed even though I had been adamant that it was not being moved from its current location less than fifteen minutes previously.

"My cousin will come and give you a price for the bookshelves, but I think you would be better off buying something freestanding for when you decide you no longer want them. You know books are going out of fashion?"

He agrees to start the work the following week. Him and his cousin and Ivor will come to move the, what feels like, eleven-tonne cast iron stove before they start.

Things don't go downhill in Italy, they go up. 'Andare a monti' literally means 'go to the mountain', it's used in the same way as we would say 'everything went downhill from then on'. I'm hoping I won't be using that phrase recounting the story of the stove move.

A phrase I am tempted to use though is: 'Ne ho fin sopra i capelli.' It means 'I have had it up to my hair'. This can be accompanied by a hand gesture indicating the top of your head. It replaces how we usually would say 'I'm sick to the back teeth', but the Italians take it higher and more extreme.

I am both getting sick to my teeth, and have it up to my hair, of building work.

I could do without dust and disturbance at the moment, but the front room and lack of a dining room are the last two main rooms that need attention. There is just the small box room, that is Ronan's dingy office, the tool room that used to be the washing machine room, and the attic space that needs to be done after that. And these rooms can wait.

The attic space will also have to wait a long time as we need to replace the roof on that wing and it will cost about €40k to do the roof and the room. I had planned to do it with the 50/50 reimbursement but that whole program is still stalled and I've already borrowed on the back of it.

The following day, I bring Mam with me to La Dogana where I am setting up for a wedding. She spends the day giving me orders about how I should set up the tables, even though I have been doing weddings for twenty years and have agreed the specifics with the venue and the couple.

We get back a few hours later to find Ronan has moved not only the sofa, TV and Mam's chair into the front room, but also the stove.

"Bloody hell Ronan what the hell have you done?"

"Can you not be pleased about something rather than telling me off?"

"That stove is a three-man job, you are not supposed to be lifting heavy stuff."

There are, of course, chips out of the corners of the recently plastered walls between the old sitting room and the new one. And Ronan has several new cuts on his arms and legs which will add to his lifetime of scars from previous renovations.

"Do you not like it?" he says.

"Yes, it looks great. But you shouldn't have done this by yourself."

"It just took a bit of engineering with some rope and a skateboard."

It looks good in the new sitting room. But Mam doesn't like the new setup.

"I am too far away from the kitchen, I can't see people coming and going and the telly is crap, there's nothing on that I want to watch."

She's frustrated, bored and, unknown to herself, missing the part of her soul that brought out the best in her. Dad.

35

ELECTRIC CHIMNEY

W edding season is kicking off at last, and a friend from a wedding band, that we haven't seen in two years because of Covid, calls in for a coffee on his way to a wedding.

He has eighty wedding bookings this year because of postponements and new bookings.

"We have to take every booking to make up for lost time. It's crazy, it's only the start of the season and I already feel tired. Oh, did you hear the news? I am a Nonno, a grandfather, our Poppy had five kids."

Mam spits out her tea. "Jesus; Mary and holy Saint Joseph."

"He means pups, Ma. Poppy is his dog."

"Look," he says, handing me a picture of the cutest puppy face.

"Poppy is a small dog, right?" I ask as my heart turns to gelato.

It's been a while since we were at their house in the woods of Narni. "Yes, she is small enough, not as small as your Looney but a medium dog."

"Should we take a pup?" I say to Ronan, surprising even myself.

"What?"

"Well, we were going to take two dogs from the kennels, and a pup will be good for Looney to play with and it might teach Paddy how to play again." But I also had another reason up my sleeve. It will give Mam something to look after, she misses having her own dog. And it will give her something to fuss over and order around, rather than me.

"Oh, I'd love a pup. It would be all mine though," says Mam. "I'd train her better than your lot. And I'll call it Toby, nothing else."

"She will be ready for you to take in two weeks," said our friend as he promptly finished his coffee and left before we could change our minds. I get it, he will be busy with weddings and cannot look after five pups all summer.

Ronan and Mam were practically jumping up and down with excitement about the idea, while I was regretting making the suggestion.

Like our friend, I had enough to do this summer with weddings without looking after a pup, but I console myself with the thought that Mam and Luca are here too, so we can spread the care. And it was a small dog, so I could take it around with me and bring it for longer walks than Looney is able to do.

But there is no way is she being called Toby, the same name Mam had called every dog we had throughout all our childhoods.

Back inside, Alex had finished installing the stovepipe in the new sitting room.

"So this size will do?" I ask, looking at the well-installed outlet that is much more discreet than I had expected. "We don't legally have to have a taller chimney or anything?"

From the outside, there is a small silver chimney with a rotating cap. It looks like we've installed a pizza oven in our TV room.

"It depends on your neighbours, they might call the police because they don't want the smoke," says Alex matter-of-factly.

"What the hell? You never mentioned that before?... And what smoke? I thought you said pellets don't smoke only when starting to light?"

He doesn't respond to my concerns, instead he just continues as if this was all my stupid idea of moving the stove to somewhere that didn't have a chimney.

"We'll see how it goes this year. Next year you may want to raise it and build a chimney," Alex says.

"Let's hope it works," I say to Ronan, as Alex strides off to the start the dining room conversion. "There is no way I am going through the whole rigmarole of building another bloody chimney when we spent a fortune blocking up three last year and restoring the one that the stove worked perfectly fine in."

"Rosie!" calls Alex from the other room. "We have a problem."

I notice our friend Lucia walking past the window towards the front door, her hand to her face. She looks upset.

My phone buzzes with a text message. It's from the drink wholesaler who is due to deliver me a van-load of alcohol the following day for our first wedding of the season later this week.

I'll need to take time translating it, but it starts with 'Pur troppo' which means 'Unfortunately.'

I have a horrible feeling things are starting to go uphill.

Alex is sitting in the big fireplace looking up the chimney and Lucia has come in the back door into the to-be dining room. She walks to me quickly, and begins to cry softly. "My check-ins."

"You need help with your guest check-ins at La Dogana? I can help with that don't worry," I say, hugging her.

"No. My check-ins. The fox got my check-ins. I know they were just check-ins, but I loved them."

This is indeed a tragedy, as she called her fluffy chickens part of her family, like us. She bought them when she went to view an alpaca she was thinking of adding to her farm.

Chickens were a better idea for this year, as the summer season was going to be hectic and it would leave her with little time to figure out how to look after the mini furry-coated-giraffe-thing, as Luca used to call them.

"I have a cousin who breeds fancy chickens, I can get you some," says Alex comforting her. "But what I can't get, is why the electricians that were here before us, have put electric wires through your chimney, Rosie."

He shines his torch up the chimney, and sure enough there are three relatively new red, blue and yellow wires short cutting their way to the other side of the fireplace through our chimney.

"Opening this fireplace will be a bigger job than you thought."

Emphasis on the 'you'. The blame seems to have jumped back to me again.

Lucia has got over her grief quickly with the idea of new, fancier arrivals.

"Here, save me ten minutes of translating and tell me what the drink supplier is saying, I think he might not be able to deliver some of the brands I wanted?"

She scans the text, "Ah no, it is worse than that, he cannot do the delivery without you having a VAT number."

"But I told him a month ago when we met that I did not have a VAT number. You have a VAT number, I could buy it through you?"

"Ah no sorry, the controllers only let agriturismo's serve produce and drink from their own estate or from within a twenty-mile radius. Don't worry, the guests can just drink wine, don't worry about it, I can get you local wine no problem," says Lucia.

"Are you crazy? An Irish wedding without a well-stocked bar is like Sunday Mass without a priest."

Alex is still sitting in the fireplace, like an ornament. "Ah, Rosie you have a lot to organise, buy the drink in the supermarket it is nearly as cheap as wholesale, I know because my sister owns a restaurant," he says.

Of course he has a relative that owns a restaurant here.

"I will think about a solution for the electric chimney, don't worry," Alex reassures. "But now I bring Lucia to get some chickens, and build a stronger fence for her against the fox guy."

36

BAD APPLES

I pledged 2020 was going to be my last summer of weddings before complete burn out kicked in. But Covid hit and all my weddings were postponed to later in the year, then to the following year and then to the following year after that.

Each time a wedding was postponed, I had to rebook and replan every element of it.

I used to love the challenge of planning events, to turn ideas and dreams into reality and being able to steer couples clear of the pot hole mistakes so many make when planning a wedding abroad.

Watching the day unfold and hearing them say 'I Do' would have me in tears. But during the last wedding season, pre-Covid, I was finding the tears were happening out of relief that the wedding was close to over, rather than the emotion of the love.

By the end of 2019 my tolerance for innocent, but bizarre requests, had shortened. I no longer found it cute or wanted to go into long explanations of why their ideas would not be practical or feasible, I just wanted to scream, "Don't be so stupid". I recognised it as edging towards burnout and middle-aged-life-is-too-short-for-this-crap.

There were some extreme things like the couple from Texas who wanted to do viewings of potential venues in Venice.

"Can you book us a car to get us around Venice to see the venues?" "No, a car is not possible."

"Why can't I get a car?"

"Because the streets in Venice are made of water."

"I don't get it. There are no roads? How do people get around?"

"By boat on the canals."

I didn't go on this viewing. I knew my ever-lowering tolerance level may have caused a drowning, so Ben, my Italian wedding planner friend who has worked closely with me on lots of my weddings for the last twelve years, offered to go.

My instinct was right.

When I called to see how it was going, his expression was of such shock that I thought he'd do a Saint Lucia on me and his eyes would fall out of his head.

"She said," he stumbled over the words he was spitting out, "She said; everything is so old here in Venice, why don't they just level it and start anew? That's what we'd do in Texas."

There would have been a drowning.

This was just after Ben dealt with a bride-to-be who calls him every day to discuss some incident. Today's issue was her mother doesn't like cheese, but they wanted to order, as a first course, pasta with mozzarella and tomatoes. So she called to ask Ben;

"What is mozzarella and tomato pasta called if you remove the mozzarella?"

"Pasta with tomato without mozzarella, is pasta with tomato," he told her and couldn't help but laugh. It was that or throw himself in a canal.

She called me to complain about his attitude as she thought he was being a smartass.

Previously, we had a bride who didn't want photos to be taken beside olive trees—they are too messy looking. "She only wants the straight lines of the vineyard at a diagonal to the left in the background," explained the groom as if this was perfectly reasonable.

I think my most bizarre request was from a bride-to-be who said, "I want a wedding ceremony at 2.30pm so that we can finish dinner early and start the party. And we must have a location with the sun setting in the background during the ceremony."

A sunset at 2.30pm? Who do you think I am, God?

Obviously I didn't say that. Now that my tolerance level has lowered I find I need to pause, take a breath and count to five before answering some questions, but I usually give a polite response.

Not all illogical requests come from ignorance or stupidity, some are just innocent and haven't been thought through.

For instance, a lot of the clients I attract would say, 'I just want a really simple wedding', meaning they wanted to spend as little as possible but still have a gorgeous wedding. Perfect. I liked couples who wanted to keep their budgets low. I always encouraged them to spend low on the wedding and use as much of their budget as possible on an amazing honeymoon.

However, the idea of 'simple' followed trends. At one point it was hay bales.

"I just want to get married in a forest with hay bales for seating."

Of course I would give a polite answer, that chairs are a simpler option, instead of the longer more erratic answer of;

Okay so how the hell do you think hay bales are going to get into the forest? They are going to have to be purchased, brought to the forest, unloaded and set up.

And have you ever tried to lift a hay bale? They are bloody heavy. And hay sticks in your ass and snags silk dresses, so you need blankets over them. So we will need to source and buy fifty blankets for the fifty bales of hay.

Hay is highly flammable and you want to put them in a forest during the dry summer with drunk people carrying cigarettes? So we would need to dowse them in flame retardant. Chairs are a simpler option, believe me.

'I just want a simple wedding' trend number 2: "I want a wedding outside, with just candles all over the lawn."

I would, of course, say that can be done, but I would need to take on another assistant for the day to look after that and would need to charge for the extra assistant. They find this hard to understand so I have to explain.

To be effective, you'll need about three hundred candles. The candles need to be in some sort of container so that they sit flat and don't set the dry summer grass on fire. Someone has to set these up, and then light them, each candle will take an average of one minute to set up and light... that is three hundred minutes which is five hours.

"We'll just do half the amount of candles then."

"That's still 2.5 hours of someone's time. And guests walking around with long floaty dresses are potentially very flammable. It really isn't a good idea."

'Simple' wedding trend number 3: "I just want simple sprigs of olive leaves going down the middle of the table with tall candles."

They send me a sample picture. I know how much time the woven centre piece takes and that it costs about one hundred euro per meter. Twenty meters of tables and you have a €2000 'simple' table arrangement that they were expecting could be done by just going out to the surrounding olive groves with clippers.

'Simple' wedding trend number 4: "Thirty euro per hour for an open bar? We'll do our own thanks. We just want to keep it simple."

Where are you getting the glasses, ice, tables, never mind the drink? Who is going to clear away and wash the glasses, clean up spills and clear away the bottles? Where are you going to keep the drinks refrigerated?

'Simple' wedding trend number 5 to save money: "We are going to do our own flowers. We'll just go out on the morning of the wedding and pick wildflowers for my bouquet and tables."

What I want to say is, "Are you crazy?"

Any non-shop bought flowers that have not been kept in cold storage are going to have critters. Critters that will climb all over your lovely white dress and tablecloths.

Morning wildflowers wilt fast once picked, and do you really see yourself skipping through meadows of wildflowers the morning of your wedding and then arranging them when hair and makeup is scheduled? And then you want to go down and decorate the tables before dinner while you are supposed to be having your photos taken?

Another cost-saving 'pot-hole' idea which usually turns out disastrous is an issue that started when digital photography became more accessible. We went through a few years when there was always an uncle who had a 'good camera' so they elected him as the wedding photographer.

Professional photographers rate wedding photography the most stressful form of photography next to war photography.

It doesn't just take a good camera; it takes capturing the perfect moment that cannot be repeated, it's making people feel comfortable in front of the camera enough so that the look in their eyes and the smile on their faces shows how much they love each other at that very moment.

Capturing the tear just before it falls, the laughs and the nerves, the fleeting look and the tender smile. It's capturing the emotion and telling the story of the couple's day and that takes practice. It's so much more than just a good camera.

I spent years chasing uncles with good cameras, who were off talking to aunts, cousins, etc that they hadn't seen in years and having drinks when the photos should have been happening.

Then there are the over-planner brides who produce a minute-by-minute schedule and want everything they have seen on Pinterest in the last three years.

A wedding planner I met at a conference told me that one such bride insisted on her, the planner, climbing under her big layers of skirt and spraying deodorant between her legs at various times of day.

The same bride had the groom scheduled to go for a shower before they sat for dinner. Her wedding took place in three different venues as she couldn't choose between them and the same went for her dress, three different dress changes. None of the guests were smiling in any of the photos.

Every now and again, I would get a request along the lines of... "We've booked this villa for a week and would like you to arrange the details."

I look on a map to see the proposed villa is three hours away from a serving airport, up a mountain and is miles away from the nearest village.

First question..."Have you told the villa owner that you intend to host a wedding there?"

"No, do we need to?"

"Emm... yes they may not have the necessary permits and licences to host events. And may not allow people who are not staying at the villa onto the premises for safety and insurance reasons."

"But we've paid a massive deposit!"

My terms and conditions in my contract grew from three pages to nine over the years, covering all eventualities. Including neither me or the venue or any vendors being responsible for people's personal safety. They're fine when it's bright out and before the bar opens, but the stupidity of people with drink in them is not to be underestimated.

I didn't take bookings for big budget weddings, even though I liked the fact that at least twenty small business owners would benefit, I just found that some of these couples felt like they owned you, you were their PA. Normal decency and politeness went out the window.

One such wedding was for an older Irish couple. I thought they would know better. We were in Tuscany for a few days before their Lake Garda wedding. The day before their wedding, we got a phone call from the Irish police to say Ronan's brother, his best friend, had been found dead.

We made the decision that we would continue to do the wedding the following day as Ronan was the photographer and then fly back the day after. There was nothing we could do for him and we needed to put our grief aside until we got back to Ireland for the funeral. We planned the funeral from Italy, to be held on the Saturday.

The couple had a party planned in Ireland for the friends and family that couldn't make it to Italy that same Saturday. They had previously asked if Ronan could send them over ten photos for a slideshow in time for their party.

I knew we would be travelling back and, at the time, it took a full day to download the photos and back them up before he even looked at them. Normally a wedding photographer would say it would be six to eight weeks before the photos were ready.

On the Saturday morning we were getting ready for the funeral when I got a text from the bride asking when would the photos arrive for her slide show.

I texted back. "Unfortunately, we had bad news, the day before your wedding, Ronan's brother died suddenly. We of course didn't want to tell you this on the day of your wedding. The funeral is today."

The response was not "So sorry to hear that and thank you very much for following through with the day and not leave us having to find a replacement photographer and planner on the day..."

No. Her response was, "But I only need ten photos. If he could just send them over as promised."

He did them, but not with the usual joy he worked on photos with. It was a mix of upset and disbelief.

It triggered the start of something—a dislike for what we did, because of the attitudes some couples got when it came to their weddings. It just took one couple of bad apples each year to slowly feed this feeling. And there was always a pair of rotten apples every year.

37

SAINTS & SWATTERS

The start of wedding season kicks off with Ronan, Luca and I running around local supermarkets filling trollies with boxes of beer and bottles of spirits and mixers. Buying an ice machine, fold out tables, glasses, straws and creating a credit buying system for guests so the bar can be cashless.

That was on top of; chasing couples for their photo lists for wedding photography jobs I am to assist Ronan with, and doing all the 'normal' wedding prep stuff like table plans, finalising menus, prepping for guests with special needs, booking pre-wedding meetings to complete the legals at the commune, prepping and sending transfer lists to the transport company and checking flights to ensure each guest gets to and from the airport.

As well as answering all the questions about timing, schedules and logistics for florists, photographers, videographers, bands, celebrants, hair stylists, makeup artists, bridal cars and caterers.

Oh and, of course, all the last-minute questions from the brides and grooms. I don't know how Jennifer Lopez did it in that movie in heels and a tight skirt. My usual look is a loose dress and comfortable shoes that I can jog in for twelve hours.

Most of my weddings have a welcome night of pizza and gelato served from a restored retro 'ape' (an Italian tuk-tuk). I always explain the Italian word 'ape' to couples since a groom asked about an inclusion of it in one of my wedding packages; "A white ape to take guests to the ceremony location."

"Does that mean some sort of King Kong character dressed in white carrying guests up the hill to the ceremony?" He was a joker, but I realised people needed to be informed that 'ape' means bee in Italian, like 'vespa' means wasp. Two forms of cute buzzy Italian transport named after buzzy insects.

Luca and I ran the pop-up bar together the arrival night until midnight as it was going to be a learning process for both of us. His girlfriend Sarah was booked to arrive the following week to work with him and relieve me of my barmaid duties.

The wedding day itself was going to be difficult as my day at the venue would start at ten in the morning, coordinating set up of catering and keeping vendors on schedule.

Then I would kick in as Ronan's photography assistant from two to seven while also coordinating, and then I would become Luca's bar assistant from 9pm until 2am.

I had it scheduled within an inch of its life. The difficult part was we were all going to be out of the house for most of the day and Mam would be on her own for the first time.

I couldn't stand the idea of my Mam eating boiled potatoes and boiled chicken in this heat, so I left a potato salad and seasoned chicken breast ready for her to have for her dinner.

"You're going to help me to death. I'm well capable. You go and do what you have to do," she said as I anxiously fussed while she peeled a pot of potatoes in preparation of a day on her own, even though I told her I'd left a plate ready in the fridge.

Luca was in the house but sleeping until 4pm and then Ronan returned at eight and drove Luca to the venue to get the bar set up and started.

It all worked well, and the wedding was fantastic. A great group; all from where I grew up in Dublin, some went to the same school as me. The familiarity of accents and humour made the first wedding after a two-year Covid hiatus, a weekend to remember not just for the bride and groom, but for me too.

Running on adrenalin worked fine until I got home. I was absolutely exhausted by the end of the night and the following morning. Needless to say, it was after nine when I work up, stiff and foggy headed.

"About time you are up, I'm starving. Dying for a cup of tea."

"Mam, in all fairness why didn't you get up and get something? You know where everything is and how to work the kettle."

"Because that's not what I'm used to. I like getting my breakfast handed to me. "

"Dad had you spoilt."

"I think he did. He'd bring me breakfast and a flower every morning. Now I have to pick my own." She's saying it with jest, but me becoming Dad's replacement or a handmaid was not on my life goals list.

There are two more weddings in the next ten days. I knew this was going to happen. I had told my brothers that May and June were going to be extremely busy for me and hoped one of them could have Mam stay with them or they could come here, but they all have their work, families and issues to deal with.

Luca's girlfriend Sarah arrives and takes over running the bar with Luca. I still need to stay until about 10pm on the arrival nights to ensure everything runs smoothly with the catering and bar.

Mam is getting grumpy with the setup. Ronan is around the house the days I am not but she's bored without me there all day to call on.

"What time will Rosie be home?"

"About ten."

"More like eleven or twelve," she says in a huff at Ronan over dinner after the third wedding of the season.

I get back exhausted but happy that another postponed wedding has come to a beautiful conclusion.

"It's midnight, why are you still up?" I say, seeing Mam sitting in her chair when I get back in.

"Where were you child? You said you would be home at 10pm, I was worried."

"Okay, Ma, this has to stop now. This is my job, it requires me to work late. Sometimes until two or three in the morning and be up and out again by nine or ten the following day. I am a 50-year-old woman, I don't need my mother sitting up waiting on me to come home and I don't need you worrying about me on my conscience as well."

"I think doing the party the day before is not a good idea."

"The welcome party?" I am laughing at her blanket decision. "It's great fun for all the guests, who is it not a good idea for?"

"For you. Working that late. That's not on, it's ridiculous."

"But Ma what do you suggest I do, it's my job?"

"I'm bored sitting in the house and in the garden all day."

"I have to do my work and you have to find ways of amusing yourself whether it be here or in Ireland. I can't be with you all day every day."

"That would drive us both nutty," she says, thinking out loud.

"Yes, it would. So please go to bed. I will come home whatever time I choose or need to come home."

"Well, I think it's stupid, out that late working, they can't be paying you enough."

"Ma, I work for myself and earn more than any of my brothers."

"Don't be ridiculous, sure Rob works for a billionaire."

It's mid-May, the fireflies and poppies are out. The seeds from the bull rushes fly like fluffy snow around the garden. This with the chorus of toads from the lake and the cicadas starting their summer noise makes this time of year in Italy with its warm summer nights magical.

"Do you know cicadas only shut up below twenty-two degrees as the sections of the diaphragm lose their elasticity? So it must be over twenty-two degrees now," says Luca who joins me outside to enjoy the stars. The only jarring sound is the owl that sounds like a distant car alarm going all night.

"What does a mosquito look like? I think I saw one today," Mam says, coming out the next morning dressed in long pants tucked into socks. A second set of socks are on her hands with her long-sleeved blouse buttoned up to her neck. "I'm not taking any chances."

"You can't dress like that every day, you will roast. Come on, I have the day free, let's go buy you some insect repellant."

I don't want to disturb Ronan who is working on editing the photos so I bite the bullet, take the car keys and for the first time drive on the motorway. And it's not as bad as I thought it would be.

Mam is in her element going around the market store that sells everything from clothes to garden furniture.

She buys herself two dresses, three fly swatters, citronella candles, an electric mosquito wall plug repellant thing, fly spray, two brands of insect repellant, two brands of after-spray, repellant wipes and a bag of repellant bracelets.

You can spot the tourists easily in the stores. They are the ones without masks. The requirement to wear masks indoors stopped on the first of May, but the Italians are not ones for taking chances with their health, so they continue to wear them indoors in public places a month later.

Masks are still required on public transport, in hospitals and pharmacies. So people need to wear them on flights out of Italy but not necessarily on flights into Italy. It depends on the departing country's rules.

On the way home, I stop off at a church. Mam has not been able to attend mass since before lockdown so while it is not mass, a visit to a quiet church to light a candle makes her happy.

She needs some of my time to do this sort of thing, to take her to the doctor or out to a church or store. But I don't have that time.

While Mam creates a small bonfire of candles for Rob, I take a stroll around to look at the art. Rob is doing well with his treatment, he has not been sick with it and his hair is growing, even though has been bald for twenty years. Which is weird!

There is a statue of a bearded saint with a machete stuck in his head. The likeness has blood running down his forehead, but he seems to not notice or care. He is frozen in time for eternity, as if chatting away to the crowd he must have been preaching to. What he was saying must have been gripping, as no one cared to say, "I think there's something in your hair, let me help you with that." I know the discomfort of having my reading glasses stuck in my hair, so I can't imagine how uncomfortable a machete must have been stuck in his head.

He goes into my favourite weird Italian saint category, along with St Lucia who gouged her own eyes out because she was so beautiful and is often depicted with them on a plate. I had first mistaken them for two olives, and thought she was just on her way to make a good martini.

And St. Agatha of Catania, who had an atrocious horrific death by torture which included her breasts being cut off. The Sicilians celebrate her feast day with cute round iced cakes with a red cherry on top.

I pray to the knifed saint for Rob. "Help the good guy out, won't you?"

Potato Salad & Lemon Chicken
Serves: 4

New potatoes (one large potato per person, or three per person, if you are like my mother).

4 Chicken fillets

3 Tbls mayonnaise (Enough to coat the potatoes)

3 Spring onions

A dollop of mustard

BBQ sauce (enough to coat each chicken fillet)

Smoked paprika (about half a tsp per chicken fillet)

1 Lemon

Half tsp of sugar per serving

Method:

Preheat the oven to 220°C (425°F).

Cut the potatoes into bite-sized cubes and boil until tender (about 10 minutes). Drain and leave aside to cool.

Dry the chicken fillets using paper towels, and season with smoked paprika and a little salt and pepper.

Finely chop the spring onions.

Heat some olive oil on a pan and sear the fillets for 2 or 3 minutes on both sides.

Transfer the fillets to parchment paper on a baking tray. Coat the top of each fillet with BBQ sauce.

Place in the oven for 10 minutes. Ensure they are cooked through.

Grate and squeeze half the lemon. Cut the other half into wedges to use as garnish.

In a bowl mix the mustard, mayonnaise, the lemon zest, the lemon juice and a half teaspoon of sugar per serving. Season with salt and pepper to taste.

Add the cooled potatoes and gently mix to coat the potato cubes with the lemon mayonnaise. Add the chopped spring onions.

Cut the cooked chicken fillets into strips and plate with the potato salad and wedge of lemon.

38

ANTS & ASHTRAYS

Mam is delighted with her new paraphernalia. The fly swatter has become an extension of her arm, frequently bashing the window where the flying insects are trying to get out.

Stuff has begun to creep out of her storage box back onto the windowsill and around her nesting chair.

"Rosie, come quick," she screeches while I'm cooking lunch, "There's crawly things." She shakes her hands after lifting her notebook off the windowsill, looking horrified.

"They are ants Ma." I'm surprised at her overreaction. "You are well used to them from your days gardening."

"In the garden yes, but not in the house."

"In hot countries they will come into the house if you leave things like this around." I pick up a barbecued rib bone from dinner two nights ago.

"I was keeping it for the new dog."

"She's a pup and you can't feed her bones. Not yet, and definitely not stored on the windowsill. You have to be careful, even with crumbs, otherwise you will have an army of ants coming in to clean them up... Effective little creatures, they have always fascinated me."

"Something is after biting me on the foot and arm. Would it be them?" she says, scratching.

"No, I don't think so." I look at the swollen mounds on her arm and foot. "It looks like mosquito bites, but you have your spray on so it can't—"

"Ah, I didn't put it on today, I put it on yesterday and thought it would last. I'll go get my bread soda paste."

Alex is back to work on the dining room. He has come up with the genius idea of building a false chimney breast over the one that is already there with enough room to re-circuit the wiring through, in front of the chimney rather than through it.

"I want a job like Mr. Roman so I can sit all day," Alex says when he hears Ronan is working on his computer. He doesn't quite appreciate that Ronan spent the day before jogging around in thirty-five degrees of heat capturing another perfect wedding. Both Ronan and I are finding our recovery time after each wedding this year takes longer than any other year.

"We're getting too old for this. And we still have a busy few months ahead. I think I am going to have to call in help. I will be dead in a month if I continue at this pace," I said to Ronan after the last big wedding.

The final decision is made the following day. Mam's foot has swollen with an angry water blister and her arm has doubled in size.

This is what I was afraid of.

"You weren't joking when you said you got a bad reaction to bites," I say, looking at the worrying swelling. "I'll bring you to the doctor, you need stronger anti-histamines than the ones you have, I think."

I call Doctor Fab Chicken and he can see Mam in half an hour, if I get her to the clinic.

"Really? That's prompt service. You'd be waiting hours for an appointment if Ireland if you could get one at all." At last Mam has been impressed by something in Italy.

Fab arrives at the clinic after us, and leads us down the maze of rooms, apologising that he still does not have his own room yet but someday soon he will. The clinic is closed, but he has opened it for us.

I can't make out what type of specialist the doctor is, who has the empty room Fab has permission to use today. Its walls are covered in shelving stuffed with fading family photos and piles of souvenir ashtrays. Some used. I browse them, recognising a lot of the towns that are from around Italy.

"His patients bring them to him from vacation as gifts," Dr Fab says when he sees me looking at them as he treats Mam to several shots of antihistamine and antibiotics.

"It seems like an odd present to bring your doctor."

"He collects them," he says matter-of-factly, pushing an ashtray on the desk to the side with five butts and ash still in it as he writes a prescription for Mam.

"Do you have antibiotics at home?" he asks.

"No. We are lucky to never have much need for antibiotics in our family, and when we do, we finish the course as instructed. It's not something we would keep lying around."

"But you have a blood pressure machine?" he asks as if it's a perfectly normal question.

"No." What does he think I own, a small hospital?

"Your mother's blood pressure is low you need to get a machine, and you need to test her blood pressure twice per day. I will give her 'Duri-six' and herbal tablets to ease the water retention around her knees and to help the circulation of her blood. It is important to take these, as it gets very hot here in Italy," he tells Mam.

Neither of us hear the name correctly of the thing he is prescribing but Mam whispers to me, "What is he giving me Durex for?"

Just as we get home I get a call, and for the first time I answer the phone to an Italian number without my stomach tightening and white noise blocking out what was being said.

"Pronto?" I say unsure what will happen next.

I understand it is a delivery.

So I proudly say "Arrivo fuori" (I arrive outside). But mispronounce it and instead say 'Arrivo fiori' which makes no sense as it means 'I arrive flowers'.

The delivery is a bottle of engine cleaner stuff Ronan has ordered for the car, to cure it of its annoying hiccups. But it doesn't work.

"Alex, do you have a mechanic cousin by any chance?" Ronan asks after another failed attempt of stopping the loud annoying beeping.

"Not a cousin, but I know one for years who is like a brother to me."

The car mechanic's workshop is a massive operation with mechanics working on every type of vehicle from vespas to articulated trucks.

"It is a family business running for fifty-six years," explains Alex as they drive in the gate past a spiralling queue of about sixty cars, vans and buses.

"Are they all waiting to be serviced? What the hell does he do that is so special?"

"It is not always this busy. They are only here because it is revisione time, there are always lots when the revisione is due in the summer."

We have figured out that this is the road-worthy test in Italy which is required to keep up to date. It's the equivalent of the MOT in the UK or Ireland.

"But I've never seen such a queue waiting for an MOT, there are a huge amount of cars to get through, that's going to take a long time. They will never fit us in this week with that amount of cars ahead of us already."

"Noooo, it will take five minutes each car, they have about forty mechanics working here."

In Ireland for the same test, they need to spend twenty minutes at least on each car; put it up on a platform, check emissions, every knob and button and can fail you over something like a window wiper or bulb in need of replacing.

"I will introduce you," says Alex, getting out of the car and walking towards an older guy with oil-embedded skin, a long bushy moustache and squinty eyes from years of having his constant flow of cigarette smoke drifting into them.

Ronan is expecting a name and a handshake but instead Alex says to the guy, squinting through his cigarette smoke.

"This is my Irish friend, don't fuck with him."

The guy nods, eyes Ronan suspiciously and walks to the admin office where his wife has a unique system of oil-encrusted, Velcroed wood blocks, each with a number on them. Our car is assigned number twenty-four and is stuck to the Velcro-striped chart that spans half the wall. The system looks so complicated and unique that even Alan Turing would find figuring it out a challenge.

Ronan has rehearsed the way to say "my car is in need of repair" like an Italian. "La mia macchina è in panne" which literally means 'my car is in cream' or creamed.

Of course, by the time he is leaving, Ronan is practically best friends with Mr and Mrs Moustache and two days later the car is ready. It cost €380 and is driving like a dream without the constant beeps nor glowing engine and oil lights on the dashboard.

It's done just in time for our two hour drive to Narni, to collect the new member of our family; our new little pup Juno.

39

THE DOG FROM NARNIA

"**W**hat the hell is that?" Mam says, practically running out of her bedroom the following day with a small pile of blackness squashed in a tissue. I know exactly what it is, but I am not telling her.

"It was on my wall and I swiped it with my fly swatter and it fell on the bed and ran and I caught it and squashed it."

"It's just a fly."

"It's not a fly, it's a scorpion, isn't it?" She says accusingly as if I put it there.

"It is." This might not be so bad, I'm thinking, it might raise her blood pressure to a reasonable level. I'm checking it twice a day with a blood pressure machine I bought at the pharmacy on the way home from the doctors. I write the reading religiously in a diary.

"Well, what does it say?" asks Mam.

"Mam, I have no clue what the numbers mean. I don't know if you are alive or dead but I succeeded in taking your blood pressure."

The swelling in her foot and arm has decreased. So I feel comfortable enough leaving her for the morning to take the nearly two-hour drive to Narni, previously known on old maps as Narnia.

It is the place that the author CS Lewis used as the inspiration name for his famous 'Chronicles of Narnia'. Although he was never there.

Supposedly, he chose the name from an old atlas he had ever since he was a child. He just liked the name. The medieval town is quite a magical place to visit. A beautiful river flows beside it and it is close to the Marmore Falls.

These man-made waterfalls are on my 'To Be Visited When I Have A Bloody Minute' list. The spectacle was created by the Romans and, at a height of one hundred and sixty-five meters, it is still the tallest man-made waterfall today.

If we were taking a male dog we'd have to call it Aslan, being from Narnia. But we have all fallen in love with the pretty female with the long eyelashes and distinctive facial markings that make her look like she's wearing winged eyeliner.

After toying with the name Biscotti, we decide to call her Juno, the Roman Queen of the Gods whose chariot was pulled by peacocks instead of horses. 'Juno and the Paycock' was a play written by Irish playwright Sean Casey, which was part of my school curriculum. I played the role of Mary in the school production.

It was after seeing video clips of the play that I realised I was crap at acting and never did it again. But it didn't stop me loving the play, nor the name Juno.

"Is that her?" I say, seeing the little head asleep under our friend's vintage vespa.

"Yep, that's your Juno," my friend says, gently pulling out the bundle of fluffy tan and black hair. She unfolds to display long legs and big paws. "Eh, I thought she was going to be a small dog?"

"Yes, well, she will probably be the size of Poppy, who is a Belgian Shepherd, the father is the bastard dog across the field who is the same size, if not smaller than Poppy."

All the other pups look smaller and without the kangaroo legs 'our' Juno has. But it's too late to do anything about it. We are already in love with the bouncing bundle. I send a photo to Karen who knows quite a lot about dogs. "She looks like she's going to be a very tall German Shepherd."

"Ah but she's not!" I'm gloating a bit as we've both had laughs in the past about Ronan having to be careful what he wishes for, as he always gets what he wants eventually, and we nearly split up over him wanting to get another German Shepherd after Asha died.

"No more big dogs that I can't feel comfortable walking by myself or I can't fit in a bag and bring everywhere with me," that was my policy, and I was sticking to it. Although, we then got Paddy, who is about the size of a greyhound but docile.

"Her mother is a Belgian Shepherd and her father is a smaller mongrel," I tell Karen.

Karen texts back; "You know dogs can be impregnated by several different dogs when they are in heat?"

"I did not know that."

"It looks like little Poppy had a fling with a very tall German Shepherd. Ronan has done it again... I don't mean impregnated the dog, I mean he got his wish... you know what I mean!"

Mam is delighted with the new arrival and is already spoiling the pup with her sitting on her lap and sleeping in her room.

It's a hot, sticky twenty-three degrees at night which is the lowest temperature forecast for the next forty-eight hours, going up to thirty-nine degrees. Mam is getting through it with a mobile air con unit and a fan going twenty-four hours a day, but won't give up her routine of hot tea in the morning and whiskey throughout the day.

It's too hot for her to go outside so she stays between the sitting room, bedroom and kitchen.

"You have to keep drinking lots of water," I tell her, giving her a full measured water bottle, which I find her watering the plants with later.

"Mam what are you doing? You need to drink that, not give it to the plants, and I keep asking you to please stop feeding the dogs off your plate," I say as I see Paddy nuzzling her hand.

"I'm not feeding him I'm just talking to him."

"Ma you have a handful of potato in your hand, under his nose."

It's then I spot the broken digestive biscuits on the ground beside her bed.

"Are you feeding the pup sugary biscuits? Stop doing that!"

"I'm not... they are only little bits. She was starving."

"Ma she is not starving, she has a bowl of dog biscuits untouched."

"They are horrible. I've tried them myself before."

"Right so when there are ants in your room and the dog has diarrhea, I'm going to stick your nose in it, not the dog's." Not that I would do that to the dog, or my mother, but she gets that I'm serious.

"Here, I've made a list of things you need to get for me and the dog." She hands me a long list of items that I know will have me hopping from one town to the next.

Except for the whiskey, none of the items are urgent, but that doesn't stop her reminding me five times a day every day about the list; "Did you not get my stuff yet no?"

On my search for her needs, I find an electrified fly swatter in the shape of a tennis racket. She is delighted with it. It's like the best present she has ever received, and the closest she has ever got to playing tennis. Every time she hits a fly or mosquito there is a spark and a 'zzztt' noise as the poor thing fizzles, "Haha got you, ye bastard," is now a regular phrase heard through the hallways.

I'm feeling overwhelmed trying to juggle Mam's needs and the needs of my business. And weddings this year are much more challenging than previous years. It's the first time a lot of people have travelled after two years of being kept away from family and friends, so they are in party mode to the extreme.

Wedding planning is stressful and the co-ordination of a big group with lots of drink and sunshine can get sloppy. Italian weddings focus on food and it has taken a while for me to 'train' the Italians into understanding this is not so much the case with Irish and UK weddings. Their focus is usually the booze.

Open bars for weddings in Italy used to be about €10 per person but then with experience of more Irish and UK weddings the price edged closer to €30 per person.

"They drank everything! We could not believe it." The Italians always said after a lot of my initial weddings in Italy, and this was after I had asked for a list of the quantity of alcohol they were bringing for the bar and told them to triple it.

Combine a lot of booze and high heels with ancient venues that have old stone steps, uneven surfaces and no handrails and there is bound to be at least one incident each year, I am always just waiting for it to happen. I've had guests fall, breaking wrists, fingers, ankles, banging their heads and a groom being carried by his mates to his bedchamber, dropping him on the way down some steps, resulting in him and his bride, still in her gown, spending their wedding night in ER while his broken leg got plastered.

I have a couple who are insisting the groom's younger brother and his mates are going to be the band and bring their own instruments. A logistical nightmare for a destination wedding. "How is that going to work?" I ask.

"Leave it to me," says the groom, as if I don't know what I am talking about. It was the same groom who asked; "Why does a bouquet cost €120 when you can buy a bunch of flowers in a supermarket for a fiver?" It's a common question from grooms, and always said in a tone as if I am trying to rip them off.

A week before the wedding. I'm asking how the band's instruments are getting to the venue; the drum kit, the keyboard, speakers and all the wiring and two guitars.

"On the guest bus."

"There won't be room," I explain. "We need four small, sixteen seaters because the hill up to the venue doesn't fit big buses. Your guest buses are full and the trunk will be full of luggage.

"We'll put the stuff in the aisle of the bus."

"No, that won't be possible, the transport company won't allow that for safety purposes."

"Can you get a price of a van then?"

I get the price of a van and book it.

Two days later the groom calls; "Eh the airline won't accept the instruments as luggage. We'll need to hire the instruments in Italy. A drum kit, a keyboard, a bass guitar and a lead guitar. Can you organise that please?"

"I think you are going to have to give me a bit more info. Also what about mics, speakers, extension leads?"

"Oh yeah, we'll need them too."

"I'll need a list."

He tuts. As if I have caused him this problem. But I think of a solution.

"What if we book a band with similar equipment, and we ask them to allow your brother's band to play a set during the night?"

He tuts again. Seriously? I'm throwing him a lifeline and he's tutting at me?

"Okay then."

I find a band willing to do it. It's a big ask. I hate asking it as I know musicians are very precious about their instruments and it's a very stretched favour.

The day of the wedding arrives. It's at an amazing ancient hilltop castle in Tuscany with a view over Florence.

After twenty years, I'm able to suss a group out within five minutes of walking into a room. "Lock up the armoury," I say to my assistant Ben.

"I am sure that's not necessary," says Ben.

"Oh, it is Ben... Do you see that group of lads over there? They'll be chasing each other with the gauntlets by, I'd say ... 11.10? 11.30pm at a stretch. And those two over there... with the groom... the guy on the left will try to get into the suit of armour for the laugh, while the other swings at him with that King Arthur style sword on the wall. Trust me, get the key and lock the door.

I love shocking Italians, it always ends up with us laughing together.

"Also, I want that ornamental vase removed, all the ornaments on the mantle replaced by flowers from the ceremony, and that very delicate chair moved out of here, and the piano locked."

Ben is on the case and works through the list of precautions with the caretaker.

The wedding ceremony and dinner went beautifully. Everyone was having a great time, including the 19-year-old brother and his mates. Of course they were, they were in Italy at a fabulous party in the Mediterranean sunshine with free booze flowing. Thankfully supplied by the caterer for this wedding and not us.

By the time the music was due to start, all five of the band of brothers were extremely drunk. One was so drunk, Ben saw him sitting on the castle wall and then disappearing. Luckily, there was a grass incline all the way down to the dry moat. He'd still be there if Ben hadn't spent an hour trying to get him out of it.

Needless to say, they played nothing.

I used to find the logistics an enjoyable challenge, but now they are just stressful disasters waiting to happen, I definitely need to get out of this soon.

40

CANDLES & CONDOMS

"Can we meet up, I have a proposal?" I text Ben, who has assisted me for twelve years at my bigger weddings, and is looking after all my long-distance weddings this summer as I can't leave Mam for the couple of nights I'd normally take to stay at the wedding venue.

Ben is forty and still has all four grandparents and both parents alive and living close to him.

He agrees to drop by on the wedding I have the following evening on his way home from his grandparent's house, where he will be for an extensive lunch with his extended family. "It is something we do every year, as there is a festival in the town."

"Oh, what is the festival? To do with a saint no doubt?"

"No, it is to forgive us our sins. It happens in a lot of towns in Italy, It's called La Perdonanza. The pardon."

"So once a year you have a festival and your sins are forgiven?"

"Exactly."

"That must have been handy in the old days when they were all killing each other."

His grandfather is ninety-seven and has dementia but he still lives at his own home with his wife, who is eighty-seven, as his carer. This same woman fell down the stairs five years ago and broke her pelvis, shoulder, arm and neck. She healed without any plates or screws involved.

Dementia has caused his grandfather to do the fascist salute every morning, which he had to do in school each day under the rule of Mussolini. Luckily, when the Nazis came into power, he missed the conscription age into the Second World War by a couple of weeks.

Ellie, Ben's wife, has a grandmother who lives independently in her own apartment with a sliding door separating her and her daughter's apartment, they share a kitchen. Her grandmother, who is in her eighties, had found porcini mushrooms while foraging and they are now going to be the ingredient the pardon lunch will be based around.

Ben and Ellie arrive at nine the following evening, which is my free time as all the guests are enjoying dinner and being looked after by the caterers. During the wedding dinner, I sit at a staff table where I have dinner with the photographer and band. Ben and Ellie aren't hungry after their three-hour lunch, so they just have a glass of wine.

The musicians are from Bologna. Their accent sounds more clipped but they say they have different accents. One has more emphasis on the 'e' and I think more 'rr' rolling. They argue about where Mozart did an exam in Bologna.

Italians do not do speeches at weddings and the speeches at this wedding have become extended which is delaying the cake cutting and the party starting.

"Why do they do speeches?" says Ellie, annoyed, as if it was her own party being delayed. "Everyone wants them to end, you can see it on their faces and they all say the same things: they are kind, caring, loving. No one stands up and says he is a fucking piece of shit."

I like Ellie.

The band are now arguing over whether granita is from Calabria or Sicily. Just as I am about to tell Ben what I wanted him to come and discuss, a bridesmaid approaches our staff table; "Rosie, do you know if there are more candles? The long ones? The ones we have are nearly used up."

"Well, dinner will be finished after the next speech, so you will be done then."

"Oh grand so, we will make do with what we have left." And she returns to her seat happily.

"Rosie what was that all about?" Ben is looking confused, as are the band.

"She wanted more candles?"

"OHHHH we had thought she said condoms!"

"The long ones," repeats the photographer, creased up laughing. The singer is crying laughing trying to catch his breath, as he repeats ..."The ones they have are nearly used up."

While the band and photographer try to recover, chatting in Italian, I turn my focus to Ben.

"Ben... would you be interested in taking over my wedding business?"

"You mean for the summer?"

"No. For good. I want to get out of wedding planning."

"Yes, of course I am interested... But you will have to do something first..."

"What is that?"

"Help me pronounce Irish names. They are crazy."

"No better time like the present," I say, handing him the table plan of the current wedding. And we begin....

Ben: "AA-ee-nnn-aaa."

Me: "It's Aine, pronounced Aww-nya. Like Yawn."

Ben: "Ah okay Yawn-ya."

I don't have time to correct him as he has moved rapidly on to the next difficult name.

Ben: "And this.... See-Obb-Hann."

Me: "That's Siobhan. Pronounced Shiv-on."

Ben: "And Gray-een-aaa."

Me: "Grainne. Say Graw-nya."

Ben: "How do I pronounce this name?"

He points to the groom's name: Padhraig.

Me: "Paw - think of a dog's paw and then rig, think of oil rig."

"Ahh okay paw-rig. I see."

It's all going well, and with Ben's help I will soon be able to step back and relax and have head space to do the things I really want to. Finish the house, look after Mam and write books.

A guest comes over to tell me the bathroom has run out of toilet paper, something I need to deal with immediately.

"Ben, will you do me a favour and look after getting the bride and groom over to the table for the cake cutting? The last speech is just ending."

"Sure," he says, being his always obliging self.

Just as I pass near the top table on my way to the bathroom with the much-needed paper, I hear Ben introduce himself to the couple.

"Hi, I am Ben and you must be Kate and Dog-oil?"

This hand over may take a little longer than expected.

41

BOOKS & BEASTS

I get one or two wedding cancellations each year. It is usually because the couple have decided to get married at home or elsewhere, but sometimes it is more tragic.

When it is tragic, I do what I can to get deposits back for the couple. However, it's not always possible, which is understandable; vendors have kept that peak date for that couple's wedding and refused other potential bookings and there is no way they could fill it with another booking once the booking season has eased.

I get a cancellation in May for a wedding in a month's time because of a very unfortunate circumstance. The couple have split up.

The bride is heartbroken, and we have got close over the last year and a half of planning. Everything has been fully paid for only the week before. I manage to get part payments back from most vendors but the catering company are refusing to give any refund. I'm sending a lot of business their way this summer, and while I know it is a loss, I feel they should give at least a percentage back. But they are not budging.

Having to unplan a wedding nearly takes as much time as planning the bloody things. I am having a particularly busy day so I am not in the mood for yet another explanation from the administrator of the catering company about why they can't give back any of the several thousand euros paid to them.

"Right, if you are not giving her a refund consider the party still on." It's the same stubborn rage I had when our landlady said she was doubling our rent. The same stubborn rage that had us pack up our van and move to Italy within three weeks during a hurricane.

"I'll have a party for my fiftieth birthday and I will pay the bride back some of the money. At least it will be something." I spit the words out.

Mam overhears me. "We're having a party?"

Parties are Mam's favourite things. I like a party but not one for me; I am not good at being the centre of attention. Whereas Mam loves it.

"It's just a veiled threat Ma," I say in a hushed voice while I'm still on hold. "To get some money back for a bride."

The secretary says she will get her boss to call me, but she says she doubts if there is anything he can do at this late stage.

The following day the catering company has still not called me back, so I email them; "Just to confirm that we are not cancelling for that date. If you are not refunding the money for the wedding, we will continue with the booking for a birthday party."

Again, I expect the caterer to cave.

But instead, they come back with "Okay".

"Okay? Bloody hell. Does this mean I have to throw a party?"

I am so annoyed that I say this out loud in front of Mam.

"You deserve a party. You are only fifty once and you didn't celebrate it at all."

"I'm not having a party, it's for forty people. I don't know forty people. And besides, it's my busiest time of the summer. "

"It's okay, I have already been on to Rob and your brothers, and they are all checking to see if they can get over. And Izzy said she wouldn't miss it for the world, so she and that chap of hers is coming. Who else said they'd come, let me check my list."

"Your list? You've invited people already?"

"Yes, you said yesterday you were having a party, so I spent the evening on the phone checking with people. You know me, I always gave yous the best birthday parties."

It's true; Mam always threw the most creative kids birthday parties at home in the 70s. Lots of sweets and cakes made by herself, not a savoury item on the table.

"Ronan said his brother, what's his name, Hal and his wife might come from Holland for it."

"Ronan is involved?" This surprises me more than anything, Ronan hates parties.

"Yes, we talked about it last night," says Mam, thumbing her way through her diary to her long list of invitees. "I think he has already spoken to him about it."

"Any word back from the caterer?" Ronan asks, coming in from the garden.

"They are not going to give the refund."

"So you are having a party then? I've already said it to Hal and Gemma and they are coming, haven't seen them in five years so that will be nice! Also Denise said just to tell her when and she'll be here."

"Denise will come? And Izzy?" My childhood best friend and my daughter. Two of my favourite females in this world. Neither have seen each other in about twenty years so it would be worth having a party for that reason alone.

"But it's for forty people, we don't know forty people."

"I bet if you make a list you will be surprised. It will be nice getting everyone we know, old friends and new together after two years of lockdowns." Ronan is continuing to surprise me at his eagerness.

"I have a wedding arriving the day after the party followed by another group arriving the day that wedding finishes. Planning a last-minute party with me as the host is bloody crazy."

"Oh, come on, you can do it. You only turn fifty once, and you deserve a bit a fun after the year you've had."

Over lunch, I play with the idea and start making a list and I reach forty no problem. I send an email and text blast and overnight we have thirty of them saying yes. People are already booking flights.

Izzy is going to come two weeks before and Dave will follow her over a few days before the party.

"It looks like we're going to have a full house. Hal and Gemma are coming for the week from The Netherlands. Denise and her mum are coming from Ireland. Izzy and Dave are coming from London, and Luca and Sarah are already here. That's max capacity. We better get this house finished," says Ronan reading the list of RSVPs to Mam.

Rob and Jenny probably won't make it—he has his medical review on the same day of the party.

Nothing quite gets you cleaning like the threat of people coming to stay. Except for Mam, she's not budging.

I'm texting Lucia cleaning questions like; "What product do you recommend for cleaning the glass in the showers with?"

The water is harder here than it is in Ireland. It leaves the glass with what looks like dusty, dried drips.

"You need to get cleaning vinegar in the shops," Lucia replies.

Having an Italian friend has been invaluable since we moved over, from negotiating our way through all the bureaucracy of buying a house, to the basics like how to clean a shower here.

Sure enough, for 80 cents there is a litre of 'aceto per pulire' (vinegar for cleaning) with the scent of lemon.

Alex has built a new fireplace in the hearth under the big chimney and mantle in the dining room. The ceiling is smooth and crisp white and the walls an ochre yellow.

"This is shit, what do you want to do with it?" says Alex, pointing at my prized red-brick wall we discovered under the plaster in the dining room and several other rooms when we started renovating. Alex and I are now friends and I'm used to his bluntness.

"Get stuffed Alex, you are not plastering over my red bricks and you are to leave the jagged plasterwork along the top of it. I like the aesthetic."

"Okay okay, but I make it nicer."

"Eh, no it's fine."

"No, I make it nicer. I do it for free. I can't look at this wall like this when I am having dinner in your house. And you need your front door done before your guests arrive. I ask my cousin to come."

"Great yes, I definitely want the front door done before next winter so now is as good as time as any."

He had somehow distracted me from focusing on the red brick wall.

I had sanded and varnished the front door myself, but it needs professional attention. One of the panels is damaged beyond repair so needs replacing, and the wooden sill along the bottom was so rotten that it crumbled away after a couple of months of opening and closing.

This was why it was possible for the autumn leaves to blow in under the door gap last year and we could see the reflection of the front garden trees in the hall tiles even when the door was closed.

We go out to the front of the house to look at the door while we watch our pets doing warm summer day activities; Juno has cornered a scorpion in the hallway, while Spooky is playing with a giant lizard in the garden. Ronan kicks the broken door panel, which Paddy is pawing at, and pulls out a grass snake. It's like we are living in a very weird petting zoo for pets.

The wrought iron work guarding the filthy cracked glass fanlight above the door, that no amount of product will clean, not even CIF, was a haven of spider nests and solid hornet cocoons.

That evening, Alex's carpenter cousin arrives to take the door away on a week-long refurbishment holiday. He also knocks out the glass so that we can clean and paint the ornate wrought iron.

"Do you want me to take off the initials from the fanlight?" asks Alex, who has another cousin who does metal work.

It was something we had considered. But looking at it now I liked it. 'LP'. The initials of the original proud owner Paulo Legume. Mr Bean. "No, let's leave him there."

It takes three men to carry each of the double doors and secure them on top of their roof rack. In its place, they nail a slab of shuttering. It makes the place look like a derelict crack den again. Not only that, but with the fan light glass now removed, the profusion of spider nests and insect community complexes that have existed there for generations is revealed.

"I'm too short to tackle it," I say with relief and a shiver up my back. "You are going to have to do it, Ronan."

"We do have an invention to help short people get to high places, I think it's called a ladder?" He's also reluctant.

"Ah but you know me. I'm no good at heights and laddery things. Cleaning the frame and evicting the inhabitants, is definitely a job for you with me at a safe distance away."

We had ten days before the party and the start of the busiest two weeks of my wedding season with back-to-back weddings.

"Ronan you need to do above the door," I say later that day, not wanting him to forget before all the spiders escape.

"I already started cleaning it, but I need to do it from outside now."

"Do you mean you cleaned it from inside? Is that what all the dirt is in the hall? I thought it blew in under the board. You didn't even move the bags and boxes near the doorway. Where did all the spider nests fall?"

"I dunno."

"Bloody hell." So the rest of my day is spent carrying all the boxes of books outside that we were storing in the hallway and de-spider-nesting them, with the help of a hoover and a brush.

The boxes of books had not been looked at since we shipped them from Ireland. Going through them brought back memories of birthdays and Christmases, book signings and gifts and bookshelves of previous houses.

To make this house complete and to feel like a home, I needed bookshelves but at a quote of €1500 from the carpenter, that was a dream that would have to wait.

42

SALAMI & STITCHES

I zzy has arrived and everyone is on cleaning duty in preparation for all our visitors.

Luca is in charge of de-cobwebbing the rooms with the large round brush thing with the long handle that the Italians have invented specifically for de-cobwebbing their high ceilings.

Having scoured all the bathrooms and made the beds, I'm in the kitchen making my Aunty Rita's salad, when Sarah comes running down the stairs. "Luca fell on a glass and he has cut his arm really badly."

Before she had finished the last word I am already on the third step of our staircase running to the second floor.

"Get Ronan, he's in the garden," I shout back.

I tear around my room, looking for something I can use as a tourniquet. I can't find something quick enough, so I bound up to the top floor. Izzy is on my heels.

Luca is lying on the bathroom floor, calm as a cucumber holding a towel to his arm. The first thing that crosses my mind in the split second of trying not to panic... That's one of my new towels...

The second thing that crosses my mind in the second split second of time; That's a very short space of time for a bath towel to be drowned in blood.

I run into his room and find a belt and see the wine glass smashed beside his bed. Another weird thought flies into my cleaning mode brain: "Should I clean up the glass first?"

Izzy is with him, and Ronan is up the stairs. I throw the belt at Ronan, he's much better in these circumstances than me.

Mam is at the bottom of the stairs calling me.

"Jezuz not now Ma, what?"

"Is he alright?"

I can see he's not. "Right, I'll get the car keys, get him down the stairs."

I'm calling doctor Fab. "Answer the phone, answer the phone, please answer the phone." I leave a voice message. "My son has cut his arm badly does the local hospital do stitches?"

I call Lucia. It's the same. No answer. I leave the same message.

I call Shelly. No answer. I leave a message.

"Why is no one near their phone?" I run towards the front door but it's barricaded. "Out the back door everyone!" I shout at the troop coming down the stairs at high speed, past the Ma and out the back.

"Which hospital?" says Ronan, jumping into the driver's seat. Izzy, holding Luca's arm, dives into the back. "The local one is five minutes away I've seen ambulances outside it, there must be doctors there."

"Sarah, you stay here with Ma, we'll call you," I shout as we speed off.

Ronan is taking the bends up the hill to the hospital door like he's driving in Formula One. Izzy is in the back with Luca managing the tourniquet.

I run to the door of the hospital. There's no one. A guy about the same age as me arrives at the bottom of the steps. "My son has a cut I need ER," I shout at him, hoping he speaks English.

"Cut? Me too," he says, pointing to his leg. He has a white gauze pad neatly tapped to his shin with some blood has seeped through. I run down the corridors calling but there's no one. Another zombie apocalypse hospital–the second time I've experienced a hospital in Italy, and both times they look abandoned. I get back to the front door.

The guy with the scrape on his shin says, "Try there." I run to the door where there is an ambulance plugged in charging. "Where is everyone?"

I know it takes twenty minutes for someone to bleed out from a wound and I've already wasted five of my son's life.

"There is no one here. We need to go to the other one."

I see the guy walk past our car and do a double take. As there is blood. Everywhere.

"Do you need a lift to the other hospital?" I call to him. "No, it is okay, I can drive but I think you should hurry," he says, looking at our car concerned.

I jump back in and we speed off towards the motorway. Except we don't. Ronan goes left rather than right. "Where the fuck are you going?" I shout.

"I don't know you are supposed to be giving me directions."

Ronan's sense of direction is terrible, but this is just ridiculous.

"You need directions to the town where you go to the supermarket three times a week? What are you a fucking goldfish?"

Another strange thought flits through my brain... This is the second time I have compared my husband to a goldfish this summer.

He turns around and we're finally going in the right direction.

Izzy and Luca are staying amazingly calm, managing the spurting with pressure and keeping his arm up. It's fifteen minutes to the hospital, Ronan has his foot down, I just pray we don't get stopped at the level crossing as that will add up to another six minutes. We don't.

We pull up to the familiar parking spot outside the bigger hospital where I brought Ronan eight months before; the place is quiet. There are three ambulance men standing around chatting. I jump out of the car and run towards them, shouting at them in Italian as we are reaching the twenty-minute deadline.

What I should have been shouting was 'tagliare'. Which means to cut. Instead I am shouting "tagliere, tagliere". Which is basically a chopping board you serve a tasty appetiser of salamis and cheese on before dinner.

"Mio figlio ha tagliere." "My son has a chopping board of tasty meats", screams the mad Irish woman running towards them with her hands covered in blood.

"Tagliere? You cut?"

They are rushing towards me and then they see Izzy. Gorgeous Izzy in her shorts and sun top, covered in more blood than me. I correct myself.

"Mio figlio ha tagliare."

"My son has to cut." I have not learnt past tense yet.

But at least they know it is my son, not me or my daughter. But it has already become apparent to them, as his arm, hand and bath towel, is completely soaked in blood at that point.

They have him in the door in seconds; we are all in the door.

"What happened?" A nurse asks in Italian.

"A broken glass. He fell," I say in Italian, breathless and shaking.

"Okay, Mamma, sit down." They give me a seat. A doctor is in with Luca.

"Can he speak Italian?"

"Yes."

"Okay, we will look after him." The words I needed to hear.

One of the ambulance men takes charge of Izzy and me, leading us into the sink where we can wash Luca's blood off us.

The admin follows me in and starts asking his details. Name, address, age, allergies. They need his ID and his EU health card. This I don't have. Ronan might have it.

No. I'm trying to think where it might be. We call Sarah. "Okay, we need Lucas ID and health card."

By phone, I am guiding her through the drawers in the kitchen where I normally keep our passports. Then I remember he travelled by himself most recently and I had given him the responsibility for all his own documents.

Fair play to Sarah, she finds his passport and his EU health card, which the admin has now asked me for five times in the space of ten minutes. Sarah takes a photo of both and we email them on to the admin, who is satisfied and stops hovering around us. I'm so glad I took the time to renew our European health cards when I was home before Christmas.

The place has little activity. Only a jogger arriving with an asthma attack, a three-box high pizza delivery, and the guy with the gash that I met outside the other hospital. They have given him a new dressing and sent him on his way.

We're standing outside the window where Luca is being treated. It's frosted glass but I can hear bits of conversation. I hear them mention 'bruciata' which I know means burnt.

"Did Luca burn himself or do they laser burn wounds closed now?" I'm concerned. I want to know what's happening with my son. He might be over eighteen, but I still want to know.

The nurse tells me it's 'profundo'. My brain is flicking quickly through my Rolodex of Italian words. Deep. I remember it means deep.

It's quite a while before he gets out.

"They had to stitch up the muscle and the artery. Before they stitched up my skin," Luca is ridiculously casual about something like this.

"I've to come back in a few days for them to change the dressing and then I think we need to do something ourselves."

"What do we need to do?"

"I don't know."

"Take the stitches out ourselves? I can do that," volunteers Ronan. He should have been a doctor. He loves this sort of stuff.

"You are not taking out his stitches, Ronan."

"Why not? It's easy to do. You just—"

"Please Ronan, not now! My stomach has had enough flips for one day. Let's just get home."

Back in the car, my heart rate has returned to normal.

"Luca, I am sure we don't have to take out the stitches ourselves and don't let your father try if he volunteers. Try to remember what it is we have to do, was it something to do with burning?"

"Burning?" asks Luca surprised.

"Yes, they mentioned 'bruciata'?"

"Ohh that was the ambulance drivers, they were hilarious, and the doctor was too. They got pizzas delivered, and they were giving out hell about the place, saying they would never order from there again as the pizza crust was burnt. So they were asking me what the English word was for burnt. And then asking me other words."

"So you were giving them a language lesson while getting your arm stitched up?"

"Yes, sort of, I suppose."

By the size of the bandage, I am thinking he is going to have one hell of a scar and a long time healing his writing hand. He won't be helping in the cleaning nor will he be doing the bar. Mam was right, housework is dangerous.

Aunty Rita's Salad

This was one of the first recipes I learnt to create when I was about ten. My Aunty Rita had brought back the idea from Switzerland. This salad gave me my first experience of garlic as it was a 'foreign exotic' thing in Irish supermarkets in the early 80s.

4-5 Carrots

3-4 Eating apples

Mayonnaise

1 Cloves of garlic

Lemon juice

Method:

Cut the clove of garlic in half, and rub it around the inside of a glass or ceramic mixing bowl.

Grate the carrots and apples into the bowl.

Add some lemon juice to save apple going brown rather than for the flavour. Add a few dollops of mayonnaise and carefully stir them all together.

You can add grated cheddar cheese for an additional taste sensation.

43

TEACHERS & KAYAKS

I zzy's boyfriend Dave has arrived. I'm walking in on crying sessions and strange one-sided conversations in not their own accents about murder, divorce and mayhem.

He's an actor too and now that Covid has lifted, the film industry has kicked off again and they both have self-tape auditions to do with short deadlines. Over-hearing heated discussions in the garden and shower room is common when living with actors.

Even though the party is just a few days away. I think we could all do with a break, so I book a morning of kayaking on the lake. I've never done it before, but Lucia recommends it.

I didn't think I would be up to it, with my 'still not one hundred percent' recovered frozen shoulders, but it shouldn't be too difficult as there is an island we can aim for that is only one and a half kilometres from where the kayaking club is on Zucco Beach. Lucia has told me to ask for her friend Angelo.

Angelo sends off a group of six men in two kayaks before prepping us with life jackets. We are smothering ourselves in factor 50, while I have packed a picnic to feed ten.

"That's a lot of stuff you want to bring," says Angelo looking at the size of the picnic hamper. "Well, we will be hungry by the time we reach the island."

"It will take about thirty minutes and there is a bar where you can buy food and drinks."

"Oh. We'll leave it here then and have it when we get back."

Angelo sets us off in our kayaks. Dave takes one to himself while Luca and Sarah have another, and Izzy and I set off on ours together. Ronan was happy to stay at home with Mam.

Angelo is a paddle board champion and paddles along ahead of us standing on his board like the god of the lake.

The lake is low, lower than it has been for years. I remember what Mick Kelly told me about how we don't have earthquakes but the ground can move in our area, ever so slightly, if the lake gets low but it hasn't done so since the fifties.

Typical, the lake reaches its lowest point in its entire history the year after we buy a house here. I'm glad we put in the ring of iron to hold the house together should the ground decide to move.

The soft sound of the paddles sloshing through the water and lake weed is so relaxing that I just enjoy the moment and forget all my worries.

Luca is having a laugh with his girlfriend and the bronzed muscular Angelo paddling alongside them. Luca has mentioned that he might go back to Ireland with Sarah for a while. He needs to find his own feet in the world now.

Hopefully, this will be a moment he thinks back on and remembers it as the beautiful place we now call home. Maybe I'll buy a kayak. It sits with me better than a motorboat. These are all the thoughts running through my head as I paddle in unison with my daughter in front of me. Her boyfriend beside us, paddling his own canoe.

The island that I didn't know existed, surprises us with an ancient castle to visit and a resort in need of some care. If I was in my old frame of mind, I would consider it for weddings.

On the way back, we are facing the undulating hills of upside-down Cyprus cones, olive groves, vineyards dotted with villas and homes tucked in between the patches of golden grains and green fields ready to turn into blaring yellow when they erupt into heads of sunflowers.

The only sound is the swish of the paddle beneath the water. A gentle breeze together with our onward motion breaks the heat of the midday sun, making a very pleasurable temperature on the glass lake.

"We live here," I say to Izzy. I'm a little awestruck by this realisation that comes over me now and then.

On return to the shore, the beach has come alive. It's a place, we discover, where to hang out on you need a bikini and a hot body.

Young adults in thonged bikinis sit at the bar and swimming pool, eating peaches, chilled watermelon and gelato.

A beach volleyball tournament is going on in an arena of soft, imported sand. Two guys about 15-years-old are rubbing oil into each other's backs, not in a sexual way—they are here to bronze up and watch the babes. Although, I do feel like pointing out to them that they have just wasted their time, as they are now sitting with their backs up against a wall.

Izzy and Dave are ahead of me, walking across the sand to the grass park area, and find a spot to sit. They choose the shaded area under the olive trees beside the 80-year-old woman in the sundress lying on her side asleep, or possibly dead.

I start to dish out our picnic. A guy walks down from the car park in wetsuit bottoms that looks like he has stuffed socks down the front. Actually, he has definitely stuffed something down the front. His wrinkled, over-bronzed torso is bare, except for the tattoo on his back, neatly between his shoulder blades. I think it is a set of angel wings but his tan is nearly as dark as the ink so it is hard to tell.

He's in his late fifties. He was probably the fittest guy in town in his thirties. Everyone greets him with joy as he struts down the grass, followed by an entourage of about five younger people. He shouts 'Ciao mamma' to the dead woman, who immediately comes alive and animated. He sits at the booth that is selling black sweatshirts with logos, possibly to do with the beach volleyball tournament.

Space is cleared for him. His mamma has managed to get up off the grass after some rolling about, and has nearly jogged down to the booth. She leans on the back of his chair and seems to talk to everyone in his entourage. I'm busy doing my Irish mammy thing of giving everyone lunchbox-sized cartons of orange juice, apples and cheese-bread I bought at the bakers.

"Can you imagine growing up here and these were all your friends?" I say to my kids, wondering if we had missed a great opportunity for them.

"I don't think it would have worked moving here when we were small. I don't think we would have fitted in with the emotional Italians," says Luca.

"I definitely don't think the schedule would have suited us," chimes in Izzy. "I know Chloe goes to school six days a week and gets tonnes of homework in the evenings, over weekends and throughout the summer. And if a child fails any of their end-of-year tests, they are automatically kept back to repeat the year. We would have been expelled in no time at all."

She's right, I don't think I could have coped dealing with the Italian school system having heard tales from other mothers during a get together of expats in Florence. Comparing their experiences, one mother said she asked if she could have her child excused from English classes as they were basic and she didn't want the child bored and religion class as they were not a religious family.

She was told, "You can get your kid excused from 'insegnamento della religione cattolica', catholic religious instruction, as Italy is a 'lay' state, but not a history of religion class. That is different. And if your child is a native English speaker, you can't get them excused from English class."

Comparisons of heated discussions they all had had with teachers of their kids English teachers ensued:

"Of course it is 'brushing your hairs', you have more than one hair on your head, no?" one teacher of English had insisted.

Another teacher marked sheep as incorrect for the plural form. "It should be 'sheeps'." The parent tackled the teacher about it and the teacher insisted the mother must be mistaken as she was taught the plural was 'sheeps' at university.

"The same teacher gave the child a nine instead of ten in an English oral exam as she spoke too quickly during it, which is rich coming from an Italian!" exclaimed one of the mothers.

"Well, my son," started another mother, "after doing an entire test and getting all the questions answered correctly, the teacher refused to give him a ten in English as it wouldn't be fair to the other students. With another teacher, he went through a period of pretending he knew nothing, as he didn't want to embarrass the teacher with the correct pronunciation of words she was saying completely wrong, but if he said it correctly, she deducted marks as she believed her way of pronouncing things like; Free-end for friend and jew-iz for juice was correct."

She continued; "I got a brew-iz while tying my sho-ez on the crew-iz—that is how she pronounces things. So at the parent teacher meeting I had to address it with her, and do you know what she said to me? She said that my pronunciation for some words was incorrect, because I was Irish and my mother tongue was not English."

They all agreed that the best line of defence with bad English school teachers is to speak to them in English at the parent-teacher meetings. "They usually look terrified and stop treating the child bad after that."

As with everything, when you sit down and start a discussion with friends—some might call it a bitching session—the bad stuff comes out more, as the shocking stuff makes the best stories.

There were, of course, stories of fabulous teachers too who embraced having a native speaker in the class to help other students and the teacher with pronunciation. Or they used it as an opportunity to help the native English-speaking child develop leadership abilities by assisting in the class.

One mother said that her child's teacher joked that the kid should get half her wages as she helped check and prepare lessons. Like everywhere, it is luck of the draw.

The school system in Italy is very academic, all kids study Dante, learn Latin and complete school well-read and with a high level of mathematical ability, ready for university. Most Italians of recent generations, seem to have at least one degree under their belt by the age of twenty-three. Many seem to stay on to do a masters or a second degree because of the shortage of jobs.

"I do love that we have a home here now though," says Izzy, flopping back on the grass. "It's so nice to come back to, it recharges my creative battery. There's bird song and stars at night, not like London. And I'm getting used to the insects flying at me. It's good to have the little guys around pollinating, we're in amongst nature here."

I look up and see the sock-cock guy's mamma struggling back from the bar with her arms wrapped around a variety of cans and bottles, including two large bottles of water. I nearly get up to help, but she manages, she is an Italian mamma looking after her boy after all, and there are at least three in his entourage half my age, who could go to her aid if she needed or allowed them.

I lie back on the grass beside Izzy, letting our lunch feast digest. There isn't a hint of a cloud in the sky, there probably won't be for months. Checking the weather app on my phone, it's 32°C here, with Monday getting up to 39°C which is worrying for Mam. Swiping across the app, I see in Ireland it is 12°C and one hundred percent chance of rain. It might get up to seventeen degrees there later in the week with only an eighty percent chance of rain, but there are no little sunshine symbols for the next ten days, only clouds with blue lines coming out of their bottoms. I'll put up with the heat, thank you very much.

However, the rising heat means mosquitoes are multiplying. Another thing not good for the mammy. I'm going to need to check out getting air conditioning for the house but first we have a party to throw.

44

THE CANCELLATION

Alex has used a hammer drill for the week, taking out loose and old mortar between the red brickwork and then refilling with a buttery mix of creamy ochre mortar, finished with a wash-down of acid. It isn't until it's done that I realise he was right; the wall did look shit beforehand.

"Do you have a ceramic or something that you like that I can embed it in the wall above the fireplace? Something nice." Alex emphasises the word 'nice'.

Our tastes are quite different but we are coming to an understanding. This is not something we have previously discussed, but he's doing it whether I like it or not. So I better find something, otherwise he might surprise me with something 'nice' of his own choosing and I'd have to explain during dinner parties, "Oh you are wondering why we have a two-foot ceramic of the national flag of Albania above our fireplace?"

I walk around the house trying to think of something. "Of course, the perfect thing!" I spot the plaster relief of a fossilised section of a field of wheat which I bought in the New York Natural History Museum thirty years ago on my first (and last) solo holiday with Ronan, in the days before the weight of your bag mattered.

That thing was heavy to carry back to Ireland. I have carted it from house to house with us for all this time and never had a place to hang. Above the chimney in our dining room would be a perfect resting place for our wheat fossil.

"This," I say, carrying the precious, ten-pound wall relief out to Alex and explain the history of it in our lives to him.

"You want this on your wall?"

"Yes," I say, doubting my taste again.

"Okay, I do it, but it stays there forever, when you move it stays."

"Well, I'm not intending to move anytime soon, and I think it deserves a home after thirty years of waiting."

Alex's cousin returns with the doors the same day Alex finishes the dining room. There's no time to lose. While the front doors and new double-glazed fanlight are being put into place, we're lifting the dining table from the 'banqueting' hallway into its own space along with the regal-looking leather cushioned chairs and my two prized Devil's Ivy plants which I bought for less than €19 each when we were living in Giovanni's.

They have now extended themselves so long, that we need to put studs in around the walls to let their trailing leafy limbs traverse above the doorways and around the walls. Along with the blue velvet armchair that I upholstered in the corner to create a cozy reading nook, and a pop art painting I did of me and Ronan twenty years ago on the wall, the room is really taking shape. Precious things are finding their place.

The front door looks terrific, although I will need to dip the handles in cola to clean them again. But it will wait until another time as now I've to rush off to collect my friend Denise, who is arriving a few days early to help with the party preparations, from the airport.

Shelly and I collect her from the evening flight and by the time we arrive back, the hallway looks like a badly managed archeological dig as Juno continues to find, dig up and carry in all the bones Paddy has buried.

But we ignore the inside of the house and enjoy a glass of wine together with Mam, Shelly and Blodwyn outside, while watching the fireflies' bums flicker.

It's 10.30pm, there's a football match happening somewhere in the distance, I can hear the players call to each other and the ref's whistle being blown. It's a balmy twenty-seven degrees, a relief from the earlier thirty-eight degrees. The toads are trilling their throats in a chorus of different octaves down by the lake.

"It reminds me of that toad chorus of Paul McCartney's number one Christmas hit when we were teenagers, remember that, Rosie?" asks Denise with her bare feet up. Her shoes are drying out from the rain she left at the Irish airport where she had to queue for four hours because of a new shortage of airport staff in Europe.

There's a warm glow of light and the laughter of my two kids and their friends coming from the house. The train passes at the bottom of the garden with people on board. It's no longer an empty filmstrip.

It's then I get the text.

"Oh my God..." I say, sitting upright.

"What's wrong?" asks Denise seeing my face drop.

"It's from the caterer... they are offering a full refund back for the wedding."

"Well, that's good."

"Yes, but it's because they have got a last-minute booking for a big event on Saturday, so if I accept they won't be doing my party. "

"What are you going to say?" asks Denise.

"I'll accept of course. The bride has lost enough money already on her big day."

I pause to think.

"I know you and Izzy have travelled all this way and Ronan's brother is coming too... but I'll have to cancel the party. We'll just do a small dinner here for you guys, if that's okay?"

I'm surprised at the disappointment I feel saying it.

"That's bollocks!" states Shelly who I have never heard curse before, never mind use one of my favourite Irish swearwords. She has obviously been hanging around with me too much. "You are going to have a bloody party. We'll rally the forces and we'll all bring a salad or something."

"I have half a cinghiale in my freezer, we can use that!" pipes up Blodwyn.

"There you go, that's the meat sorted," says Shelly. "I know Helga has a garden full of zucchini and lettuce since that strong wind knocked over her seed jars in the spring. I have a tonne of tomatoes. And I'm sure you have some drink left over from the bar," says Shelly.

"If not, we can just go to the hooch stop," says Blodwyn.

"The hooch stop?" asks Denise.

"Yes, there's a wine shop up the road that has a petrol pump style thing and they fill up a gallon container of very good local wine for a tenner. Two of them and your wine is sorted for your party."

"I'll do potatoes," says Mam her eyes lighting up at the thought of having a big crowd to peel potatoes for. "And you can make a pot of one of those nice pasta dishes you make. The one that strangles priests is one of my favourites. Did she ever make it for you Shelly, no?"

Did my mother just compliment my cooking?

"So there's no need to cancel, between us we'll make a party better than any caterer, won't we girls?" says Blodwyn, holding her glass up for a cheers.

"Cheers!" shouts Mam. "It will be no trouble for you Rosie, there's only thirty people, that's only double the amount of people you used to cook Christmas dinner for back in Ireland. Rosie does quite a good Christmas dinner, do you know that?" Mam says to Blodwyn.

Was that another compliment? Did she bang her head or something?

"My roast potatoes and Yorkshire puddings are better though." And there it was, Mam was back to her old self again. I don't need to take her to Doctor Fab Chicken to get her head checked.

By the end of the night Shelly, Denise and Blodwyn are writing lists and making calls.

"I've texted the bride who had to cancel and told her the good news, she's delighted. I've also told the caterer to go ahead with the cancellation of my party booking."

The first thing to do the next morning is to buy the wine. "If it is just down the road, I'll come for the walk with you," says Mam. "I'll bring me wheelchair for a walk."

At the wine shop we get two white, and two red, five-litre plastic containers filled with wine.

"It's bloody heavy," I say, carrying two out of the shop to hand to Denise. Before going back for my two.

"Here put them in the wheelchair," says Mam. "I'll push it home, I can do with the walk." So we fill Mam's wheelchair full of wine with the woman of the shop standing at the door laughing in disbelief.

"It's the miracle of the wine and the wheelchair, I can walk again!" laughs Mam, pushing along the wine-filled chair.

"I think we should rename the wheelchair the hooch train," she says as we get close to our house and need to cross the road. Cars on each side volunteer to stop as they see the little old dear pushing her wheelchair full of wine ready to cross the road. Typical Italian respect for the elderly and wine.

"We will need jugs or carafes for the wine." I send out a text to our yoga group, and we get a few offers back. As we are having the party at Lucia's, where the wedding was to be, we have the use of her catering kitchen, crockery and cutlery. All we need now are the guests.

45

SURPRISES

I awake the day of the party.

"Hello Greg," I call out to the little gecko that enjoys hanging out on my bedroom ceiling. I love geckos, they have such cute toes.

Over breakfast I get a text from Ruth, "Is it okay if I bring a couple of friends to your party?"

I'm thinking it an odd request, a couple of friends could mean several. Perhaps she has friends staying, and I wouldn't want Ruth to miss the party as her yoga group has helped me make friends here.

"No problem, let me know their names and I'll put them on the table plan."

"Thanks Rosie. Didn't realise there was a seating plan. Elena and Marco. They don't speak English."

Now this is very odd. I recognise the names; they are her neighbours, Elena does some cleaning for her and she recommended

Marco to me for carpentry work when we were starting to renovate.

I wanted to keep this intimate with family and friends, not strangers. And who am I going to sit them beside if they don't speak English?

I text her back. "If they are family and it means you guys can't come no problem. But I do want to keep this intimate so I'm not trying to fill seats if you know what I mean, I am sure you understand."

"If it's going to cost extra, we'll pay."

She seems determined. I decide to dismiss it as just something odd. Maybe the couple are having some sort of crisis in their lives and lovely Ruth is trying to bring them some happiness, that would be her style.

"Sorry just re-read my text and it sounds horrible. If you can't come because of this arrangement, then I want them there. You are a big part of making us welcome in Italy. Looking forward to meeting them."

Ronan has borrowed Sherwin's car to collect his brother and his wife from the airport, as I need our car to take everyone up to La Dogana to start prepping the food, before I go and buy supplies for the wedding party arriving the following day.

I arrive back to La Dogana in the afternoon to music playing and a hive of activity. Mam is peeling enough potatoes to feed Hannibal's army of Celts when they were in this spot fighting the Romans, two thousand years ago.

Lucia is preparing the starter of chopped up peaches with stracciatella with Denise, Helga is washing salad, and Blodwyn is mincing cinghiale for the lasagne, while Izzy and Dave are setting up the tables with Luca and Sarah.

I can't believe this is all coming together so well. The tables just need some decoration, so I do what I tell brides not to do and go pick some flowers along the road for the tables, when I see Shelly's car.

"Oh, I wasn't expecting to see you here, I thought you would be at home getting ready," she says.

"We're just finishing up. I'm going to pop home for an hour and get ready shortly. What are you doing here?"

"Oh ermmm," she says, fumbling in the boot of her car. "I brought you this."

She holds out a tall plastic pink jug. "You said you needed jugs for wine, so I thought I'd bring it up to you."

"Oh, thanks Shelly, but you shouldn't have driven all this way to bring me... this," I say holding the jug, not wanting to point out the obvious large crack.

"Okay, I'll be off then." And she drove away leaving me with the cracked jug.

With the flowers on the gingham table-clothed table, place cards in place, wine chilling, salads done, potatoes peeled, cinghiale lasagne made, we go home to get ready.

We arrive back to find one of my favourite wedding singers, Renoir, setting up his speakers and guitar. "What are you doing Renoir? I invited you as a guest."

"My music is my gift to you, happy birthday."

"Well, it's not really my birth—" But I stop myself as Alex walks in with his wife carrying a gift bag and helium balloons. "Guys you really shouldn't have, it's not really my birthday."

"Oh, come on Rosie. Why you say that? It is your birthday party to celebrate your birthday year. Stop saying it's not your birthday we are here to celebrate."

More gifts arrive as more guests appear, I really hadn't expected that. Ronan is late arriving back from the airport, but at last I see his car pull up.

"Hal, Gemma!" I call to my brother-in-law and his wife, who I hadn't seen in five years. "It's been too long, was your flight delayed?" I say hugging them.

"Not their flight but, these," Ronan says open the other back door.

"Rob and Jenny, you made it!"

"We thought we'd surprise you. Doctors are really happy with my progress, so they gave me the all clear to travel. And to be honest, I would have come anyway whatever they said."

Renoir is playing my favourite songs, Lucia is dishing out the lasagne, while Luca and Sarah are doing a fantastic job keeping everyone's glasses topped up.

All the familiar faces of the people I love from my past in Ireland and my new life in Italy are here mingling and dancing together.

Denise and Izzy with Patricia the postwoman and Mick Kelly the architect, Shelly and Sherwin, Blodwyn and Helga along with Ruth our yoga teacher who brought us all together, Ben and Ellie, Louise the Irish makeup artist with her family, and of course Karen and John without whom, we'd probably be in Spain or still in Ireland. Mam is at the top of the table with her electric tennis racket providing a mini fireworks display.

There are only two unfamiliar faces, Ruth's surprise guests. She has introduced them to me and they seem to be enjoying themselves, but just as we tidy away the plates, Shelly and Ruth ask Renoir for the mic. The crowd hush. "Rosie, as you are celebrating your birthday in Italy, we thought it would be nice to add an extra Italian touch with a little surprise."

With that, Ruth's mysterious carpenter takes the mic and stubs out his cigarette. Was he going to make a speech in Italian about how to build a bookcase? He paused, closed his eyes, took a deep breath that expanded his chest, opened his mouth and out flooded 'Nessun Dorma' in the most beautiful operatic voice. And as he bellowed the closing "Vincerò, Vinceroò" out came Ruth carrying a massive carrot cake she had home-baked, my favourite, with fifty candles glowing.

Shelly followed, carrying a white cake. It wasn't until she had put it down on the table, that I saw it was in the shape of a book with the cover of my newly released book iced on the front. I immediately want to hide it... half the people here don't know I write and are in the book.

"I came with the cake earlier to put it in the fridge, I wasn't expecting you to be here, so I handed you the broken jug I had in the back since Sherwin and I went camping last month. I had to drive around the block three times with the air con going full blast waiting for you to leave! The design was Ronan's idea," said Shelly, laughing.

Thank God, both Ruth and Shelly's crazy spells of the last twelve hours were now explained.

And as everyone started to sing happy birthday, the tears came. I was filled with the love from the friends and family I was surrounded by in the most beautiful place in the world; Home.

46

FULL CIRCLE

Water levels in the Po are three quarters down in the worst drought in seventy years and levels of the Arno and Tiber are more than half down. Over thirty percent of national crop production is now threatened.

I'm reading the news in Italian with the help of a dictionary, trying to get some words to stick.

Nearly a million people in Italy currently have Covid, most of the people in hospital with Covid are now in ordinary wards, but that doesn't reach headlines.

Things are opening up again, on the town hall's website they have an announcement that the 'lice market' will be back this summer.

I am getting messages from friends in the States, concerned about how we are coping with the heat as we don't have AC. The house is built with foot-deep stone walls and we use the shutter method.

We have both inside and outside shutters and once you master the air flow, it helps to keep the temperature under control. Except on the top floor, which is roasting. Closing the shutters during the day to shades the rooms, but there is still air flow.

I can't stand the big clunky units you need to attach to the house for air con but we've priced it anyway. At €3k for only two rooms, we feel we need to rethink things.

The front room that is now our sitting room and never gets the sun, is wonderfully cool. I lie on my velvet sofa reading a book while Mam sits in her electric chair with her feet up, a fan beside her and the windows open. But it is going to get hotter and Mam can't just stay in one room for the next five months.

We completed our last wedding at Dogana until September. I have other weddings during July and August in other parts of Italy, but they don't require bar service, so Sarah is packing her bags to go home to Ireland.

"Mam," says Luca when he gets me on my own in the kitchen. "I'm going back to Ireland with Sarah. Her parents are okay for me to stay at their house, and Sarah has got me a job at the pizzeria she's going back to work at."

"Oh, a summer job, that's a good idea."

I continue to make my tea. Luca is still standing there. I feel there's something else coming.

"So when will you be coming back?"

"I'm not. I'm moving back to Ireland for good."

I drop my tea bag, but hide my reaction to the bombshell I was not expecting. "What about your art college in Florence?"

"I need to be around friends, and to think about what I want to do for a career. I tried that, but it's not for me. I don't know what I want to do."

My breathing has got shallower.

"When are you going?"

"I've my flight booked for the fourth of July."

"That's in two days' time?"

"If he's going, I'll go back with him," pipes up Mam, shuffling in behind. "It's going to get too hot here, and I just escaped from a swarm of flying ants. There are too many insects. I'll happily go back to my little house and little car in Ireland and have my independence. I'm perfectly happy to live there for the summer and come back here in the winter."

All of a sudden we were going from a full house bursting at the seams, to just Ronan and me within the space of two weeks.

Dropping the three of them at the airport was our usual last-minute dash with no time to be emotional. Mam was happy to be getting away from the heat and 'bitey flying things' and Luca and Sarah were happy to be going back to a cooler Ireland where they had some work lined up.

As we wave them through security, the first question I ask myself is if I made a complete mess of bringing up my kids. My TV star daughter is between jobs, in other words unemployed, while my son is leaving his art studies in Florence to work in a takeaway pizzeria in Ireland, with zero ambition to do anything else other than hanging out with his friends.

On the way home in the car, Ronan is easing my worries reaffirming that this is good for Luca. I'm nodding.

Yes, yes, he needs to be around his friends and people his own age.

Yes, yes, he has a summer job and can gain some independence.

Yes, yes, it will be good for him.

But a silence falls on my soul. I look at the golden hay rolly-pollies in the fields, the nodding heads of sunflowers as far as my eyes can see–for once they are looking at me—wanting me to smile back.

I think of the first visits to Italy, when we saw our first field of sunflowers and how we pulled over and took a picture of me in my happy place. I think of the fireflies and how they were magical beings to three-year-old Luca. Him tasting an olive for the first time and how we drove for hours on a Wednesday after-noon looking for somewhere to sell us a genuine Italian pizza, Luca's favourite food. Years later we laughed at our naivety; Looking for a restaurant open between 3pm and 7pm, and a pizza oven fired up on a Wednesday?

On the journey home I see Orvieto and remember all the towns we have visited, precariously balanced on fairytale hilltops. The towns he fell in love with and we promised to return to... His favourite being his namesake; Lucca, with its roundy square, and the city walls we cycled around the top of, stopping to eat the best coconut gelato we ever had.

And Gubbio, with its shops of antique crossbows, swords and suits of armour and meteor evidence.

Florence where he experienced the art of the greats, the Duomo and the Arno.

Getting lost in Siena and not being able to find the car for three hours in the rain, but where we saw the most amazing cathedral ceiling of stars, which I tried to recreate on his bedroom ceiling when he was still little. I wish digital phones were around then, so I would have captured the starry ceiling and the map of Winnie the Pooh's Hundred Acre Woods I painted on his wall. We then found the equally magical hundred acres of olive woods at La Dogana which led us to living by Lake Trasimeno.

Did we do the right thing uprooting him as a teenager and moving him to a country where he had no friends and didn't know the language? We're not sure, but we did it out of love, and love is never wasted. Good experiences are never wasted. They are banked.

Going back is good for him yes, yes.

He needs it yes, yes.

But... My baby has flown the nest.

When will he return? We don't know. When will he call or text? We don't know, he's not a big communicator. My life has revolved around trying to help him find his happiness in Italy but I haven't succeeded.

I hope he looks back on it and thinks, wow that was amazing and realises how brave he was to push himself to learn Italian and to study here.

Yes, he has dropped out, and yes, he has no official piece of paper to show for his work, but experiences are never wasted I remind myself again.

We arrive home, worried that Juno would have thrashed the place in the five long hours we were gone. But the house is not destroyed and the dogs are happy to see us.

I go from room to room but everywhere is too hot, except for the tranquilla room. There, my blue velvet sofa and terracotta rag rolled walls feel cool. I sit alone, without my Mam or Luca. Ronan finds me looking glum.

"There's no one you have to look after or think about now, but yourself."

He goes to buy ingredients for dinner. I sit, my head relaxes.

I see on my phone that Ben is responding to emails. I don't have to stress about weddings anymore; he is gradually taking over. I don't have to stress about Mam relying on me for company and chat and I don't have to stress about Luca being depressed and lonely on the second floor anymore. I don't have to stress about Izzy being lonely in London. I no longer need to keep up a front and be like a robot trying to act human.

I don't have to stress about anyone... but I can think about them. I allow myself to think of Dad, and allow myself to accept Luca has grown and left home. My stomach jerks again and again and loud sobs erupt.

I am alone but it is good for me yes, yes.

I will be better for it yes, yes.

I will become me again yes, yes.

It's going to be strange. But maybe it's time to breathe a little deeper and learn the Italian way of 'dolce far niente' – the sweetness of doing nothing.

But not yet, I need to keep myself busy for a few days, to distract myself during the adaption to this new quiet life.

Now that the building work is finished and all the rooms have a proper identity, it will be easier to place things and just have the furniture that is supposed to be in each room, and I want to start right now.

The large sideboard with the display cabinet is still in the tranquilla room along the wall where I want a big bookcase.

"It is fascist style," Lucia's mother had told us when we first bought the house. At the time, I wasn't too sure what to do with it but I didn't want to throw it out. Now I know exactly what to do with it.

"This has to go," I say to Ronan, pointing at the cabinet as soon as he returns.

"Go where?"

"Into the hallway, grab that end."

And together we push and shunt the heavy wood cabinet from the tranquilla room to the hallway. It fits perfectly where the dining table was only two weeks ago.

I pull out the dusty box of things I found left in the house. Paolo, the original owner's war medal, the collection of wooden spoons, black and white postcards, the calligraphy ink slab from Japan, his policeman's handbook, an undeveloped roll of film, the photo of his dog that looks very like Juno, the memorial coin, broken costume jewellery, the designer espresso cup, set of Murano glasses and the funniest 'learn English course' book. They all go into the display cabinet alongside my 'A Rosie Life in Italy' series. These items and this house has fuelled the content for these books. And the income from these books has funded the more recent renovations of this house. A full circle of support displayed in the cabinet.

Dusted and polished, Ronan places our family photos on the glass side shelves of the 'fascist' sideboard; his parents, my dad, my sister Eileen all smile proudly at us.

Alongside them I place the photo I found of Paolo Legume, Mr Bean. His smile is the proudest.

"******

To get updates on the house, life in Italy and book releases, join Rosie's mailing list on www.rosiemeleady.com

If you enjoyed this book PLEASE leave a review on Amazon or Good Reads, it stops my books disappearing into a black hole.

Pre order 'A ROSIE LIFE IN ITALY 5' on www.rosieme leady.com.

ACKNOWLEDGMENTS

Many thanks to:

Lucy Hayward

Rosemary Beard

Suzy Pope

Sara Pietrelli

Marco Merella (cover illustration)

ABOUT THE AUTHOR

Dubliner Rosie Meleady was a magazine publisher and editor for twenty years. She won the International Women in Publishing Award 1996 at the ripe old age of 24. She couldn't attend the award ceremony in London as she decided it would also be a good day to give birth.

She enjoys writing whatever makes her laugh. She lives happily ever after in Italy running writers retreats, while renovating the villa and writing long into the night.

Follow Rosie on her blog: www.rosiemeleady.com

ALSO BY ROSIE MELEADY

A Rosie Life In Italy 1: Why Are We Here?

A Rosie Life In Italy 2: What Have We Done?

A Rosie Life In Italy 3: Should I Stay or Should I Go?

'A ROSIE LIFE IN ITALY 5 available for pre-order (www.
rosiemeleady.com)

Hero-scope series

Spiced and Seasoned Contemporary Romantic Comedies

The Cosmo Club

Coming soon:

Laura's Lion

Bell's Bull

Wendy's Wolf

Deadly Wedding Cozy Mystery series

A Nun-Holy Murder

A Brush With Death

More coming soon!

Check out www.rosiemeleady.com for house and book updates.

Made in the USA
Las Vegas, NV
08 December 2022

61429125R00206

Made in the USA
Las Vegas, NV
08 December 2022

61429125R00206